THE
INDISPENSABLE
CAT

LOGE DE CONCIERGE

JOYEUX NOËL !
On peut déposer
les cadeaux dans
le vestibule

Un Voisin Qui Vient
C'est Bien
Un Voisin Généreux
C'est Mieux

GRAND

BRILA

JEAN·CLAUDE SUARÈS

THE INDISPENSABLE CAT

STEWART, TABORI & CHANG
PUBLISHERS

NEW YORK

LA PARESSE

p. 1 Rudyard Kipling, illustration for *The Cat That Walked by Himself.*
p. 2 Robert Sivard, *Le Chat du Concierge.* Collection of Dr. and Mrs. Paul Bauer, 983 Park Avenue, New York, NY
p. 3 Drawing by Théophile Steinlen.
p. 4 Felix Vallotton, *La Paresse.*
p. 5 Drawings by Théophile Steinlen.

Published and distributed in the United States by Stewart, Tabori & Chang, 575 Broadway, New York, New York 10012.

Distributed in the English language elsewhere in the world (except Canada and Central and South America) by Melia Publishing Services, P.O. Box 1639, Maidenhead, Berkshire SL6 6YZ England. Canadian and Central and South American accounts should contact Sales Manager, Stewart, Tabori & Chang.

Library of Congress Cataloging-in-Publication Data

Suarès, Jean-Claude.
  The indispensable cat.

  Includes index.
    1. Cats—Literary collections. 2. Cats in art.
I. Title.
PN6071.C3S8 1983   760'.04432   82-10512
ISBN 0-941434-21-4 (hardcover)
ISBN 1-55670-357-0 (paperback)

Design by J. C. Suarès
Editorial supervision by Leslie Stoker
Art and photo research by Don Hamerman
Production by Carole Ginesi
Captions by Roberta Newman
Initial letters from cat alphabet by Debi Gardiner

Printed in Italy
3H/1P94

Excerpt on p.48 from *Anne Frank: The Diary of a Young Girl* by Anne Frank. Copyright 1952 by Otto H. Frank. Reprinted by permission of Doubleday & Company, Inc.

Excerpt on p.84 from "An Elegy to Oscar" from *H. P. Lovecraft, Selected Letters, Vol. II* (1968). Permission granted by Arkham House Publishers, Inc., Sauk City, Wisconsin.

Excerpt on p.152 from "The Cat That Walked by Himself" from *Just So Stories* by Rudyard Kipling. Reprinted by permission of Doubleday & Company, Inc. and The National Trust of Great Britain and Macmillan London Limited.

Excerpt on p.158 from *The Tiger in the House* by Carl Van Vechten, copyright 1936 by Alfred A. Knopf, Inc.

Excerpt on p.179 from "The Cat and the Moon" from *Collected Poems* by William Butler Yeats. Reprinted with permission of Macmillan Publishing Company, Inc., copyright 1919 by Macmillan Publishing Company, Inc., renewed 1947 by Bertha Georgie Yeats. Also with permission of M.B. Yeats, Anne Yeats and Macmillan London Limited.

CONTENTS

INTRODUCTION   7

PART ONE: THE TIGER IN
    THE HOUSE   15

Cats as Human Companions   15
How It All Began   18
Making Friends   24
Man's Better Friend   66

PART TWO: MOUSERS,
MODELS, MOVIE STARS   93

Working Cats   93
Mice for Breakfast, Lunch, and Dinner   102
Cats in Advertising   120
Cats in Posters   126
The Silver Screen   134
On the Run   140
Comic-Strip Cats   146

PART THREE:
A DARK MIRROR   151

The Cat as Symbol   151
The Almighty Cat   158
Sentenced to Death   170
Beware of the Cat   177

Breeds   182
Index to Literature   188
Index to Art   189

INTRODUCTION

My cat is one year, two months, and four days old (a Capricorn); he is twenty-nine-and-a-half inches long from the tip of his nose to the end of his tail, which is eleven inches long. He stands ten-and-a-half inches at the shoulder and weighs ten pounds, four ounces. He has a seven-inch neck, and his longest whiskers are three-and-a-quarter inches long. His coat consists of short orange tan hair spotted with brownish orange stripes. He is undoubtedly the cleanest creature in the house and certainly the only one who eats no more than necessary. He can jump onto a five-foot-high surface (or about five times his height) from a sitting position without exerting himself whatsoever. He can stop a bug in midair with a single punch on a good day. He survives the coldest winters and the hottest summers with very little suffering. He is *Felis catus*, the domestic cat, according to the encyclopedia, the descendant of both *Felis libyca*, a small African wild cat, and *Felis silvestris*, the wild cat of Europe. Otherwise he is a short hair domestic according to his file card at the veterinarian's, an American short hair according to *Cats Magazine*, and an alley cat according to my mother, who doesn't like animals.

In the past twenty-four hours he has spent seven hours and twenty minutes sleeping on my bed and another five hours sleeping on a couch. He looked out the window of the living room for twenty-five minutes and sunbathed at the kitchen window for an hour and a half. He also spent ten minutes chasing a fly (that he didn't catch) and another eight minutes playing with a small twenty-five dollar shaving brush (which is still missing). The rest of the time he spent inspecting the apartment, walking in and out of closets, and climbing on chairs and bookshelves without ever disturbing a vase or a plant.

He ate once at 9:15 A.M. for six minutes and promptly licked himself thoroughly, a daily chore that takes him sixteen minutes on the average: five minutes to lick his paws, four minutes to lick the fur on his chest, four-and-a-half minutes to lick his shoulders, and the rest of the time to clean his tail and his ears, something he accomplishes by first moistening his paws and then brushing them against his ears.

Socks, the White House Cat

The first cat in three presidential administrations to reside in the White House, Socks is a short-hair, domestic black and white male. He moved in with the Clintons in January, 1993.
Nina Duran, Collection of the Artist

This is your typical apartment cat, the result of several hundred years of evolution in the company of man. In many ways he seems to have adjusted to city life better than humans, since unlike them, he is content within the confines of that small space. Like man, he is resolute in the prospect of living his entire life in the company of the other. This is something an observer from another planet would find quite fascinating, since cat and man have no common language and, more important, no mutual survival techniques: the cat does not scout for man's prey in order to share the carcasses of slain game, nor does he protect his herds or his property. The visitor would conclude that their relationship is based on a purely psychological need on the part of man. The entry in his intergalactic journal might read:

> Men and women keep big cats in zoos and small cats in their homes. They feed them well and give them cute names like "Fluffy" or "Pumpkin." They ask only one thing in return: that they be loyal companions. They let them sleep on their beds at night and talk about them to their friends all the time, when they are not talking about movies. To some humans, the cat is a very important element in their lives; this is typically manifested when they are planning to live in a new house. Invariably, you overhear them deciding on some basic acquisitions: a bed, a sound system, a cat. All indispensable.

Attributed to Razon Tsuneyki

Taken from a Japanese album of 1857, this design of a small round cat was originally intended as a model for ornamental carvings on knives, sheaths, sword handles, and related items.

There are several schools of thought as to how man and beast first found themselves under the same roof. It happened no doubt shortly after man gave up several thousand years of nomadic wanderings and decided to settle down on the riverbanks of the Nile. By that time, of course, the dog had already been domesticated. But did man seek the cat, or did the cat seek man's warm shelter, as some thinking goes? The answer to this question is irrelevant. After all, many creatures have wandered in and out of man's house but either were not welcomed or decided not to stay. We don't consider ducks, geese, chickens, goats, sheep, and cows pets, just domesticated animals. What is relevant, then, is why and how the cat and man found themselves comfortable enough with each other to extend their relationship for five thousand years.

Man's limited living space is, in fact, a natural extension of *Felis libyca*'s natural habitat. A small space is easier to patrol. The small wild cat of Africa simply needs a low place with high grass to stalk prey from, a high place to sleep safely in, and a hidden place to have kittens in. He found that he could survive better in a small area. He often picked a cluster of trees near a river or a lake and seldom left it unattended. Here he could watch the area from the highest branch and have his kittens in the trunk of a dead tree; he need only leave the area at night to hunt nearby. He learned that he could conceal his presence from potential enemies by burying his feces and that there would be less chance of his scent carrying downwind if he licked himself thoroughly after every meal.

The cat's tall tree has been replaced by the cupboards high above the kitchen stove, and the dead hollow tree trunk is now the broom closet. He'll rid the place of mice if they exist, but otherwise will be satisfied to teach his young how to hunt by chasing a Ping-Pong ball across the carpet. He will defend his turf against newcomers and intruders with amazing ferocity. He still buries his feces thoroughly and licks himself clean, but he's forgotten why. If he ever stopped, however, he would most certainly find himself on the sidewalk with his belongings neatly packed, waiting for a Checker cab to take him back to Africa.

Drawing by Steinlen

Don't let Garfield, that sloppy, overweight, violent, clumsy comicstrip character, fool you: cats *are* quite obsessed with their dignity. Do they ever neglect their grooming? forget to use the cat litter? lose their balance? overeat? They are very dignified creatures, indeed. Dignified, that is, until you happen to place an empty shopping bag in the middle of the room. Within three minutes of the bag's appearance, your cat has climbed into it and established permanent residence. He will occasionally venture a peek at the outside world. But otherwise, don't try to evict him—that paper womb has reduced him to a babbling idiot. Do you call that dignity? security in a paper bag that says A&P on the outside and that only moments ago was used to carry four cans of soup, a carton of milk, a bag of Dorito Corn Chips, and a head of lettuce across Lexington Avenue?

All cats find comfort in small enclosed spaces, it seems, driven by a strong instinct, the same strong instinct that makes them inexplicably afraid of water, jealous of their turf, restless at night, and unafraid of heights.

So don't listen to stories of how this cat or that one is the "most unusual in the world." . . . All cats are very much the same, precisely because they all share the same instincts that shape what sometimes seem like strange behaviors.

After you've listened to a thousand stories about incredible cats from the cat owners you meet, you'll find out two things:

1. Most cats are alike, and the weird things they do are not so unusual when you find that all cats do them.
2. Cat owners are much stranger than their pets, and most of them like to believe things about their pets that are terribly exaggerated, or simply not true.

You can pretty much guess just how eccentric a cat owner is by the names he/she has forced on the cat. Space does not allow for a complete listing of those names and their meanings, but here are some examples of often-used names and some clues about the people behind them:

Prometheus, Wotan, Zeus, Jupiter, and other names from the Bible, the Iliad, the Odyssey, the Book of the Dead, and so on: my cat is more than what you see; he is a reincarnation, a deity, a mythical being.

Socrates, Voltaire, Melville, Shakespeare, Proust, and other names of great authors, thinkers, and philosophers: this is the cat of an educated person who studied freshman literature and took two philosophy courses in college, among other things.

Henry, Patterson, Lucy, Albert, Junior, Baby, Sweety, Pumpkin, Licorice, Daisy, and other common first names: this is my cat, but I also consider him my child. I would send him to college if I could.

Fritz, Felix, Krazy Kat, Pussycat Princess, Chessie, Figaro, Heathcliff, and other names of famous cats in comics, movies, television, and so on: this is my pet, and I'm damn proud of him (a healthy attitude).

Catastrophe, Biafra, Chicken, Fido, Polyester, and other contemptuous names (such as all dog names): he's my cat, and I can name him anything I want; he'll never know the difference anyway (a not-so-healthy attitude).

After years of feeding, grooming, nursing, petting, cuddling, and loving your cat, the Nagging Question still remains: Does he recognize you? Some cat lovers are convinced that their animal knows them, that the cat waits for *them* every day, loves *them* exclusively, and would not fail to pick

William Thompson Bartoll, *Girl and Cat*

By holding her cat tightly, this mid-nineteenth-century girl contained her high spirits and impatience. In this way, the artist was able to portray her, like so many other youngsters who had their pictures painted, for the pleasure of her parents as well as for posterity. *Abby Aldrich Rockefeller Folk Art Center, Williamsburg, Virginia.*

Charles Sheeler,
Feline Felicity

American artist Charles Sheeler (1883–1965) created this beautiful, detailed study in black conté crayon of a striped cat asleep on a Shaker-style chair with a cane seat. *Fogg Art Museum, Harvard University, Louise E. Bettens Fund.*

them out on a crowded beach a hundred miles away if the need arose. Others take a more cynical view. Cats can't tell people apart, they insist; cats are either friendly to *all* people or none. Don't feel flattered if a cat settles comfortably in your lap, they warn; he is only thinking of himself. Furthermore, that purr you hear is not for you, it is a selfish rumbling of self-satisfaction that's meant to be shared with no human.

I've searched everywhere for the answer to the Nagging Question. I've interviewed veterinarians, animal psychologists, zoologists, animal fanatics, and bloodthirsty vivisectionists. I've consulted books, pamphlets, microfilm, microfiche, and even hieroglyphics. I've finally found the answer, and I have the Rare Manuscript Division of the New York Public Library to thank for it.

It happened one afternoon about ten minutes before closing time. I had looked up from a large medieval book on the history of the Black Plague to find an ancient librarian trying to get my attention. He was a small, serene-looking, grayish man. He wore a dark gray suit, a gray sweater with buttons down the front, and a gray tie. He had noticed me examining manuscript after manuscript in the past few weeks, he said, and had come to sense my growing frustration and therefore offered to help. I explained that the object of my research was cats and, more specifically, the Nagging Question, which I described to him while pointing out that I had come nowhere close to an answer.

He turned out to be a cat fancier himself, professing that he had enjoyed the company of no less than a hundred cats in his own lifetime. He vowed to help and soon disappeared behind a set of ancient wood cabinets. He returned with a rumpled manila folder, which he placed on the lectern in front of me. It was a dusty, worn, faded folder that did not bear the customary library file numbers or even a typewritten label. Only a pencilled inscription gave any kind of clue at all: the folder contained, it seemed, an unpublished manuscript by one Professor Antoine Barbizon of the French Academy entitled "Do Cats Recognize People" and the date, 1941. I could judge by the thickness of the manuscript, some 900 pages on onionskin paper, that Professor Barbizon had done a lifetime of research on the subject and that the manuscript had never found its way into book form probably because of its completion during the war year 1941, when paper was scarce and only government publications and patriotic novels such as *Les Aventures de Jean et Fritz* were published.

The more I leafed through the manuscript, the more I felt I was only a few minutes away from finding out the answer to the Nagging Question. Time was running out, however, and the folder would soon have to go back to its place in the wooden cabinets, so I reverted to my old college system of term-paper research and turned to the last page of the manuscript. I knew that a scholar of the stature of Professor Barbizon would not have completed a mammoth study of this kind without including a conclusion.

Herein, then, and in Professor Barbizon's own words, is the last paragraph of his work, the answer to the Nagging Question, the final word, showing once and for all that cats *do* recognize you:

> . . . Therefore I must conclude that when it comes to recognizing the individuals who keep them, cats have learned to behave just like the humans they've been kept by for five millenia: they recognize you all right, but what is misleading is that they sometimes pretend not to; so they'll go about their business hoping that you'll assume that they are too busy to notice you. As to the other great Nagging Question, Do cats miss us when we're gone? the answer is similar: they do. But just like humans, they prefer to call instead of writing letters. It is unfortunate that no one ever thinks of leaving their forwarding phone number with their cat.

PART ONE

THE TIGER IN THE HOUSE

ats and people have lived together for something less than fifty centuries. That's not very long, as such relationships are measured. Dogs have been a part of human culture for at least twice as long. In man's stable of domesticated animals, cats are the most recent arrivals, the newest family on the block. It should come as no surprise, then, that humans and felines behave somewhat tentatively toward each other: cats and people are still just getting acquainted.

As virtually any cat owner will affirm, one generally gets to know a cat only on the cat's terms. The famous feline independence is an effective bar to the sort of slobbery chumminess that dog owners enjoy with their pets. Cats are aloof and self-sufficient; they just don't seem to need people in quite the same way dogs do, nor in quite the same way that people need them.

This, indeed, is one of the main reasons we find cats so fascinating: they seem to act the way we wish *we* could act. Who doesn't envy the cat's ability to sit calmly, casually washing himself one leg at a time, while all hell breaks loose around him? What woman doesn't envy the cat's unstudied elegance? What athlete doesn't yearn for the fluid grace of a cat at full gallop? What young boy doesn't envy the tomcat's defiant swagger? Cats remind us of our better selves, the cool, collected, confident and coordinated people who exist mostly in our imaginations. As Carl Van Vechten once wrote, "There is, indeed, no single quality of the cat that man could not emulate to his advantage."

But the cat's independence has a dark side, too. His aloofness usually strikes us as something to be envied, but it can also seem like a challenge, a threat. Over the five thousand years of our shared existence, man has lapsed into periods of great cruelty toward cats. Although felines have more than once been worshiped as gods on earth, they have also been brutally persecuted by institutions as mighty as the Catholic Church. We fear cats because we can't quite seem to understand them and because they sometimes make us wonder if they don't understand us all too well.

Pierre August Renoir,
Woman with a Cat

French Impressionist painter Pierre Auguste Renoir's (1840–1919) fascination with surface, light, and texture is evident in *Woman with a Cat*. Renoir handles the cat's coat as well as the cloth behind it as a collection of fleeting impressions of color and light.
National Gallery of Art, Gift of Mr. and Mrs. Benjamin Levy.

How It All Began

preceding overleaf:
Harry Warnecke, *Cat Crossing the Street in Traffic*

On a warm summer afternoon in 1925, a mother cat decided to carry her kittens across New York's busy Centre Street. When Harry Warnecke, a New York *News* photographer arrived, the cat and her kittens had already reached their home. Not wanting to miss such a wonderful shot, Warnecke convinced a cooperative policeman to hold up traffic while he restaged the scene. After two attempts, he got this result.
New York Daily News *Photo.*

Gefferson Gaunnut, *Two Children,* American, 1843

Museum of Fine Arts, Boston.

Cats awaken emotions—both good and bad—very near the core of us. They prompt us to think and act in new and sometimes unsettling ways. And that, of course, is why they make such interesting companions.

No one is really certain how or why cats first came to live with men, but the subject has produced some fascinating speculation over the years. One of the most intriguing examples is a story written eighty years ago by Rudyard Kipling. Called "The Cat that Walked by Himself," Kipling's story is a modern-day semimythic explanation for the cat's unique position in human society. Kipling explores the cat's fiercely independent character by tracing it back to its earliest beginnings at the dawn of civilization. (For an excerpt from "The Cat that Walked by Himself," see page 152.)

The Cat in Kipling's story is the last of the wild animals (the others are the Dog, the Horse, and the Cow) to give up the ways of the Wild Wet Woods and agree to serve Man, the new king of beasts, in exchange for his protection. After the other animals have all settled into their new lives, the Cat arrives at the mouth of the humans' cave and says, "I am not a friend, and I am not a servant. I am the Cat who walks by himself, and I wish to come into your Cave."

The Cat is eventually admitted to human society, but the terms of his initiation are stricter than those of any other animal. As a consequence, the Cat comes to occupy a sort of halfway position between the wild and civilization. "He will kill mice," as Kipling concluded, "and he will be kind to Babies when he is in the house, just as long as they do not pull his tail too hard. But when he has done that, and between times, and when the moon gets up and night comes, he is the Cat that walks by himself, and all places are alike to him. Then he goes out into the Wet Wild Woods or up the Wet Wild Trees or on the Wet Wild Roofs, waving his wild tail and walking by his wild lone."

Kipling's story may be a good approximation of what actually happened back in the earliest days of the man/cat alliance. The wild cats of Egypt, who provided the breeding stock for the first domesticated felines, were solitary predators who had little communal life. Like the lions and tigers we are familiar with today, these protocats hunted to satisfy their own hunger and relied on individual skills and cunning to overpower their prey. Unlike dogs, who in the wild formed quite elaborate social structures to govern everything from hunting to the raising and educating of the young, wild cats were essentially loners. It is thus only natural that, after entering human society, cats should retain some of

M·S·T·2

Brigitte Bardot

French *charmeuse*, actress
and future animal activist
socializes with a cat on the set
of one of her earlier pictures,
Mademoiselle Striptease.
Culver Pictures

Artist Unknown, *Henry Wriothesely, Third Earl of Southampton, in the Tower of London*

Henry Wriothesely, the third Earl of Southampton (1573–1624), is best remembered as William Shakespeare's patron, but he was also a colorful and influential political figure. He accompanied the second Earl of Essex, Queen Elizabeth I's right-hand man, on his expeditions to Cadiz and the Azores, and he later collaborated in a plot, staged by Essex, to depose the Queen's councils. For his part in this intrigue, Southampton was sentenced to death and held in the Tower of London, where this portrait was painted, until Elizabeth's death. Released by King James I, Elizabeth's successor, in 1603, he went on to equip John Smith's expedition to the New World settlement at Jamestown.
The Granger Collection.

J. B. Greuze,
The Woolwinder

The Woolwinder (1759) seems to reflect the glorification of peasant life that was common to the mid-eighteenth century as well as the movement away from rococo representations of aristocracy. Here, an idealized girl stares off into space, ignoring the kitten who toys with her wool.
Copyright © The Frick Collection, New York.

their most elemental characteristics. Indeed, most of the feline qualities we value can be traced to behavior that was important to survival in the wild.

Still, the modern house cat is only a very, very distant descendant of his untamed forebears. Man and evolution have combined to bend the cat's nature to man's will. The elements of wildness that endure in the house cat's nature are elements that have proved themselves useful to human beings. The cat's predatory instincts remain sharp because the cat's principal role in human society over the centuries has been as an exterminator of pests. We have molded the cat's heritage and made him our own.

Making Friends

The cat's original role in human society may have been partly as a companion. In "The Cat that Walked by Himself," Kipling's protagonist originally proves his worthiness to the Woman by playing peacefully with her baby, and we can probably assume that something similar happened in Egypt thousands of years ago. By being inquisitive, quick on their feet, and nearly indestructible, cats have all the qualities necessary to good baby-sitters. "The cat is the nurse's favorite," as Champfleury wrote, "and the baby's earliest friend." Despite their deadly skill as hunters, cats are patient playmates who tolerate pokes, tail pulls, and strangleholds from children too young to know better. Cat fancier Helen M. Winslow wrote at the turn of the century about a placid kitten who allowed his young mistress to wash him in the bathtub and carry him by the ears. A college professor once told a story of his even-tempered mother cat who allowed his two-year-old daughter to suckle along with her litter of newborn kittens.

Of course, cats are popular with grown-ups, too—and with no grown-ups more than with writers. Cats and literature have always had something of an intimate relationship, for reasons that seem to have to do with the very nature of the art. Carl Van Vechten once said that "the cat is as nearly as possible what many a writer would like to be himself." Since cats are independent, punctual, even-tempered, and clean, it's easy to believe that Van Vechten may have been right. Aldous Huxley was even more direct. When asked for advice by a young man who said he hoped to enter the profession, Huxley said, "If you want to write, keep cats."

Dozens of important writers over the centuries have lived as though they were in complete agreement with Huxley's advice. Henry James is said to have enjoyed writing with a cat perched on his shoulder. Ernest Hemingway kept as many as thirty cats in his house and even converted the ground floor of a tower

William Coupon, *Aborigine and Cat*

Photographed during a mourning ceremony at the Daly River Aboriginal Reserve in Australia, an aborigine with an ochred face poses with an unidentified local cat.
Copyright © William Coupon.

Morris Hirshfield, *Nude on Sofa with Three Pussies*

Many characteristics of nineteenth-century folk art, such as aerial perspective, attention to detail, and an unconventional personal vision, are kept alive by twentieth-century primitive painters. In this painting by naïve artist Morris Hirshfield, a reclining nude enjoys the company of three white kittens, who play with the sprig of flowers she dangles from her hand.

The Regis Collection, Minneapolis, Mn.

Janet Nelson, *Man with Cat*

For centuries cats have provided companionship and solitude.

Copyright © Janet Nelson.

Jeanette MacDonald

The soprano, best known for her movie partnership with Nelson Eddy, poses with a Maurice Chevalier look-alike.

Culver Pictures

he owned into a sanctuary for them. He also allowed his special favorites to eat at the table with him. Charles Dickens's cat Williamina (originally called William, but renamed after giving birth to kittens) used to sprawl on Dickens's writing table and bat out his candle with her paw, hoping to persuade her master to put down his pen and play.

The great French essayist Montaigne believed strongly that cats led secret lives and once asserted that "cats undoubtedly talk and reason among themselves." The fourteenth-century Italian poet Petrarch was so devoted to his cat that when the poet died, the cat was killed, mummified, and buried with him. Dr. Johnson used to trudge out into the alleys of London to buy oysters for his Hodge. Mark Twain adored cats and wrote about them again and again.

Cell Mates

When poet Christopher Smart was confined to a London madhouse in the eighteenth century, his only companion was Jeoffry, his cat. Smart wrote about Jeoffry in a long poem called "Jubilate Agno" ("Rejoice in the Lamb"), part of which is reproduced here.

For I will consider my Cat Jeoffry.
For he is the servant of the Living God duly and daily serving him.
For at first glance of the glory of God in the East he worships in his way.
For is this done by wreathing his body seven times round with elegant quickness.
For then he leaps up to catch the musk, which is the blessing of God upon his prayer.
For he rolls upon prank to work it in.
For having done duty and received blessing he begins to consider himself.
For this he performs in ten degrees.
For first he looks upon his fore-paws to see if they are clean.
For secondly he kicks up behind to clear away there.
For thirdly he works it upon stretch with the fore-paws extended.
For fourthly he sharpens his paws by wood.
For fifthly he washes himself.
For sixthly he rolls upon wash.
For seventhly he fleas himself, that he may not be interrupted upon the beat.
For eighthly he rubs himself against a post.
For ninthly he looks up for his instructions.
For tenthly he goes in quest of food.
For having consider'd God and himself he will consider his neighbor.
For if he meets another cat he will kiss her in kindness.
For when he takes his prey he plays with it to give it a chance.
For one mouse in seven escapes by his dallying.
For when his day's work is done his business more properly begins.
For he keeps the Lord's watch in the night against the adversary.
For he counteracts the powers of darkness by his electrical skin & glaring eyes.
For he counteracts the Devil, who is death, by brisking about the life.
For in his morning orisons he loves the sun and the sun loves him.
For he is of the tribe of Tiger.

Cecilia Beaux, *Man with a Cat (Henry Sturgis Drinker)*

Cecilia Beaux (1863–1942) was one of the foremost American woman painters of the late nineteenth and early twentieth centuries. Broad, lively, expressionistic brush strokes characterize her portrait of Henry Sturgis Drinker and his sleeping orange cat.
National Museum of Fine Arts, the Smithsonian Institution. Bequest of Henry Ward Ranger, through the National Gallery of Design.

Calvin Coolidge and Timmie

President Calvin Coolidge is pictured here with Timmie, the pet cat of Bascom Timmons, a Washington journalist during the 1920s. Timmie was in love with the president's canary. The feeling was probably not mutual.
Culver Pictures.

Theodore Roosevelt and Slippers

Slippers, a cat with extra toes, or polydactylism, was the White House feline during Teddy Roosevelt's administration. At press conferences and official functions, Slippers was often the center of attention.

Colette, who may well be the greatest cat lover that literature (or the world, for that matter, has ever known) filled her books and stories with memorable felines. She also filled her house with them and gave them wonderful names: Mini-mini, Kro, Kapok, Muscat, La Touteu, Petiteu, Pinichette, Minionne, Toune, La Chatte, One and Only, and La Chatte Dernière. When La Chatte Dernière died in 1939, Collete was so brokenhearted she vowed never to replace her, and she remained catless for the last fifteen years of her life.

Cats have been popular with other great figures as well. Sir Isaac Newton loved cats and owned a barn that was ruled by two of them. He is also said to have invented the cat door, that great triumph of engineering which allows cats to come and go as they please. Louis Pasteur, Albert Einstein, and Albert Schweitzer were also devoted to felines, finding in them a pleasant antidote to the pressures and frustrations of their work.

America's presidents have shared the White House with cats a number of times over the course of our 200-year history. Tad Lincoln had a pet named Tabby. Theodore Roosevelt looked after two cats, a six-toed gray cat named Slippers and a rambunctious kitten named Tom Quartz. Calvin Coolidge didn't have a cat, but he did have a canary that fell in love with one; the president's songbird, named Caruso, became so enamored of a reporter's kitten, named Timmie, that Coolidge had no choice but to make a gift of his pet to the reporter. In the Kennedy White House, young Caroline and John-John looked after Tom Kitten, a favored cat who merited an obituary in a Washington-area paper when he died: "Unlike many humans in the same position," the paper eulogized, "he never wrote his memoirs of his days in the White House and never discussed them for quotation, though he was privy to many official secrets."

White House Cat

On January 6, 1903, President Theodore Roosevelt took time out from his White House duties to write a letter to his son Kermit describing the hijinks of the boy's kitten, Tom Quartz.

Dear Kermit,

We felt very melancholy after you and Ted left and the house seemed empty and lonely. But it was the greatest possible comfort to feel that you both really have enjoyed school and are both doing well.

Tom Quartz is certainly the cunningest kitten I have ever seen. He is always playing pranks on Jack and I get very nervous lest Jack should grow too irritated. The other evening they were both in the library—Jack sleeping before the fire—Tom Quartz scampering about, an exceedingly playful little creature—which is about what he is. He would race across the floor, then jump upon the curtain or play with the tassel. Suddenly he spied Jack and galloped up to him. Jack, looking exceedingly sullen and shame-faced, jumped out of the way and got upon the sofa and around the table, and Tom Quartz instantly jumped upon him again. Jack suddenly shifted to the other sofa, where Tom Quartz again went after him. Then Jack started for the door, while Tom made a rapid turn under the sofa and around the table and just as Jack reached the door leaped on his hindquarters. Jack bounded forward and away and the two went tandem out of the room—Jack not co-operating at all; and about five minutes afterwards Tom Quartz stalked solemnly back.

England's Queen Victoria kept a cat named White Heather at Buckingham Palace; when the queen died, White Heather was taken up by her successor, King Edward VII, at least temporarily guaranteeing the future of the line. Frederick the Great, King Louis XV, and Pope Leo XII all loved cats. The pope's favorite was a small, grayish red animal with black stripes, whose name was Micetto. Pope Leo kept Micetto snuggled in his robes when he gave audiences to the supplicants who made pilgrimages to the Vatican. When the pope died, Micetto was adopted by the French ambassador, Chateaubriand, who did his best to make the kitten feel at home in more modest surroundings. "I am trying," Chateaubriand wrote, "to make it forget exile, the Sistine Chapel, the sun on Michelangelo's cupola, where it used to walk, far above the earth."

Chateaubriand's countryman, the Cardinal Richelieu, was obsessed with cats and used to allow a dozen or so of his favorites to play on his bed before he retired in the evening. "He had one of his chambers fitted up as a cattery," one historian wrote, "which was entrusted to overseers. . . . Abel and Tessandier came, morning and evening, to feed the cats with pâtés fashioned of the white meat of chicken." Richelieu provided generously for his pets in his will, but others didn't share his enthusiasm for the animals, and shortly after his death his cats were burned.

A Cat of Quality

Most cat owners ascribe human qualities and emotions to their pets, a weakness to which English philosopher Jeremy Bentham (1748–1832) was not immune. Bentham, one of the chief expounders of utilitarianism, seemed to have little patience with cats that did not live up to his standrds of utility. Bentham's friend John Bowring once described the philosopher's relationship with a favorite pet.

Bentham was very fond of animals, particularly "pussies", as he called them, when they had domestic virtues, but he had no particular affection for the common race of cats. He had one, however, of which he used to boast that he had "made a man of him", and whom he was wont to invite to eat macaroni at his own table. This puss got knighted, and rejoiced in the name of Sir John Langbourne. In his early days he was a frisky, inconsiderate, and, to say the truth, somewhat profligate gentleman; and had, according to the report of his patron, the habit of seducing light and giddy young ladies, of his own race, into the garden of Queen's Square Place: but tired at last, like Solomon, of pleasures and vanities, he became sedate and thoughtful—took to the church, laid down his knightly title, and was installed as the Reverend John Langbourne. He gradually obtained a great reputation for sanctity and learning, and a Doctor's degree was conferred upon him. When I knew him, in his declining days, he bore no other name than the Reverend Doctor John Langbourne: and he was alike conspicuous for his gravity and philosophy. Great respect was invariably shown his reverence: and it was supposed that he was not far off from a mitre, when old age interfered with his hopes and honours. He departed amidst the regrets of his many friends, and was gathered to his fathers, and to eternal rest, in a cemetery in Milton's garden.

John Sloan, *Sunbathers on a Roof*

This etching, commissioned by the College Society of Print Collectors, was executed by John Sloan in 1941. After twenty summers in Santa Fe, New Mexico, Sloan created this plate from his memories of sweltering summers in New York City. This languid couple, basking on one of New York's "tar beaches," is accompanied by an equally lethargic black cat.
Reprinted from the collections of the Library of Congress.

Despite the ingratitude they sometimes receive at the hands of ignorant humans, cats seem to enjoy and even prosper in relationships with their two-legged companions. Although they are not so slavishly affectionate as dogs, cats still develop strong attachments to people. Cats have been known to rescue families from burning houses (by awakening them as the smoke began to fill the rooms) and to notify their masters that dangers of one sort or another (rain-storms, tornadoes) were approaching. Other cats become deeply devoted to individuals after being treated kindly by them. An old sea captain named George H. Grant once told the story of a cat that he had saved from a sinking ship. The cat was so grateful that it refused to leave Grant's shoulder for several days. Another sailor had a similar experience: after he had removed a fishhook from the lip of a cat, the cat brought him a freshly caught fish every day for many months.

Scientific studies have shown that cats are actually good for their human masters: people who care for pets live longer and have fewer heart attacks than people who don't, and their pets live longer, too. Stroking a cat relieves stress in both the stroker and the cat, making both of them healthier. Caring for a cat can also provide a core of stability to a household, an opportunity for its human occupants to focus their attention on something besides themselves. Cats have proven themselves especially beneficial as companions for the elderly. Because of the relative simplicity of their needs, cats can be cared for even by the infirm. Nursing homes have discovered that the morale and even the health of their residents improve when pet-care programs are introduced. Cats and people are good for each other.

Feline Affection

An anonymous writer in the scientific journal Nature *describes a remarkable example of a cat's affection for her master.*

In 1887, I was absent from Madras two months, and left in my quarters three cats, one of which, an English tabby, was a very gentle, affectionate creature. During my absence the quarters were occupied by two young gentlemen who delighted in teasing and frightening the cats. About a week before my return, the English cat had kittens, which she carefully concealed behind book-shelves in the library. On the morning of my return I saw the cat and patted her as usual, and then left the house for about an hour. On returning, I found that the kittens were located in the corner of my dressing-room, where previous broods had been deposited and nursed. On questioning the servant as to how they came there, he at once replied, "Sir, the old cat, taking one by one in her mouth, brought them here." In other words, the mother had carried them one by one in her mouth from the library to the dressing room, where they lay quite exposed. I do not think I have heard of a more remarkable instance of reasoning and affectionate confidence in an animal, and I need hardly say that the latter manifestation gave me great pleasure. The train of reasoning seems to have been as follows, "Now that my master has returned, there is no risk of the kittens being injured by the two young savages in the house, so I will take them out for my protector to see and admire, and keep them in the corner in which all my former pets have been nursed in safety."

Philippe Halsman,
Wanda Landowska at the
Harpsichord, 1944

The cat seated on top of this harpsichord listens to the music with the same intense concentration as Wanda Landowska, the musician.
Copyright © Philippe Halsman.

Colette

French writer Colette (1873–1954) said, "Our perfect companions never have fewer than four feet." Colette portrayed her quadrupedal friends in a particularly loving way. In fact, she was so devoted to her cats, both real and fictional, that when La Chatte Dernière died in 1939, Colette refused to replace it out of respect. *Archives Nationaux, Paris.*

Raymond Chandler

Raymond Chandler (1888–1949), the creator of one of America's favorite "hard-boiled" detectives, Philip Marlowe, was also a cat owner. Although cats do not play a significant part in Chandler's mysteries, cats did share his life.
©John Engstead.

Ernest Hemingway

Wherever he went in his varied and adventurous life, the great American writer Ernest Hemingway (1898–1961) loved to be surrounded by cats. In fact, he owned forty of them! Although he was always in search of a new experience, Hemingway constantly sought out feline companionship.
©Peter Buckley.

Pablo Picasso

Unlike many artists, Picasso (1881–1973) was not a solitary individual. According to the diaries of Fernande Olivier, Picasso's mistress during the early part of his career, the artist owned two cats, one dog, and a monkey.
Archives Nationaux, Paris.

Charlie Chaplin

One of America's greatest comic artists uses a twig to hold kitty's attention.
Culver Pictures

Drawing by Mark Twain

Mark Twain and His Cats

Mark Twain or Samuel Langhorne Clemens (1835–1910), surely one of America's greatest writers, was an absolutely devoted lover of cats. Indeed, cats permeated his work and his life. Among his fictional felines were Tom Quartz, from the novel *Roughing It*, a cat who distinctly preferred gold mining to the more mundane pursuit of rat catching, and Catasauqua from *Letters from the Earth*, a Manx who wanted no surname because it was an ostentation for a tailless cat to have one. Here, Twain is pictured with just a few of his many cats. *Mark Twain Memorial, Hartford, Ct.*

At the Zoo

Mark Twain loved cats and wrote about them often. In The Innocents Abroad, *he describes an extraordinary feline he discovered while traveling in France. Twain's diminutive cat had defied the natural order by setting up housekeeping with the biggest beast of all.*

In the great Zoological Gardens [of Marseille] we found specimens of all the animals the world produces, I think. . . . The boon companion of the colossal elephant was a common cat! This cat had a fashion of climbing up the elephant's hind legs, and roosting on his back. She would sit up there, with her paws curved under her breast, and sleep in the sun half the afternoon. It used to annoy the elephant at first and he would reach up and take her down, but she would go aft and climb up again. She persisted until she finally conquered the elephant's prejudices, and now they are inseparable friends. The cat plays about her comrade's forefeet or his trunk often, until dogs approach, and then she goes aloft out of danger. The elephant has annihilated several dogs lately, that pressed his companion too closely.

Thomas Eakins, *Amelia C. Van Buren and Cat*

Dissatisfied with what his own eye could see, American realist painter Thomas Eakins became a photographer and enlisted the camera to aid him in his quest for accuracy. These photographs of Amelia C. Van Buren and a cat, taken in 1891, were studies for a portrait Eakins executed later that year.
Philadelphia Museum of Art, Philadelphia, Pa.

Thomas Eakins, *Self-Portrait*

The Metropolitan Museum of Art, David H. McAlpin Fund, 1943.

Cats are sometimes said to be fair-weather friends—affectionate enough under comfortable circumstances but quick to disappear when the going gets rough—but there is plenty of persuasive evidence to the contrary. Anne Frank's wretched exile was made more endurable by the abiding presence of two cats, one of them her beloved Mouschi. The English poet Christopher Smart, who was imprisoned in a London madhouse from 1759 to 1763, had no other companion for those years than his cat Jeoffry, whom he immortalized in a poem called "Jubilate Agno." When the Earl of Southampton was locked up in the Tower of London, following the so-called Great Protestation of 1621, he was often visited by his favorite cat, who somehow managed to find its way into its master's cell by climbing down the chimney.

Other cats have made even more remarkable efforts to reunite themselves with human companions from whom they have been separated, whether by accident or not. A New York veterinarian, who was forced to abandon his cat before moving to California, discovered the same cat on his doorstep five months later. The cat had apparently made a trip of several thousand miles. The vet had no doubt that it was the same cat, because it had an easily identifiable lump on its spine as the result of an injury suffered several years before. Another cat, named Pooh, tramped the 200 miles between Newton, Georgia, and Spartanburg, South Carolina, to rejoin its family, which had moved away. When I was a child, a cat of ours returned to our door two weeks after jumping from my mother's car in a parking lot a few miles away.

Friends in Hiding

When Anne Frank and her family were in hiding from the Nazis during World War II, Anne's cat Mouschi was both a companion and, occasionally, a nuisance. The following passage is excerpted from the diary Anne kept during the period, published two years after her death as The Diary of a Young Girl.

Wednesday, 10 May, 1944

We were sitting in the attic doing some French yesterday afternoon when I suddenly heard water pattering down behind me. I asked Peter what it could be, but he didn't even reply, simply tore up to the loft, where the source of the disaster was, and pushed Mouschi, who, because of the wet earth box, had sat down beside it, harshly back to the right place. A great din and disturbance followed, and Mouschi, who had finished by that time, dashed downstairs.

Mouschi, seeking the convenience of something similar to his box, had chosen some wood shavings. The pool had trickled down from the loft into the attic immediately and, unfortunately, landed just beside and in the barrel of potatoes. The ceiling was dripping, and as the attic floor is not free from holes either, several yellow drips came through the ceiling into the dining room between a pile of stockings and some books, which were lying on the table. I was doubled up with laughter, it really was a scream. There was Mouschi crouching under a chair, Peter with water, bleaching powder, and floor cloth, and Van Daan trying to soothe everyone. The calamity was soon over, but it's a well-known fact that cats' puddles positively stink. The potatoes proved this only too clearly and also the wood shavings, that Daddy collected in a bucket to be burned. Poor Mouschi! How were you to know that peat is unobtainable?

Fernando Botero, *The Cat*

Contemporary Colombian artist Fernando Botero is known for the large, fleshy figures in his paintings, who are often accompanied by equally inflated pets like this cat.

Courtesy of Mr. Julio Mario Santo Domingo III.

Tsugouharu Foujita

Tsugouharu Foujita gained an international reputation for combining Japanese brushwork and linear images with elements of Western art. Born in Japan, Foujita lived most of his adult life in France. He was noted, particularly, for his paintings of cats.

this page:
Nude
Musée Royal des Beaux Arts de Belgique, Brusssels.

overleaf:
Reclining Nude with Cat
Petit Palais Musée, Geneva, Switzerland.

following overleaf:
Mrs. E. C. Chadbourne
Collection of the Art Institute of Chicago.

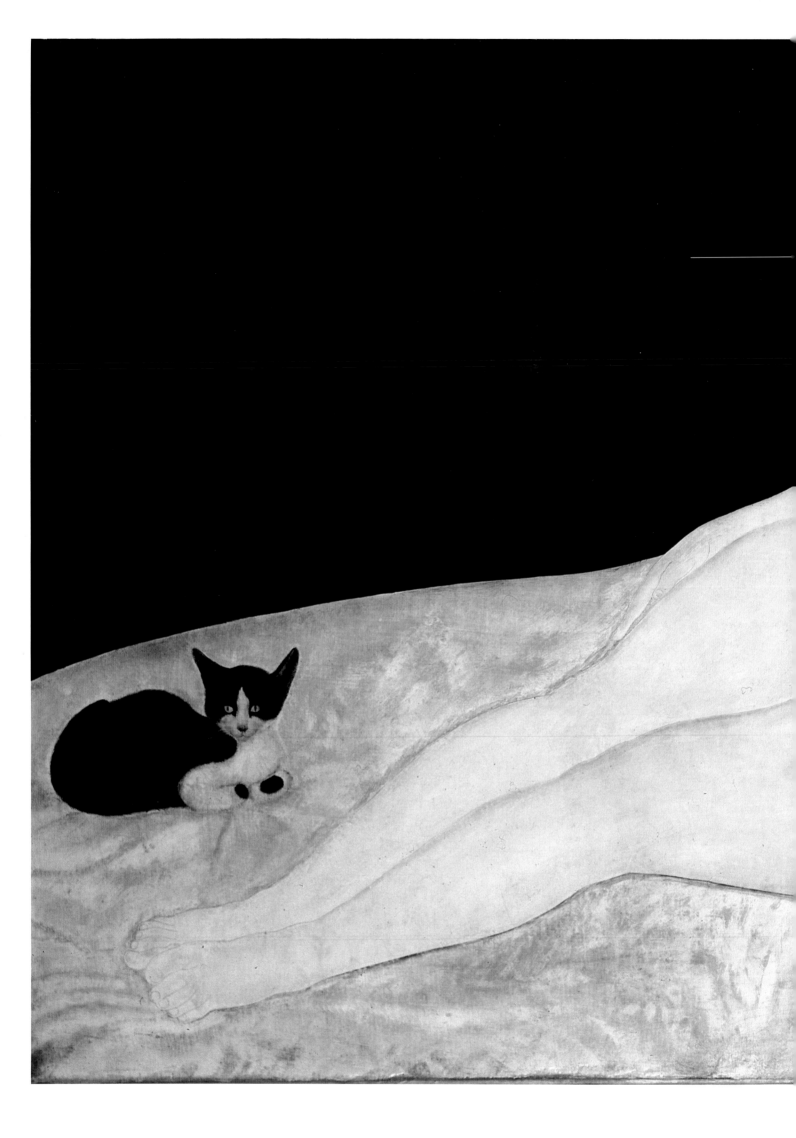

A cat's devotion to its owner can even extend beyond the grave. In France, a cat named Fripon followed its mistress's coffin to the grave and then returned every Sunday—at first with its master and later alone—to pay respects. In certain parts of Europe, it was once customary for cats to be decked in black mourning ribbons when a human member of the houschold died.

Of course, relationships between cats and people aren't always so solemn. "My cat has taken to mulled port and rum punch," a gregarious owner once wrote. "Poor old dear! he is all the better for it." Cats don't have weaknesses for many human bad habits, but every now and then they do slip from the straight and narrow path of feline propriety. Colette's Kiki-la-Doucette "knew the difference between tap water and mineral water and ate peas one by one." Cats have also been known to become impossibly vain, staring at their own reflections for hours on end. Cats are even said to have a tendency to get "stuck" in mirrors: they become so fascinated by looking at themselves that they can't seem to tear themselves away.

Cats can also be acutely sensitive to human emotions. When cat owners marry, they sometimes find their pets acting like jealous children. *Time* magazine reported the case of one cat who regularly urinated on the side of the bed where his mistress's new husband slept. Other cats use newcomers' chairs or clothes as litter boxes, or spend days sulking in darkened corners. Sometimes their behavior becomes so upsetting that their owners feel compelled to seek professional advice: there are about a dozen cat psychiatrists in this country, some of whom charge fees as high as fifty dollars an hour. Other owners take matters into their own hands with varying degrees of success. A friend of mine once tried to cure his Siamese of stealing a new puppy's toys by giving the cat some catnip whenever it tried to make off with something that belonged to the puppy. My friend had been hoping that the cat would prefer the catnip to the toys and so leave the toys alone; but, of course, the cat came to associate his therapy with a catnip reward and made more trouble than ever before.

Dr. Johnson's Cat

Samuel Johnson loved cats, although his biographer, James Boswell, was apparently allergic to them. Here Boswell describes Dr. Johnson's affection for his pet, Hodge.

I never shall forget the indulgence with which he treated Hodge, his cat; for whom he himself used to go out and buy oysters, lest the servants having that trouble should take a dislike to the poor creature. I am, unluckily, one of those who have an antipathy to a cat, so that I am uneasy when in the room with one; and I own, I frequently suffered a good deal from the presence of the same Hodge. I recollect him one day scrambling up Dr. Johnson's breast, apparently with much satisfaction, while my friend, smiling and half-whistling, rubbed down his back, and pulled him by the tail; and when I observed he was a fine cat, saying, 'Why, yes, Sir, but I have had cats whom I liked better than this;' and then, as if perceiving Hodge to be out of countenance, adding, 'but he is a very fine cat, a very fine cat indeed.'

William Morris Hunt,
Girl with Cat

A follower of the Barbizon School, American-born artist William Morris Hunt (1824–1879) studied painting and sculpture in Europe for a number of years before returning to work in New England. The play of light and dark, or chiaroscuro, which defines the forms in this painting, gives them a sculpturesque yet ethereal quality.
Museum of Fine Arts, Boston.

above left:
Anonymous, *Girl with
a Grey Cat,* American,
ca. 1840

Museum of Fine Arts, Boston.

above right:
**Attributed to Beardsley
Limner,** *Child Posing with
Cat,* American, ca. 1790

*Abby Aldrich Rockefeller Folk
Art Center, Williamsburg, Va.*

right:
Joseph Whiting Stock,
Mary Jane Smith,
American, 1838

*Abby Aldrich Rockefeller Folk
Art Center, Williamsburg, Va.*

left:

**Attributed to Samuel
Miller,** *Girl in a
Green Dress,* American,
ca. 1845

*N.Y. State Historical Association,
Cooperstown, N.Y.*

Pierre Auguste Renoir,
Le Jeune Garçon au Chat

Cats, with their flighty and often unpredictable personalities, made excellent subjects and models for the French impressionists, who were fascinated by the interaction of light and color and the fleeting impressions they create. In this way, Renoir's *Le Jeune Garçon au Chat* embodies the very soul of impressionism.
Courtesy Christie's, London, with the kind assistance of Mr. John Lumley, Private Collection.

Pierre Bonnard,
Children and Cat

Small areas of strong color define the forms in French modernist Pierre Bonnard's (1867–1947) work. *Children and Cat* evokes a feeling of childhood innocence.
The Phillips Collection, Washington, D.C.

Théophile Steinlen,
La Fillette au Chat

*Petit Palais Musée, Geneva,
Switzerland.*

Thomas Hart Benton,
Jessie, One Year Old, 1940

*Collection Jessie Benton Lyman,
Los Angeles, California.*

Cat and dog owners often argue with one another about the comparative intelligence of their pets. Cats, the dog owners say, prove the inferiority of their intellectual gifts when they fail to respond to human commands. Dogs, the cat owners counter, are not so much intelligent as slavish, dumbly complying with such demeaning orders as "heel," "go fetch," "roll over," "play dead," and so on.

Of course, these arguments are foolish. Scientists say that the intellects of dogs and cats, though different, are approximately equal. The differences arise not from discrepancies in IQ, but from the fact that dogs and cats have very different backgrounds, when you consider evolution. While Fido's primitive ancestors hunted in packs and developed an elaborate communal life, Tabby's forebears primarily hunted alone and were strong enough individually not to require the security and stability of an extended social group. As a consequence, Fido adapts easily to the give and take of life in a human pack, while Tabby is constantly testing the limits of her bondage and asserting her jungle-bred independence at every opportunity. "A dog," one proverb says, "will remember a three days' kindness three years, while a cat will forget a three years' kindness in three days." This saying, which has been used by both dog and cat owners to support their claims of intelligence for their pets, probably has at least some basis in fact: it points to the primitive origins of behavior we now take for granted.

When we talk about our pets' intelligence, we are really talking more about ourselves than about them. We are most likely to call intelligent those types of behavior that most resemble what we think of as intelligent behavior in ourselves, or behavior that is flattering to us. This is probably not the best way to judge any animal's intelligence, but the urge to do so is almost irresistible. When a cat proves, by running down into the basement and hiding behind the furnace, that he knows it's time for his weekly calcium pill, it's impossible not to feel a little thrill of pride and admiration. Indeed, cats can be almost breathtakingly ingenious. J. K. Huysmans used to say that his cat greeted him with purrs only if he made it home before eleven o'clock at night; if he arrived any later than that, the cat made her displeasure known by giving him the cold shoulder. Other cats have learned to open doors, turn on water taps, ring doorbells, open cupboards, and lift the tops off cookie jars. Carl Van Vechten once wrote of a cat who warmed himself by plopping down on a heating register and turning on the switch.

Cats also have a reasonably well-developed language that they use both to communicate among themselves and to make their wishes known to their human companions. Champfleury claimed to hear sixty-three separate notes in the feline mewing repertoire. Other resourceful investigators have painstakingly counted out vowels, consonants, and diphthongs, hoping to uncover some underlying structure. Even without descending into linguistic theory, it's possible to learn a great deal about what cats have to say. Every cat owner is familiar with his pet's special cries, shrieks, purrs, and meows, which may signify varying degrees of danger, hunger, happiness, and alarm. I once had a cat who told me he wanted to come in by making a sound outside the door that only the dog could hear. The dog would then make a high-pitched sound that was known in our house as the "kitty bark," which signaled us to open the door and let in the cat.

Not all dogs are quite so considerate when it comes to cats. One dog owner told the story of a pet who was distinctly jealous of a new kitten in the house. One evening, when the kitten was receiving what the dog felt was an inordinate amount of attention, the dog walked over to a catnip mouse bought for the kitten, squatted over it, and urinated.

There are other cat haters who are every bit as adamant, if not nearly so ingenious. Tyrants, for some reason, don't think much of felines. Napoleon was once found half-naked, sweating profusely, and slashing his sword in the direction of a cat concealed behind a curtain in his bedroom. King Henry III of France is said to have fallen unconscious upon seeing a cat. Genghis Khan, Julius Caesar, and Mussolini are all said to have hated cats as well. Perhaps the cat's uncompromising independence is intolerable to men bent on conquering the world. Cats infuriate and even paralyze tyrants because they represent such blatant denials of their will. Cats submit to no one and cannot be conquered, which must surely give tyrants fits.

One needn't be a tyrant, though, not to like cats. Some people have very sound medical reasons for avoiding them. A great many people are allergic: eyes become red and watery, noses run, lungs wheeze, and bodies break out in great itching hives whenever they come into close contact with cats. These people react to feline dander, which is a combination of cat hair, saliva, and flecks of skin, prompting the victim's immunological system to swing into action after sufficient contact. Boswell was apparently allergic. "I am, unluckily, one of those who have an antipathy to a cat," he wrote in his *Life of Johnson*, "so that I am uneasy when in the room with one." Some sufferers are so sensitive that they are uneasy even when they are *out* of the room. Carl Van Vechten quotes a fascinating story, told by a Dr. Mitchell: "My father, the late Professor John K. Mitchell, having placed a small cat in a closet with a saucer of cream,

preceding overleaf:
**Joseph Hilliard Davis
(active 1832–1838),**
*Family Group with Cat,
Child, and Vase*

American folk artists often portrayed whole families, not just individuals or children. Each figure in this family group seems to be pasted onto the decorative background, creating a two-dimensional effect. *Museum of Fine Arts, Boston.*

Kittens Through the Looking Glass

Dinah, Alice's pet cat, makes appearances in both Alice's Adventures in Wonderland *and* Through the Looking-Glass, *by Lewis Carroll. In this excerpt from* Through the Looking Glass, *Dinah cares for her two kittens, Kitty (who is black) and Snowdrop (who is white).*

The way Dinah washed her children's faces was this: first she held the poor thing down by its ears with one paw, and then with the other paw she rubbed its face all over, the wrong way, beginning at the nose: and just now, as I said, she was hard at work on the white kitten, which was lying quite still and trying to purr—no doubt feeling that it was all meant for its good.

But the black kitten had been finished with earlier in the afternoon, and so, while Alice was sitting curled up in a corner of the great armchair, half talking to herself and half asleep, the kitten had been having a grand game of romps with the ball of worsted Alice had been trying to wind up, and had been rolling it up and down till it had all come undone again; and there it was, spread over the hearth-rug, all knots and tangles, with the kitten running after its own tail in the middle.

"Oh, you wicked little thing!" cried Alice, catching up the kitten, and giving it a little kiss to make it understand that it was in disgrace. "Really, Dinah ought to have taught you better manners! You *ought*, Dinah, you know you ought!"

Stereograph, *Fast Friends Passing Through the Gates of Sleepyland*

From the 1850s until about 1920, stereoscopy was all the rage. With a special viewer, the stereoscope, one could look at a pair of photographs printed on a single card, called the stereograph, and see a three-dimensional picture. Each half of a stereograph approximated the image of an object or scene as one eye alone sees it. The stereoscope combined the two halves to simulate human binocular vision, or the ability to perceive one three-dimensional image even though one eye does not see exactly the same thing as the other.

Steroscopy made its first appearance in England in the late 1830s. But it did not gain its incredible popularity until 1851, when it impressed Queen Victoria at the Crystal Palace Exposition in London. For the most part, stereographs portrayed subjects that were favorites of middle-class Victorian society. This one is a 1905 variation on the "cute child with cat" motif, published by Underwood and Underwood.

asked Mr. H. to come and look at some old books in which he would be interested. He sat down, but in a few minutes grew pale, shivered and said, 'There is a cat in the room.' Dr. Mitchell said, 'Look about you. There is no cat in the room. Do you hear one outside?' He said, 'No, but there is a cat.' He became faint and, complaining of nausea, went out and promptly recovered."

A handful of other diseases also link the feline and human species. Cats and people have been living together long enough to have developed the ability to do one another serious harm. Feline leukemia may or may not be passed from cats to humans, although it is certainly passed, by a virus, from cat to cat. Pregnant women are usually warned by their doctors to avoid contact with cats, who may be carriers of a parasitic disease called toxoplasmosis. Cats pick up the disease from other animals and pass it through their feces. The illness, if untreated, can cause blindness and brain damage in the woman's unborn child. Other illnesses are passed in the opposite direction, from humans to cats: because cats keep themselves tidy by rigorously licking their fur, they are vulnerable to any hazardous materials that may accumulate there, and as man's pollution of the atmosphere has increased, the danger to cats has risen.

Whether because they are sick, injured, ill-tempered, or just plain unwanted, millions of cats are abandoned every year all over the world. A great many of these cats die, but many others survive to become part of the enormous, shifting population of indigent felines. *Time* magazine estimates that there are 15 million homeless cats in the United States alone, although the number is almost certainly higher. One source estimates that there are twelve strays for every cat with a proper home. Some of these unwanted cats end up in shelters and humane societies, but shelters are enormously expensive to operate, and in times of economic hardship, they tend to be high on the list of forgotten charities. In recent years many shelters have been forced to close. Cat owners thus have a responsibility to make sure their pets are neutered and thus unable to expand the population of unwanted kittens. We may sometimes think it cruel to deprive our pets of their "sexuality," but it is far more cruel to behave in a way that spreads new sorrow throughout the world.

All relationships come to an end, of course. In the case of cats and people, the end of the relationship is brought about most often by the end of the cat. Since the average life expectancy for a cat is only a fraction of that for a human, most cat lovers find they have known a great many cats over the course of their lives. As we look back, each of those cats conjures up its own associations in our memory. Thinking about one of them can bring back an entire flood of images and feelings. The cats of our youth may no longer be with us, but cats that have once been companions are a part of our lives forever.

A Beloved Cat

One of the most enduring tributes to the human–feline relationship is Charles Dudley Warner's memoir "Calvin."

Calvin is dead. His life, long to him, but short for the rest of us, was not marked by startling adventures, but his character was so uncommon and his qualities were so worthy of imitation, that I have been asked by those who personally knew him to set down my recollections of his career.

His origin and ancestry were shrouded in mystery; even his age was a matter of pure conjecture. Although he was of the Maltese race, I have reason to suppose that he was American by birth as he certainly was in sympathy. Calvin was given to me eight years ago by Mrs. Stowe, but she knew nothing of his age or origin. He walked into her house one day out of the great unknown and became at once at home, as if he had been always a friend of the family. He appeared to have artistic and literary tastes, and it was as if he had inquired at the door if that was the residence of the author of *Uncle Tom's Cabin*, and, upon being assured that it was, had decided to dwell there. This is, of course, fanciful, for his antecedents were wholly unknown, but in his time he could hardly have been in any household where he would not have heard *Uncle Tom's Cabin* talked about. When he came to Mrs. Stowe, he was as large as he ever was, and apparently as old as he ever became. Yet there was in him no appearance of age; he was in the happy maturity of all his powers, and you would rather have said in that maturity he had found the secret of perpetual youth. And it was as difficult to believe that he would ever be aged as it was to imagine that he had ever been in immature youth. There was in him a mysterious perpetuity.

After some years, when Mrs. Stowe made her winter home in Florida, Calvin came to live with us. From the first moment, he fell into the ways of the house and assumed a recognized position in the family,—I say recognized, because after he became known he was always inquired for by visitors, and in the letters to the other members of the family he always received a message. Although the least obtrusive of beings, his individuality always made itself felt.

His personal appearance had much to do with this, for he was of royal mould, and had an air of high breeding. He was large, but he had nothing of the fat grossness of the celebrated Angora family; though powerful, he was exquisitely proportioned, and as graceful in every movement as a young leopard. When he stood up to open a door—he opened all the doors with old-fashioned latches—he was portentously tall, and when stretched on the rug before the fire he seemed too long for this world—as indeed he was. His coat was the finest and softest I have ever seen, a shade of quiet Maltese; and from his throat downward, underneath, to the white tips of his feet, he wore the whitest and most delicate ermine; and no person was ever more fastidiously neat. In his finely formed head you saw something of his aristocratic character; the ears were small and cleanly cut, there was a tinge of pink in the nostrils, his face was handsome, and the expression of his countenance exceedingly intelligent—I should call it even a sweet expression if the term were not inconsistent with his look of alertness and sagacity.

It is difficult to convey a just idea of his gayety in connection with his dignity and gravity, which his name expressed. As we know nothing of his family, of course it will be understood that Calvin was his Christian name. He had times of relaxation into utter playfulness, delighting in a ball of yarn, catching sportively at stray ribbons when his mistress was at her toilet, and pursuing his own tail, with hilarity, for lack of anything better. He could amuse himself by the hour, and he did not care for children; perhaps something in his past was present to his memory. He had absolutely no bad habits, and his disposition was perfect. I never saw him exactly angry, though I have seen his tail grow to an enormous size when a strange cat appeared upon his lawn. He disliked cats, evidently regarding them as feline and treacherous, and he had no association with them. Occasionally there would be heard a night concert in the shrubbery. Calvin would ask to have the door opened, and

From *The Histoire of Four-Footed Beasties*

The cat, along with other animals, is described in an early natural history, *The Histoire of Four-Footed Beasties*, which was collected from the writings of Conrad Genser and other authors and compiled by Edward Topsall in 1685.

Artist Unknown, *Tinkle, a Cat*

Cats often served as subjects for nineteenth-century American folk artists such as the unknown painter of *Tinkle, a Cat*. Unlike many other naïve paintings of this period, this one does not show the cat with its owner. Tinkle, whose name may derive from the bells attached to its collar, was probably a pet cat with an owner devoted enough to paint this portrait or to commission it. *Courtesy, Shelburne Museum, Shelburne, Vermont.*

then you would hear a rush and a "pestzt," and the concert would explode, and Calvin would quietly come in and resume his seat on the hearth. There was no trace of anger in his manner, but he wouldn't have any of that about the house. He had the rare virtue of magnanimity. Although he had fixed notions about his own rights, and extraordinary persistency in getting them, he never showed temper at a repulse; he simply and firmly persisted till he had what he wanted. His diet was one point; his idea was that of the scholars about dictionaries—to "get the best." He knew as well as anyone what was in the house, and would refuse beef if turkey was to be had; and if there were oysters, he would wait over the turkey to see if the oysters would not be forthcoming. And yet he was not a gross gourmand; he would eat bread if he saw me eating it, and thought he was not being imposed on. His habits of feeding, also, were refined; he never used a knife, and he would put up his hand and draw the fork down to his mouth as gracefully as a grown person. Unless necessity compelled, he would not eat in the kitchen, but insisted upon his meals in the dining-room, and would wait patiently, unless a stranger were present; and then he was sure to importune the visitor, hoping that the latter was ignorant of the rule of the house, and would give him something. They used to say that he preferred as his tablecloth on the floor a certain well-known church journal; but this was said by an Episcopalian. So far as I know, he had no religious prejudices, except that he did not like the association with Romanists. He tolerated the servants, because they belonged to the house, and would sometimes linger by the kitchen stove; but the moment visitors came in he arose, opened the door, and marched into the drawing-room. Yet he enjoyed the company of his equals, and never withdrew, no matter how many callers—whom he recognized as of his society—might come into the drawing-room. Calvin was fond of company, but he wanted to choose it; and I have no doubt that his was an aristocratic fastidiousness rather than one of faith. It is so with most people.

The intelligence of Calvin was something phenomenal, in his rank of life. He established a method of communicating his wants, and even some of his sentiments; and he could help himself in many things. There was a furnace register in a retired room, where he used to go when he wished to be alone, that he always opened when he desired more heat; but never shut it, any more than he shut the door after himself. He could do almost everything but speak; and you would declare sometimes that you could see a pathetic longing to do that in his intelligent face. I have no desire to overdraw his qualities, but if there was one thing in him more noticeable than another, it was his fondness for nature. He could content himself for hours at a low window, looking into the ravine and at the great trees, noting the smallest stir there; he delighted, above all things, to accompany me walking about the garden, hearing the birds, getting the smell of the fresh earth, and rejoicing in the sunshine. He followed me and gamboled like a dog, rolling over on the turf and exhibiting his delight in a hundred ways. If I worked, he sat and watched me, or looked off over the bank, and kept his ear open to the twitter in the cherry trees. When it stormed, he was sure to sit at the window, keenly watching the rain or the snow, glancing up and down at its falling; and a winter tempest always delighted him. I think he was genuinely fond of birds, but, so far as I know, he usually confined himself to one a day; he never killed, as some sportsmen do, for the sake of killing, but only as civilized people do—from necessity. He was intimate with the flying squirrels who dwell in the chestnut trees—too intimate, for almost every day in the summer he would bring in one, until he nearly discouraged them. He was, indeed, a superb hunter, and would have been a devastating one, if his bump of destructiveness had not been offset by a bump of moderation. There was very little of the brutality of the lower animals about him; I don't think he enjoyed rats for themselves, but he knew his business, and for the first few months of his residence with us he waged an awful campaign against the horde, and after that his simple presence was sufficient to deter them from coming on the premises. Mice amused him, but he usually considered them too small game to be taken seriously; I have seen him play for an hour with a mouse, and then let him go with a royal condescension. In this whole matter of "getting a living," Calvin was a great contrast to the rapacity of the age in which he lived.

I hesitate a little to speak of his capacity for friendship and the affectionateness of his nature, for I know from his own reserve that he would not care to have it much talked about. We understood each other perfectly, but we never made any fuss about it; when I spoke his name and snapped my fingers, he came to me; when I returned home at night, he was pretty sure to be waiting for me near the gate, and would rise and saunter along the walk, as if his being there were purely accidental,—so shy was he commonly of showing feeling; and when I opened the door he never rushed in, like a cat, but loitered, and lounged, as if he had had no intention of going in, but would condescend to. And yet, the fact was, he knew dinner was ready, and he was bound to be there. He kept the run of dinner-time. It happened sometimes, during our absence in the summer, that dinner would be early, and Calvin, walking about the grounds, missed it and came in late. But he never made a mistake the second day. There was one thing he never did,—he never rushed through an open doorway. He never forgot his dignity. If he had asked to have the door opened, and was eager to go out, he always went deliberately; I can see him now, standing on the sill, looking about at the sky as if he was thinking whether it were worth while to take an umbrella, until he was near having his tail shut in.

His friendship was rather constant than demonstrative. When we returned from an absence of nearly two years, Calvin welcomed us with evident pleasure, but showed his satisfaction rather by tranquil happiness than by fuming about. He had the faculty of making us glad to get home. It was his constancy that was so attractive. He liked companionship, but he wouldn't be petted, or fussed over, or sit in any one's lap a moment; he always extricated himself from such familiarity with dignity and with no show of temper. If there was any petting to be done, however, he chose to do it. Often he would sit looking at me, and then, moved by a delicate affection, come and pull at my coat and sleeve until he could touch my face with his nose, and then go away contented. He had a habit of coming to my study in the morning, sitting quietly by my side or on the table for hours, watching the pen run over the paper, occasionally swinging his tail round for a blotter, and then going to sleep among the papers by the inkstand. Or, more rarely, he would watch the writing from a perch on my shoulder. Writing always interested him, and, until he understood it, he wanted to hold the pen.

He always held himself in a kind of reserve with his friend, as if he had said, "Let us respect our personality, and not make a 'mess' of friendship." He saw, with Emerson, the risk of degrading it to trivial conveniency. "Why insist on rash personal relations with your friend?" "Leave this touching and clawing." Yet I would not give an unfair notion of his aloofness, his fine sense of the sacredness of the me and the not-me. And, at the risk of not being believed, I will relate an incident, which was often repeated. Calvin had the practice of passing a portion of the night in the contemplation of its beauties, and would come into our chamber over the roof of the conservatory through the open window, summer and winter, and go to sleep on the foot of my bed. He would do this always exactly in this way; he never was content to stay in the chamber if we compelled him to go upstairs and through the door. He had the obstinacy of General Grant. But this is by the way. In the morning, he performed his toilet and went down to breakfast with the rest of the family. Now, when the mistress was absent from home, and at no other time, Calvin would come in the morning, when the bell rang, to the head of the bed, put up his feet and look into my face, follow me about when I rose, "assist" at the dressing, and in many purring ways show his fondness, as if he had plainly said, "I know that she has gone away, but I am here." Such was Calvin in rare moments.

He had his limitations. Whatever passion he had for nature, he had no conception of art. There was sent to him once a fine and very expressive cat's head in bronze, by Frémiet. I placed it on the floor. He regarded it intently, approached it cautiously and crouchingly, touched it with his nose, perceived the fraud, turned away abruptly, and never would notice it afterward. On the whole, his life was not only a successful one, but a happy one. He never had but one fear, so far as I know: he had a mortal and a reasonable terror of plumbers. He would never stay in the house when they were here. No coaxing could quiet him. Of course he didn't share our fear about their charges, but he

John Kay, *The Favourate Cat and De La-tour, Painter*

Scottish caricaturist and miniature painter, John Kay executed more than nine hundred portraits. This one, an etching with aquatint made in 1813, represents the French pastel artist Maurice Quentin De La-tour and a rather odd cat wearing spectacles and a medallion engraved with the initials "I.K.," standing for "Iohannes Kay." Is this a caricature of the artist's cat or is it the way Kay, with his clever sense of humor, chose to portray himself?

The FAVOURATE CAT
and DE LA-TOUR
PAINTER

must have had some dreadful experience with them in that portion of his life which is unknown to us. A plumber was to him the devil, and I have no doubt that, in his scheme, plumbers were foreordained to do him mischief.

In speaking of his worth, it has never occurred to me to estimate Calvin by the worldly standard. I know that it is customary now, when anyone dies, to ask how much he was worth, and that no obituary in the newspapers is considered complete without such an estimate. The plumbers in our house were one day overheard to say that, "They say that *she* says that *he* says that he wouldn't take a hundred dollars for him." It is unnecessary to say that I never made such a remark, and that, so far as Calvin was concerned, there was no purchase in money.

As I look back upon it, Calvin's life seems to me a fortunate one, for it was natural and unforced. He ate when he was hungry, slept when he was sleepy, and enjoyed existence to the very tips of his toes and the end of his expressive and slow-moving tail. He delighted to roam about the garden, and stroll among the trees, and to lie on the green grass and luxuriate in all the sweet influences of summer. You could never accuse him of idleness, and yet he knew the secret of repose. The poet who wrote so prettily of him that his little life was rounded with a sleep, understated his felicity; it was rounded with a good many. His conscience never seemed to interfere with his slumbers. In fact, he had good habits and a contented mind. I can see him now walk in at the study door, sit down by my chair, bring his tail artistically about his feet, and look up at me with unspeakable happiness in his handsome face. I often thought that he felt the dumb limitation which denied him the power of language. But since he was denied speech, he scorned the inarticulate mouthings of the lower animals. The vulgar mewing and yowling of the cat species was beneath him; he sometimes uttered a sort of articulate and well-bred ejaculation, when he wished to call attention to something that he

Anonymous, *Man with Cat with Sunglasses*

This photograph of Kentucky grocer Lon Dodd and his two cats was probably made in the 1920s or 30s. No record of the photographer or the circumstances exists. Might we assume that the bespectacled kitty had "star quality" and simply was not interested in being recognized?
Kentucky Library, Western Kentucky University.

considered remarkable, or to some want of his, but he never went whining about. He would sit for hours at a closed window, when he desired to enter, without a murmur, and when it was opened he never admitted that he had been impatient by "bolting" in. Though speech he had not, and the unpleasant kind of utterance given to his race he would not use, he had a mighty power of purr to express his measureless content with congenial society. There was in him a musical organ with stops of varied power and expression, upon which I have no doubt he could have performed Scarlatti's celebrated cat's-fugue.

Whether Calvin died of old age, or was carried off by one of the diseases incident to youth, it is impossible to say; for his departure was as quiet as his advent was mysterious. I only know that he appeared to us in this world in his perfect stature and beauty, and that after a time, like Lohengrin, he withdrew. In his illness there was nothing more to be regretted than in all his blameless life. I suppose there never was an illness that had more of dignity and sweetness and resignation in it. It came on gradually, in a kind of listlessness and want of appetite. An alarming symptom was his preference for the warmth of a furnace register to the lively sparkle of the open wood fire. Whatever pain he suffered, he bore it in silence, and seemed only anxious not to obtrude his malady. We tempted him with the delicacies of the season, but it soon became impossible for him to eat, and for two weeks he ate or drank scarcely anything. Sometimes he made an effort to take something, but it was evident that he made the effort to please us. The neighbors—and I am convinced that the advice of neighbors is never good for anything—suggested catnip. He wouldn't even smell it. We had the attendance of an amateur practitioner of medicine, whose real office was the cure of souls, but nothing touched his case. He took what was offered, but it was with the air of one to whom the time for pellets was past. He sat or lay day after day almost motionless, never once making a display of those vulgar convulsions or contortions of pain which are so disagreeable to society. His favorite place was on the brightest spot of a Smyrna rug by the conservatory, where the sunlight fell and he could hear the fountain play. If we went to him and exhibited our interest in his condition, he always purred in recognition of our sympathy. And when I spoke his name, he looked up with an expression that said, "I understand it, old fellow, but it's no use." He was to all who came to visit him a model of calmness and patience in affliction.

I was absent from home at the last, but heard by daily postal card of his failing condition; and never again saw him alive. One sunny morning, he rose from his rug, went into the conservatory (he was very thin then), walked around it deliberately, looking at all the plants he knew, and then went to the bay window in the dining room and stood a long time looking out upon the little field, now brown and sere, and toward the garden, where perhaps the happiest hours of his life had been spent. It was a last look. He turned and walked away, laid himself down upon the bright spot in the rug, and quietly died.

It is not too much to say that a little shock went through the neighborhood when it was known that Calvin was dead, so marked was his individuality; and his friends, one after another, came in to see him. There was no sentimental nonsense about his obsequies; it was felt that any parade would have been distasteful to him. John, who acted as undertaker, prepared a candle-box for him, and I believe assumed a professional decorum; but there may have been the usual levity underneath, for I heard that he remarked in the kitchen that it was the "dryest wake he ever attended." Everybody, however, felt a fondness for Calvin, and regarded him with a certain respect. Between him and Bertha there existed a great friendship, and she apprehended his nature; she used to say that sometimes she was afraid of him, he looked at her so intelligently; she was never certain that he was what he appeared to be.

J. A. D. Ingres,
*Madame Ingres' Kitten
Asleep in Her Arms*

Warm and intimate, this is not the type of work usually associated with Ingres, the neoclassic painter.
Musée Ingres, Mantauban, France.

When I returned, they had laid Calvin on a table in an upper chamber by an open window. It was February. He reposed in a candle-box, lined about the edge with evergreen, and at his head stood a little wine-glass with flowers. He lay with his head tucked down in his arms—a favorite position of his before the fire,—as if asleep in the comfort of his soft and exquisite fur. It was the involuntary exclamation of those who saw him, "How natural he looks!" As for myself, I said nothing. John buried him under the twin hawthorn trees—one white and the other pink—in a spot where Calvin was fond of lying and listening to the hum of summer insects and the twitter of birds.

Perhaps I have failed to make appear the individuality of character that was so evident to those who knew him. At any rate, I have set down nothing concerning him but the literal truth. He was always a mystery. I did not know whence he came; I do not know whither he has gone. I would not weave one spray of falsehood in the wreath I lay upon his grave.

Tributes to Lost Friends

The passing of beloved cats sometimes provides poetic inspiration for the animals' bereft human companions. Over the centuries a number of poets—some of them great, others not so—have been moved to pen some truly moving verse tributes to the memories of their lost friends. Several of these poems are reproduced here. All of them call to mind the sentiment expressed in an epitaph on a gravestone in a pet cemetery:

No. Heaven will not ever Heaven be
Unless my cats are there to welcome me.

Last Words to a Dumb Friend
Thomas Hardy

Pet was never mourned as you
Purrer of the spotless hue,
Plumy tail, and wistful gaze
While you humoured our queer ways,
Or outshrilled your morning call
Up the stairs and through the hall—
Foot suspended in its fall—
While expectant, you would stand
Arched to meet the stroking hand;
Till your way you chose to wend
Yonder, to your tragic end.

Never another pet for me!
Let your place all vacant be;
Better blankness day by day
Than companion torn away.
Better bid his memory fade,
Better blot each mark he made,
Selfishly escape distress
By contrived forgetfulness,
Than preserve his prints to make
Every morn and eve an ache.

From the chair whereon he sat
Sweep his fur, nor wince thereat;
Rake his little pathways out
Mid the bushes roundabout;
Smooth away his talons' mark
From the claw-worn pine-tree bark,
Where he climbed as dusk embrowned,
Waiting us who loitered round.

Strange it is this speechless thing,
Subject to our mastering,
Subject for his life and food
To our gift, and time, and mood;
Timid pensioner of us Powers,
His existence ruled by ours,
Should—by crossing at a breath
Into safe and shielded death,
By the merely taking hence
Of his insignificance—
Loom as largened to the sense,
Shape as part, above man's will,
Of the Imperturbable.

As a prisoner, flight debarred,
Exercising in a yard,
Still retain I, troubled, shaken,
Mean estate, by him forsaken;
And this home, which scarcely took
Impress from his little look,
By his faring to the Dim
Grows all eloquent of him.

Housemate, I can think you still
Bounding to the window-sill,
Over which I vaguely see
Your small mound beneath the tree,
Showing in the autumn shade
That you moulder where you played.

Elegy
John Greenleaf Whittier

Bathsheba: To whom none ever said scat,
No worthier cat
Ever sat on a mat
Or caught a rat:
Requies-cat.

Drawing by Steinlen

On a Cat
That Was Killed as She Was Attempting to Rob a Dove House
Ibn Alalaf Alnaharwany

Gottfried Mind, *Minette Washing*

Poor Puss is gone!—'tis Fate's decree—
    Yet I must still her loss deplore;
For dearer than a child was she,
    And ne'er shall I behold her more!

With many a sad, presaging tear,
    This morn I saw her steal away,
While she went on without a fear,
    Except that she should miss her prey.

I saw her to the dove-house climb,
    With cautious feet and slow she stept,
Resolved to balance loss of time
    By eating faster than she crept.

Her subtle foes were on the watch,
    And marked her course, with fury fraught;
And while she hoped the birds to catch,
    An arrow's point the huntress caught.

In fancy she had got them all,
    And drunk their blood and sucked their breath;
Alas! She only got a fall,
    And only drank the draught of death.

Why, why was pigeon's flesh so nice,
    That thoughtless cats should love it thus?
Hadst thou but lived on rats and mice,
    Thou hadst been living still, poor Puss!

Cursed be the taste, howe'er refined,
    That prompts us for such joys to wish;
And cursed the dainty where we find
    Destruction lurking in the dish.

Cat Tombstone

When a cat died of natural causes at home in ancient Egypt, its human family shaved their eyebrows and lamented loudly. After the appropriate interval of mourning, the eyes of the deceased were closed and its whiskers were pressed to its lips in order to prepare it for mummification. Then the feline was decently buried, often in an elaborate sarcophagus. And the ceremonious internment of cats is still practiced in the United States. This cat tombstone reflects America's interest in feline burial.
Courtesy, Shelburne Museum, Shelburne, Vermont.

Elegy to Oscar, a Dead Cat
H. P. Lovecraft

Damn'd be this harsh mechanick age
    That whirls us fast and faster,
And swallows with Sabazian rage
    Nine lives in one disaster.

I take my quill with sadden'd thought,
    Tho' falt'ringly I do it;
And having curst the Juggernaut,
    Inscribe: OSCARVS FUIT!

Drawing by Steinlen

Monody on the Death of Dick, an Academical Cat
George Huddesford

Though no funereal cypress shade thy tomb,
For thee the wreaths of Paradise shall bloom,
There, while Grimalkin's mew her Richard greets,
A thousand Cats shall purr on purple seats.
E'en now I see, descending from his throne,
Thy venerable Cat, O Whittington!
The kindred excellence of Richard hail,
And wave with joy his gratulating tail.
There shall the worthies of the whisker'd race
Elysian Mice o'er floors of sapphire chase,
Midst beds of aromatic marum stray,
Or raptur'd rove beside the Milky Way.
Kittens, than eastern houris fairer seen,
Whose bright eyes glisten with immortal green,
Shall smooth for tabby swains their yielding fur,
And to their amorous mews, assenting purr;—
There, like Alcmena's, shall Grimalkin's son
In bliss repose,—his mousing labours done,
Fate, envy, curs, time, tide, and traps defy,
And caterwaul to all eternity!

Mother Goose's Cats

There are several cats in the nursery rhymes known to children of all ages as the works of Mother Goose. The rhymes are of uncertain origin, but they date from at least the seventeenth century.

Ding dong bell, ·
Pussy's in the well.
Who put her in?
Little Johnny Green.
Who pulled her out?
Little Tommy Stout.
What a naughty boy was that,
To drown a poor Pussy Cat,
Who never did any Harm,
And killed the mice in his father's barn.

High diddle, diddle,
The Cat and the fiddle,
   The cow jumped over the moon.
The little dog laughed
To see such sport
   And the dish ran away with the spoon.

Pussy Cat, Pussy Cat, where have you been?
   I've been to London to look at the queen.
Pussy Cat, Pussy Cat, what did you there?
   I frightened a little mouse under her chair.

Six little mice sat down to spin;
Pussy passed by and she peeped in.
What are you doing, my little men?

Weaving coats for gentlemen.
Shall I come in and cut off your threads?
No, no, Mistress Pussy, you'd bite off our heads.
Oh, no, I'll not; I'll help you to spin.
That may be so, but you can't come in.
Says Puss: You look so wondrous wise,
I like your whiskers and bright black eyes;
Your house is the nicest house I see;
I think there is room for you and for me.
The mice were so pleased that they opened the door,
And Pussy soon had them all dead on the floor.

I love little Pussy,
   Her coat is so warm,
And if I don't hurt her,
   She'll do me no harm.

So I'll not pull her tail,
   Nor drive her away,
But Pussy and I
   Very gently will play.

She shall sit by my side,
   And I'll give her some food;
And Pussy will love me
   Because I am good.

The Master Cat

Gustave Doré,
Puss in Boots

To accompany Charles Perrault's version of the classic fairy tale "Puss in Boots," French illustrator Gustave Doré (1833–1883) created this equally timeless drawing.

"Puss in Boots" is a classic fairy tale. Although there are many variations from different countries, this story of an intrepid cat was immortalized by the French writer Charles Perrault (1628-1703) in his book of fairy tales *Contes du Temps Passe* (1697). The moral from "Puss in Boots" is excerpted below.

Moral
It's a pleasant thing, I'm told,
   To be left a pile of gold.
But there's something better still,
   Never yet bequeathed by will.
Leave a lad a stock of sense—
Though with neither pounds nor pence—
   And he'll finish, as a rule,
   Richer than the gilded fool.

A Certain Smile

One of the best known cats in all of literature is the Cheshire Cat, encountered by Alice in the course of her adventures in Wonderland. The following passage is excerpted from Lewis Carroll's classic tale.

The Cat only grinned when it saw Alice. It looked good-natured, she thought: still it had *very* long claws and a great many teeth, so she felt that it ought to be treated with respect.

"Cheshire Puss," she began, rather timidly, as she did not at all know whether it would like the name: however, it only grinned a little wider. "Come, it's pleased so far," thought Alice, and she went on. "Would you tell me, please, which way I ought to go from here?"

"That depends a good deal on where you want to go," said the Cat.

"I don't much care where—" said Alice.

"Then it doesn't matter which way you go," said the Cat.

"—so long as I get *somewhere*," Alice added as an explanation.

"Oh, you're sure to do that," said the Cat, "if you only walk long enough."

Alice felt that this could not be denied, so she tried another question. "What sort of people live about here?"

"In *that* direction," the Cat said, waving its right paw round, "lives a Hatter: and in *that* direction," waving the other paw, "lives a March Hare. Visit either you like: they're both mad."

"But I don't want to go among mad people," Alice remarked.

"Oh, you can't help that," said the Cat. "We're all mad here. I'm mad. You're mad."

"How do you know I'm mad?" said Alice.

"You must be," said the Cat, "or you wouldn't have come here."

Avoid Large Places at Night

Born to Greek and Irish parents, Lafcadio Hearn (1850–1904) adopted the customs, language, and culture of Japan as his own. Living among the Japanese people, he collected and retold many of their traditional fairy tales and ghost stories. "The Boy Who Drew Cats" is one of the most charming and haunting.

A long, long time ago, in a small country-village in Japan, there lived a poor farmer and his wife, who were very good people. They had a number of children, and found it very hard to feed them all. The elder son was strong enough when only fourteen years old to help his father; and the little girls learned to help their mother almost as soon as they could walk.

But the youngest child, a little boy, did not seem to be fit for hard work. He was very clever, —cleverer than all his brothers and sisters; but he was quite weak and small, and people said he could never grow very big. So his parents thought it would be better for him to become a priest than to become a farmer. They took him with them to the village-temple one day, and asked the good old priest who lived there, if he would have their little boy for his acolyte, and teach him all that a priest ought to know.

The old man spoke kindly to the lad, and asked him some hard questions. So clever were the answers that the priest agreed to take the little fellow into the temple as an acolyte, and to educate him for the priesthood.

The boy learned quickly what the old priest taught him, and was very obedient in most things. But he had one fault. He like to draw cats during study-hours, and to draw cats even where cats ought not to have been drawn at all.

Whenever he found himself alone, he drew cats. He drew them on the margins of the priest's books, and on all the screens of the temple, and on the walls, and on the pillars. Several times the priest told him this was not right; but he did not stop drawing cats. He drew them because he could not really help it. He had what is called "the genius of an *artist,*" and just for that reason he was not quite fit to be an acolyte;—a good acolyte should study books.

One day after he had drawn some very clever pictures of cats upon a paper screen, the old priest said to him severely: "My boy, you must go away from this temple at once. You will never make a good priest, but perhaps you will become a great artist. Now let me give you a last piece of advice, and be sure you never forget it. *Avoid large places at night;—keep to small!*"

The boy did not know what the priest meant by saying, "*Avoid large places;—keep to small.*" He thought and thought, while he was tying up his little bundle of clothes to go away; but he could not understand those words, and he was afraid to speak to the priest any more, except to say good-by.

He left the temple very sorrowfully, and began to wonder what he should do. If he went straight home he felt sure his father would punish him for having been disobedient to the priest: so he was afraid to go home. All at once he remembered that at the next village, twelve miles away, there was a very big temple. He had heard there were several priests at that temple; and he made up his mind to go to them and ask them to take him for their acolyte.

Now that big temple was closed up but the boy did not know this fact. The reason it had been closed up was that a goblin had frightened the priests away, and had taken possession of the place. Some brave warriors had afterward gone to the temple at night to kill the goblin; but they had never been seen alive again. Nobody had ever told these things to the boy;—so he walked all the way to the village hoping to be kindly treated by the priests.

When he got to the village it was already dark, and all the people were in bed; but he saw the big temple on a hill at the other end of the principal street, and he saw there was a light in the temple. People who tell the story say the goblin used to make that light, in order to tempt lonely travelers to ask for shelter. The boy went at once to the temple, and knocked. There was no sound inside. He knocked and knocked again; but still nobody came. At last he pushed gently at the door, and was quite glad to find that it had not been fastened. So he went in, and saw a lamp burning,—but no priest.

He thought some priest would be sure to come very soon, and he sat down and waited. Then he noticed that everything in the temple was gray with dust, and thickly spun over with cobwebs. So he thought to himself that the priests would certainly like to have an acolyte, to keep the place clean. He wondered why they had allowed everything to get so dusty. What most pleased him, however, were some big white screens, good to paint cats upon. Though he was tired, he looked at once for a writing-box, and found one, and ground some ink, and began to paint cats.

He painted a great many cats upon the screens; and then he began to feel very, very sleepy. He was just on the point of lying down to sleep beside one of the screens, when he suddenly remembered the words, *"Avoid large places;—keep to small!"*

The temple was very large; he was all alone; and as he thought of these words,—though he could not quite understand them—he began to feel for the first time a little afraid; and he resolved to look for a *small place* in which to sleep. He found a little cabinet, with a sliding door, and went into it, and shut himself up. Then he lay down and fell fast asleep.

Very late in the night he was awakened by a most terrible noise,—a noise of fighting and screaming. It was so dreadful that he was afraid even to look through a chink of the little cabinet: he lay very still, holding his breath for fright.

The light that had been in the temple went out; but the awful sounds continued, and became more awful, and all the temple shook. After a long time silence came; but the boy was still afraid to move. He did not move until the light of the morning sun shown into the cabinet through the chinks of the little door.

Then he got out of his hiding-place very cautiously, and looked about. The first thing he saw was that the floor of the temple was covered with blood. And then he saw, lying dead in the middle of it, an enormous, monstrous rat,—a goblin-rat,—bigger than a cow!

But who or what could have killed it? There was no man or other creature to be seen. Suddenly the boy observed that the mouths of all the cats he had drawn the night before, were red and wet with blood. Then he knew that the goblin had been killed by the cats which he had drawn. And then also, for the first time, he understood why the wise old priest had said to him, *"Avoid large places at night;—keep to small."*

Afterward that boy became a very famous artist. Some of the cats which he drew are still shown to travelers in Japan.

Anonymous, *Children Playing Games on a Winter Day* **(Sung Dynasty)**

The cat made its first known appearance in Chinese art during the Sung dynasty (A.D. 960–1279). One reason for its considerably late arrival, more than 2,000 years after its counterparts in Indian art, may be explained by the legendary belief that the cat was the only creature who failed to mourn the Buddha's death. In Sung art, aristocratic youngsters were often accompanied by pet cats. *The Granger Collection.*

D rawings by Edward Lear

Nonsensical Cats

The nineteenth century's great master of nonsense, Edward Lear (1817–1888) wrote several silly songs about cats, the most famous of which was "The Owl and the Pussycat." Lear's greatest friend in life was Foss, his cat, who lived with the writer for seventeen years.

I.

The Owl and the Pussy-Cat went to sea
   In a beautiful pea-green boat,
  They took some honey, and plenty of
    money,
  Wrapped up in a five-pound note.
The Owl looked up to the stars above,
  And sang to a small guitar,
"O lovely Pussy! O Pussy, my love,
  "What a beautiful Pussy you are,
   "You are,
   "You are!
"What a beautiful Pussy you are!"

II.

Pussy said to the Owl, "You elegant fowl!
  "How charmingly sweet you sing!
"O let us be married! too long we have tarried
  "But what shall we do for a ring?"
They sailed away for a year and a day,

To the land where the Bong-tree grows,
And there in a wood a Piggy-wig stood,
  With a ring at the end of his nose,
   His nose,
   His nose,
With a ring at the end of his nose.

III.

"Dear Pig, are you willing to sell for one shilling
  Your ring?" Said the Piggy, "I will."
So they took it away, and were married next day
  By the Turkey who lives on the hill.
They dined on mince, and slices of quince,
  Which they ate with a runcible spoon;
And hand in hand, on the edge of the sand,
  They danced by the light of the moon,
   The moon,
   The moon,
They danced by the light of the moon.

T his page from a letter written by Edward Lear includes a drawing of his cat Foss.

nor any summer place so everlastingly green
& lovely. The view of the Lecco mountains
from my windows is enough to make a blacking=
= brush squeak with delight; & downstairs
there is a garden with the loveliest flowers

all green

I am thankful to say my health continues
much better than it was, though I am now too
infirm to walk.

Yours ever,

Edward Lear.

Edward Lear.
æt 73.½

His cat Foss,
æt 16.

PART TWO

MOUSERS, MODELS, MOVIE STARS

For much of their shared history with people, cats have had to earn their keep. They have served as mousers, playmates, models, and even stars. The relationship between cats and humans has thus had an economic component that has affected, at least in a small way, the course of civilization.

One of the earliest artistic representations of a cat is an Egyptian painting showing a domesticated feline in chains. The cat in bondage wasn't a prisoner; he was a slave. The ancient Egyptians used cats to help them hunt, and they valued their new partners to such an extent that they tied them up to prevent them from running away. The precaution was certainly worth it: another painting, on a tomb at Thebes, depicts a hunting cat with one bird in its mouth and two more beneath its feet. Men quickly discovered that the cat's natural hunting instincts could be used for their own benefit.

Cats have never been used as hunters to the extent that dogs have been, but still they have had to work. Cats who once sustained themselves by catching rodents and other small mammals in the wild, now earn a place in human society by killing mice, rats, and other pests that threaten human economies and societies—a natural adaptation of their basic predatory instincts. In ancient Egypt, the periodic flooding of the Nile brought plagues of vermin that endangered the livelihood and even the lives of the Egyptians, who were quick to understand the cat's usefulness in restoring a healthy balance. Thus, the entry of cats into human society was originally prompted by a very powerful human need for the assistance cats could provide.

The skills cats use in combating vermin are as much a part of them as their purr. Even very young cats have the predatory instinct. All cats exhibit essentially the same stalking and pouncing behaviors, and all cats refine their natural instincts in essentially the same ways. When young kittens reach a certain age, their mother begins to bring killed prey back to the nest. Later on, once the kittens have grown accustomed to seeing dead mice and birds around the nursery, the mother begins to bring back live prey. Killing techniques are taught as a kind of play, so as the months go by the kittens gradually accumulate and hone their hunting skills. They also acquire the necessary stealth and patience.

Working Cats

A Dinner Scene in January, from a Flemish Book of Hours

During the late Middle Ages and early Renaissance, it was common for the rich of France and Flanders to commission books of hours, which contained prayers for each month of the year and different times of the day. This devotional material was always richly and beautifuly illustrated with illuminations of domestic scenes from the patron's manor. The cat, an incarnaton of the corn spirit, the symbol of eternal life, is welcome at this dinner scene from a Flemish book of hours, suggesting that the patron has had a successful harvest.
The Granger Collection.

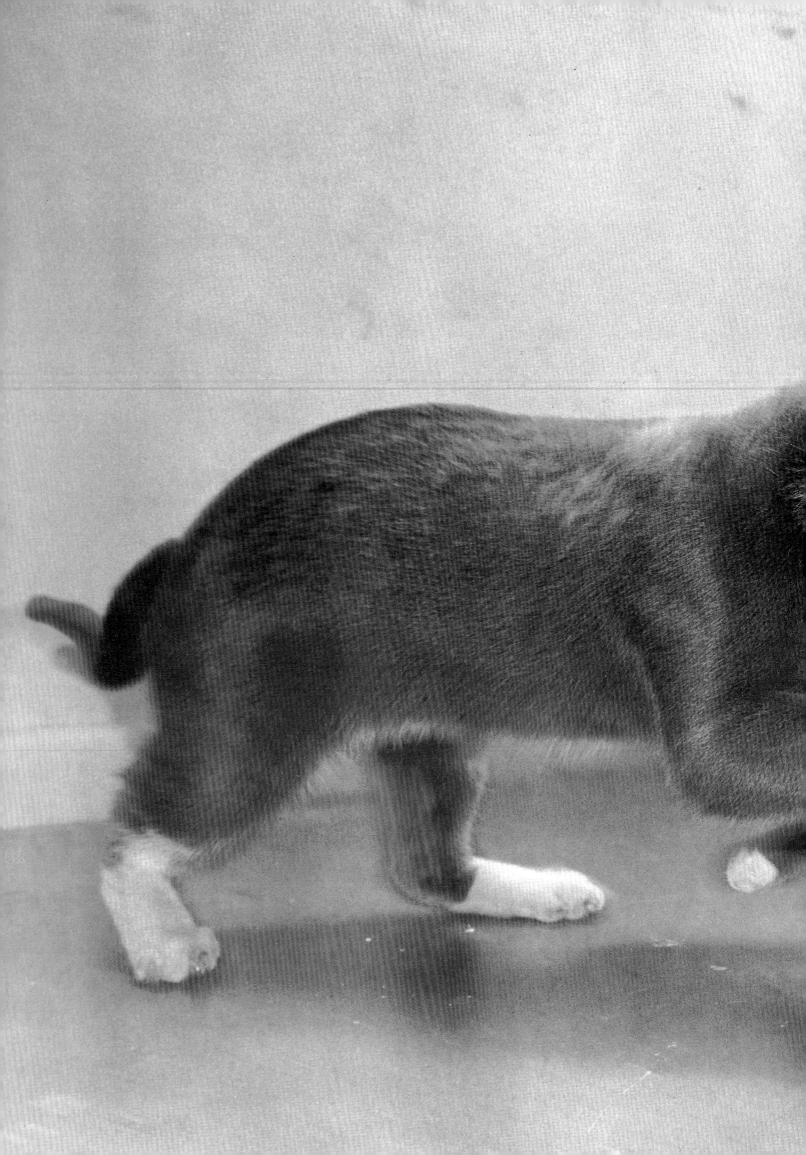

The first cats kept by the ancient Egyptians were such effective mousers that the animals quickly came to be regarded as a precious natural resource. Laws were enacted making it illegal to take cats out of the country, and they seem to have been effective for several centuries. But such a powerful weapon could not be kept secret forever, and eventually someone—probably a Phoenician sailor—managed to smuggle a few cats out of Egypt, beginning their gradual spread across Europe. The smugglers no doubt came to appreciate the usefulness of having cats on board a ship: with the mouse and rat population kept at bay, precious stores and cargoes in the hold could be preserved throughout a journey.

As cats spread throughout Europe and Asia, their role in the economy of their new homes increased. Cats were used by farmers to protect the grain harvests from the ravages of vermin, which brought the animals a position of great importance at the foundation of agriculture. In tenth-century Wales, Prince Hoel the Good enacted laws establishing the official values of different kinds of animals, including cats. Some of his laws appear in the excerpt below.

The Legal Value of a Cat

Hoel Dha (Howell the Good), king of Wales in the tenth century, placed a great value on cats, as he proved when he enacted the following laws.

The Vendotian Code XI.
The worth of a cat and her teithi (qualities) this is:—
1st. The worth of a kitten from the night it is kittened until it shall open its eyes, is one penny.
2d. And from that time until it shall kill mice, two pence.
3d. And after it shall kill mice, four legal pence; and so it shall always remain.
4th. Her teithe are to see, to hear, to kill mice, and to have her claws.
. . . The "Dimentian Code." XXXII. . . .
1st. The worth of a cat that is killed or stolen. Its head to be put downward upon a clean, even floor, with its tail lifted upward and thus suspended, whilst wheat is poured about it until the top of its tail be covered and that is to be its worth. If the corn cannot be had, then a milch sheep with a lamb and its wool is its value, if it be a cat that guards the king's barn.
2d. The worth of a common cat is four legal pence.
3d. The teithi of a cat, and of every animal upon the milk of which people do not feed, is the third part of its worth or the worth of its litter.
4th. Whosoever shall sell a cat (cath) is to answer that she devour not her kittens, and that she have ears, teeth, eyes, and nails, and be a good mouser.
The "Gwentian Code." . . .
3d. That it be perfect of ear, perfect of eye, perfect of teeth, perfect of tail, perfect of claw, and without marks of fire. And if the cat fall short in any of these particulars, a third of her price had to be refunded. As to the fire, in case her fur had been singed the rats could detect her by the odor, and her qualities as a mouser were thus injured. And then it goes on to say:—
4th. That the teithi and the legal worth of a cat are coequal.
5th. A pound is the worth of a pet animal of the king.
6th. The pet animal of a breyer (brewer) is six score pence in value.
7th. The pet animal of a taoog is a curt penny in value.

"The worth of a kitten," the prince decreed, "from the night it is kittened until it shall open its eyes is a legal penny. And from that time, until it shall kill mice, two legal pence. And after it shall kill mice, four legal pence; and so it always remains." (The value of a lamb, by way of comparison, was only a penny.) In Saxony 200 years later, a man convicted of killing someone else's cat was required to pay the bereaved owner sixty bushels of corn. In 1750, in Paraguay, a mousing cat was valued at a pound of gold.

The enormous trade explosion that accompanied the Crusades increased Europe's population not only of cats but also of rats. The rats brought plague, and the cats killed the rats, but the Europeans did not at first appreciate the connection. Cats were even suspected for a very long time of *causing* the plague, leading to mass exterminations and the flourishing of superstitions. People were driven by fear to kill the animals that were in actual fact their only protectors against the Black Death.

As difficult as it is for us to comprehend today, just a few centuries ago cats were held to be fully sentient individuals, and thus responsible for their own actions. As a consequence, they could be tried in courts of law, or called upon to serve as witnesses. Even when they weren't present, they could still affect the dispensation of justice. In one fascinating case, in France in 1540, a bishop attempted to excommunicate some local mice, who had been blamed by peasants for destroying that year's corn crop. The mice were summoned to appear in court, but they didn't arrive on the appointed date. A lawyer appointed by the court to represent the mice in their absence had argued that the mice had wanted to appear, but that local cats had prevented them from traveling on the roads. The judge apparently found this argument eminently reasonable, because the case against the mice was dismissed.

Rat Watch

Three cats, five eyes. Walter de la Mare explains this odd arithmetic in a poem called "Five Eyes."

In Hans' old mill his three black cats
Watch the bins for thieving rats.
Whisker and claw, they crouch in the night,
Their five eyes smouldering green and bright:
Squeaks from the flour-stacks, squeaks from where
The cold wind stirs on the empty stair,
Squeaking and scampering everywhere.
Then down they pounce, now in, now out,
At whisking tail, and sniffing snout;
While lean old Hans he snores away
Till peep of light at break of day;
Then up he climbs to his creaking mill.
Out come his cats all grey with meal—
Jekkel, and Jessup, and one-eyed Jill.

Raoul Dufy, *Woodcut*

Dessins sans paroles

des Chats

par

Steinlen

Collection
Rodolphe Salis

PARIS
ERNEST FLAMMARION
EDITEUR
26 Rue Racine
Près L'Odéon

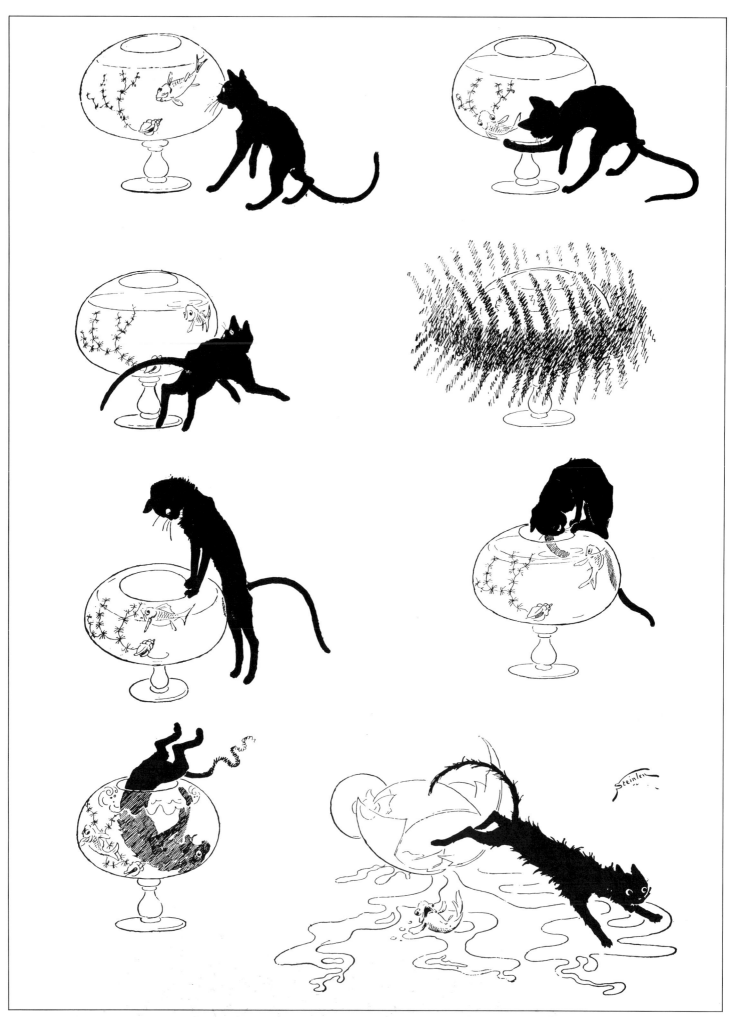

Horrible Fin d'un Poisson Rouge

Une Brouille

Paresse

Un Effet de la Gourmandise

Histoire Navrante d'un Chat et d'un Petit Cochon d'Inde

The Japanese understood the cat's value as a predator, but they were reluctant to demean their treasured pets by actually making them kill mice. Mousing was too low an occupation for an animal of such considerable qualities, so when rodents infested Japanese crops, planters kept their cats indoors. To combat the pests, the planters used *images* of cats: statues, paintings, tokens, and other symbols were displayed prominently near precious grain crops in the hopes that the rats would be as frightened of symbolic tormentors as they were of real ones. When the rats failed to be fooled, cats fell into disrepute, although in later years they were finally put to work doing what they were meant to do.

Cats are most successful at tasks that are consistent with their natural instincts. They may make terrible soldiers, but they are excellent exterminators, and it is in that capacity that cats have made their most important contribution. It is not an exaggeration to say that the history of human civilization might be very different if cats had not had a part in shaping it. Egyptian culture might not have flourished if the country's crops had repeatedly been ravaged by mice and rats and if cats had not been there to stop them. The devastation of Europe in the plagues that swept across it might have been even worse if cats had not helped bring the pestilence to an end. Life in many modern cities might be untenable if cats were not on hand to keep the rat population in check.

Ode on the Death of a Favourite Cat Drowned in a Tub of Gold Fishes
Thomas Gray

'Twas on a lofty vase's side
Where China's gayest art had dyed
  The azure flowers, that blow;
Demurest of the tabby kind,
The pensive Selima, reclined,
  Gazed on the lake below.

Her conscious tail her joy declared;
The fair round face, the snowy beard,
  The velvet of her paws,
Her coat, that with the tortoise vies,
Her ears of jet, and emerald eyes,
  She saw; and purr'd applause.

Still had she gazed; but 'midst the tide
Two angel forms were seen to glide,
  The genii of the stream:
Their scaly armour's Tyrian hue
Through richest purple to the view
  Betray'd a golden gleam.

The hapless nymph with wonder saw:
A whisker first, and then a claw,
  With many an ardent wish,

She stretch'd, in vain, to reach the prize
What female heart can gold despise?
  What cat's averse to fish?

Presumptuous maid! with looks intent
Again she stretch'd, again she bent,
  Nor knew the gulf between.
(Malignant Fate sat by, and smiled)
The slipp'ry verge her feet beguiled,
  She tumbled headlong in.

Eight times emerging from the flood
She mew'd to ev'ry wat'ry God,
  Some speedy aid to send.
No Dolphin came, no Nereid stirr'd:
Nor cruel Tom, nor Susan heard.
  A fav'rite has no friend!

From hence, ye beauties, undeceived,
Know, one false step is ne'er retrieved,
  And be with caution bold.
Not all that tempts your wand'ring eyes
And heedless hearts is lawful prize.
  Nor all that glitters, gold.

Nathaniel Hone,
Kitty Fisher

As an aristocratic woman sits for her portrait, she is oblivious to the small cat who is about to make a seafood dinner out of a bowl of goldfish. *Northampton Historical Society.*

**Martin Drolling
(1752–1817),**
The Woman and the Mouse

In the never-ending struggle
to build a better mousetrap,
this woman, who believes that
she has constructed one, displays her catch to the surprise
and delight of a small child
and a rather befuddled cat.
*Musée des Beaux Arts, Or-
léans, France.*

Monument to a Cat

Few cats, real or legendary, have won the fame and notoriety of Dick Whittington's magical mouser. A monument stands at Highgate Hill, in north London, where Whittington "turned again" to seek his fortune in the city. Whittington, who was lord mayor of London three times in the fifteenth century, owed all his success to his adept feline. *Keystone Press Agency, London and New York.*

Arthur Rackham,
Dick Whittington

Dick Whittington and his magic cat have served as subjects for many English artists. This early twentieth-century silhouette was created by the famous book illustrator Arthur Rackham.

When people weren't busy killing their cats or dragging them into court, they continued to appreciate their usefulness as mousers. Nowhere is this more evident than in the story of Dick Whittington. Whittington was a semifictional character who is known to have served three terms as the mayor of London, the first of them beginning in 1397. According to legend, Whittington was born and raised in poverty and traveled to London as a boy, hoping to make his fortune in a city whose streets he believed to be paved with gold.

Dick Whittington's Cat

Dick Whittington's cat, according to legend, was one of the great mousers of all time. Following is an excerpt from the tale that bears his name.

The King and Queen were seated at the upper end of the room, and a number of dishes were brought in for dinner. They had not sat long when a vast number of rats and mice rushed in, helping themselves from almost every dish. The captain wondered at this, and asked if these vermin were not very unpleasant.

"Oh, yes," said they, "very destructive; and the King would give half his treasure to be freed of them, for they not only destroy his dinner, as you see, but they assault him in his chamber, and even in bed, so that he is obliged to be watched while he is sleeping for fear of them."

The captain jumped for joy; he remembered poor Whittington and his cat, and told the King that he had a creature on board the ship that would dispatch all these vermin immediately. The King's heart leapt so high at the happiness this news gave him that his turban dropped off his head. "Bring this creature to me," said he; "vermin are dreadful in a Court, and if she will perform what you say I will load your ship with gold and jewels in exchange for her."

The captain, who knew his business, took this opportunity to set forth the merits of Mrs. Puss. He told His Majesty that it would be inconvenient to part with her, as, when she was gone, the rats and mice might destroy the goods in the ship—but to oblige His Majesty he would fetch her.

"Run, run!" said the Queen; "I am impatient to see the dear creature."

Away went the captain to the ship, while another dinner was got ready. He put Puss under his arm, and arrived at the place soon enough to see the table full of rats.

When the cat saw them she did not wait for bidding, but jumped out of the captain's arms, and in a few minutes laid almost all the rats and mice dead at her feet. The rest of them in their fright scampered away to their holes.

The King and Queen were quite charmed to get so easily rid of such plagues, and desired the creature who had done them so great a kindness might be brought to them for inspection. Upon which the captain called: "Pussy, pussy, pussy!" and she came to him. He then presented her to the Queen, who started back, and was afraid to touch a creature who had made such a havoc among the rats and mice. However, when the captain stroked the cat and called "Pussy, pussy," the Queen also touched her and cried "Putty, putty," for she had not learned English. He then put her down on the Queen's lap, where she, purring, played with Her Majesty's hand, and then sung herself to sleep.

The King, having seen the exploits of Mrs. Puss, and being informed that her kittens would stock the whole country, bargained with the captain for the whole ship's cargo, and then gave him ten times as much for the cat as all the rest amounted to.

Hamlet

Hamlet, the Algonquin cat, was as much a part of the literary circle that haunted the Algonquin Hotel as were the writers and artists themselves. *Copyright © Bill Hayward.*

He didn't find riches in London, but he did find a cat, which he bought for a penny and kept as a protector and companion in the rat-infested room where he boarded. Whittington was later persuaded to "invest" his pet in a trading voyage that his employer was sponsoring. In the course of the voyage, the cat was bought by the king of a country entirely overrun by voracious rodents. The cat put an end to the problem in short order, and the king was so grateful that he paid Whittington ten times the value of the rest of the cargo put together. The cat's predatory skills thus made Dick Whittington a very rich man, enabling him to marry his employer's daughter and to become an extremely important man in London society.

The Dick Whittington story is a charming reminder of the value placed on cats by people who understand their usefulness in controlling pests and thus of the cat's working relationship with his human companions. That relationship continues to this day. In Great Britain cats for many years have been scheduled as employees on official postal system payrolls: the government allocates money for the support of "Post Office cats," who in return are expected to keep mice from gnawing through letter pouches and eating up the mail. The venerable Algonquin Hotel in New York City, scene of some of the greatest literary convocations, has had a cat in residence ever since the 1930s. Not many years ago, guests who complained to the desk about mice in their rooms were not surprised to be greeted a few moments later by a bellboy carrying Rusty, the hotel's mascot and official mouser.

In Borneo in 1961, hundreds of stray cats from Singapore were airlifted into the rice fields to save the crop from destruction by rats. In medieval Japan, cats were considered a great luxury and thus served primarily as toys for the wealthy.

Barnyard Mousing

Cats are extremely patient hunters, a fact that doesn't always work to their advantage. Here Henry David Thoreau describes an incident in which his pet, Min, was outwitted by a rooster.

Min caught a mouse, and was playing with it in the yard. It had got away from her once or twice and she had caught it again, and now it was stealing off again, as she was complacently watching it with her paws tucked under her, when her friend, Riorden, a stout cock, stepped up inquisitively, looked down at the mouse with one eye, turning its head, then picked it up by the tail, gave it two or three whacks on the ground, and giving it a dexterous toss in the air, caught the mouse in its open mouth. It went, head foremost and alive, down Riorden's capacious throat in the twinkling of an eye, never again to be seen in this world; Min all the while, with paws comfortably tucked under her, looking on unconcerned. What did one mouse matter, more or less, to her? The cock walked off amid the currant-bushes, stretched his neck up and gulped once or twice, and the deed was accomplished. Then he crowed lustily in celebration of the exploit. It might be set down among the *Gesta gallorum*. There were several human witnesses. It is a question whether Min ever understood where that mouse went to. She sits composedly sentinel, with paws tucked under her, a good part of her days at present, by some ridiculous little hole, the possible entry of a mouse.

Théophile Steinlen, *Des Chats*

Des Chats, a turn-of-the-century album of picture stories without words best illustrates Steinlen's elegant and amusing felines. The following six pages are from this work.

William Hogarth,
The Graham Children

In reaction to the spun-sugar style of French Rococo painters such as Watteau and Fragonard, the first important English school of art since the Middle Ages was born. William Hogarth (1697–1764), the first of this school, made his mark in the 1730s with pictures showing "modern, moral subjects," in order to teach the virtues of middle-class values. Surely the family cat, a pet and a worker, exemplified the moral subject.
Tate Gallery, London.

Currier and Ives, *Three Little White Kitties (Their First Mouse)*

On seeing its first mouse, only one of these white kittens displays a truly adventurous nature. Another hides beneath a parlor curtain and the third, even more timid, seeks refuge behind his mother. As a result of mid-nineteenth-century economic progress in America, cats such as the ones in this Currier and Ives lithograph no longer had to earn their keep as mousers and had become "parlorized" household pets. This explains their befuddled reaction to the mouse.

Cats in Advertising

Throughout history, the cat has been portrayed as an image of sexuality, a demon, an instrument of Satan, and an omen of good luck. Given its symbolic background, it is no wonder that today the cat plays a prominent role in one of our more important mythologies, advertising. Despite its bad reputation in medieval society, the cat often appeared on signs that hung outside inns and public houses. When a family's name included the word "cat," it was used on heraldic shields and banners.

The commercial cat came into its own during the nineteenth century when it appeared in countless magazine advertisements for everything from stoves to broomsticks and medicines. Since then, the cat has maintained its role in the symbolic language of advertising.

The continued importance of the cat in the commercial world may be explained, in part, by its mythic history. For example, the expression of sexuality is an inextricable part of modern advertising. The cat appears in perfume, lingerie, and jewelry ads to suggest a sexual ideal to which women should aspire.

Commercial cats adorn the labels of liquor bottles and shoe polish cans. And cats have appeared on cigar labels, orange crates, and of course, cat food packaging.

The resilient nature of feline feet make them the perfect model for Cat's Paw Rubber Heels and Soles. This sign appears in shoe repair shop windows all over America. *Copyright © Don Hamerman.*

A large black cat, perhaps a lucky "Matagot," looms gigantic over a pack of English cigarettes.

ATTENTION!
Something Important for every Purchaser of

DRY GOODS,
to see at

E. G. SOUTHWICK & CO.'S,
NORTHAMPTON,   MASS.

ATTENTION!
Something Important for every Purchaser of

DRY GOODS,
to see at

E. G. SOUTHWICK & CO.'S,
NORTHAMPTON,   MASS.

USE
"ACME SOAP"
LEADER IN
QUALITY

Cats appeared in advertisements for such unlikely items as soap, dry goods, stove blacking, and even the Metropolitan Life Insurance Company. *Northampton Historical Society.*

The well-appointed black-and-white pied cat on this turn-of-the-century lemon-crate label serves several purposes. The healthy, serene animal seems to demonstrate the nutritious quality of the fruit in the crate; while the cat's origin recalls wholesomeness, its majestic attitude suggests that the product it endorses may be, in some way, regal.

TOM

OROSI FOOTHILL CITRUS ASSOCIATION
OROSI, TULARE CO.
CALIFORNIA

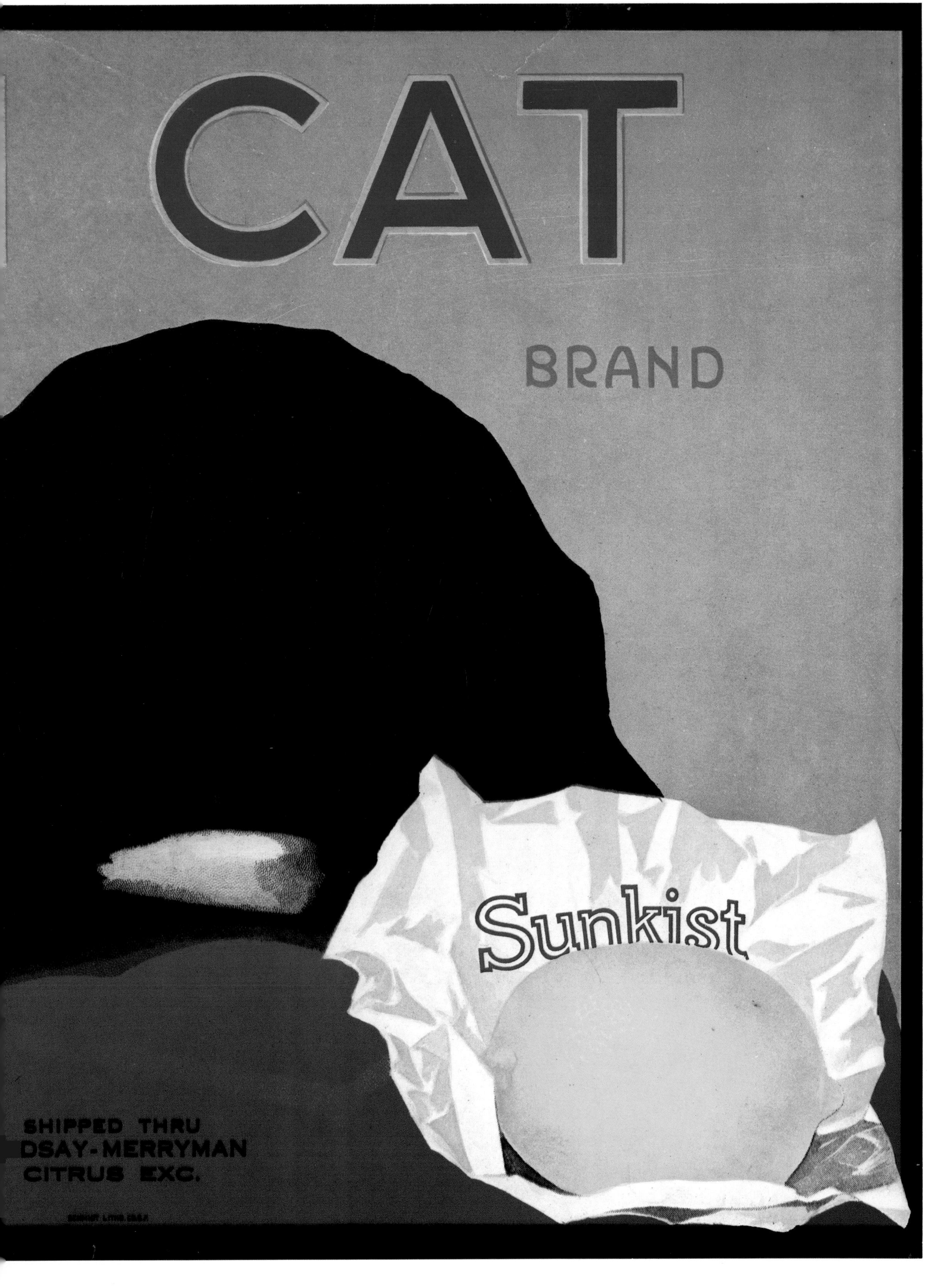
CAT
BRAND
Sunkist
SHIPPED THRU
DSAY-MERRYMAN
CITRUS EXC.

MERRY XMAS IS

21 EDWARD PENFIELD
PELHAM MANOR N.Y.

Cats in Posters

Brooklyn-born Edward Penfield (1866–1925) was one of America's finest graphic artists. During his career, he designed a myriad of magazine covers, posters, and advertisements. As the art editor of *Harper's Magazine*, *Harper's Weekly*, *Harper's Bazaar* from 1890 to 1901, he learned to use commercial lithographic techniques to his own artistic ends, working either with flat colors and patterns influenced by Bonnard or with Lautrec-like splatters. On his *Harper's* covers and posters, Penfield often used the images of the elegant young woman and the Ivy League college man of the "gay 90s," frequently in the company of one or more dignified, graceful, and grinning cats. Edward Penfield is only one in a tradition of artists who used cats in posters. The posters on pages 126 to 131 are by Penfield.

	APRIL					MAY					JUNE			
Sun		4	11	18	25	Sun		2	9	16	23/30	Sun		6	13	20	27
Mon		5	12	19	26	Mon		3	10	17	24/31	Mon		7	14	21	28
Tue		6	13	20	27	Tue		4	11	18	25	Tue	1	8	15	22	29
Wed		7	14	21	28	Wed		5	12	19	26	Wed	2	9	16	23	30
Thu	1	8	15	22	29	Thu		6	13	20	27	Thu	3	10	17	24	
Fri	2	9	16	23	30	Fri		7	14	21	28	Fri	4	11	18	25	
Sat	3	10	17	24		Sat	1	8	15	22	29	Sat	5	12	19	26	

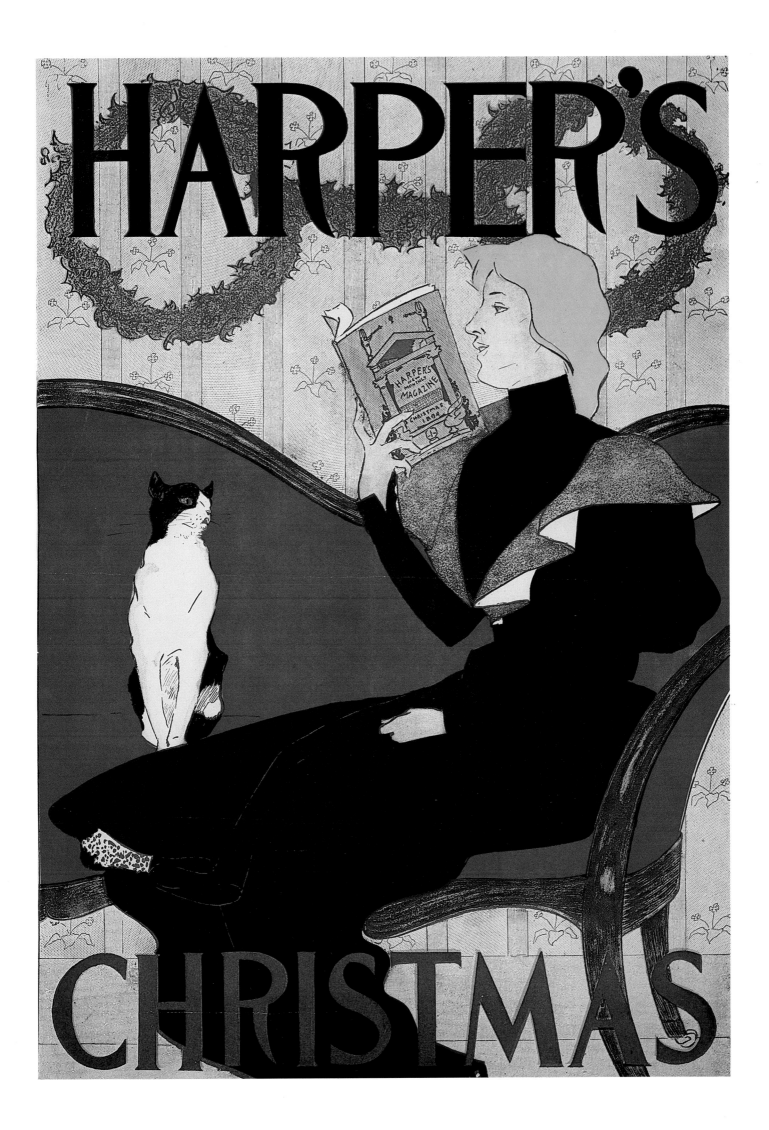

Edouard Manet, *Les Chats*

In 1870, the first important study of cats, *Les Chats*, was published by the French journalist Jules Husson, under the pen name Champfleury. Edouard Manet, a friend of Husson's created this lithograph for the cover. It appeared on the cover of each subsequent edition.

J. ROTHSCHILD, ÉDITEUR, 43, RUE S⁼-ANDRÉ-DES-ARTS, PARIS

CHAMPFLEURY

LES CHATS

HISTOIRE — MŒURS — ANECDOTES

ILLUSTRÉ   ILLUSTRÉ
PAR   PAR

E. Delacroix   Ed. Manet

Brenghel   Ok'Sai

Viollet-le-Duc   Mind, Ribot

UN VOLUME ORNÉ DE NOMBREUSES GRAVURES

5 FRANCS

Théophile Steinlen, Poster Advertising Sterilized Milk

What better way to illustrate the benefits and pleasures of drinking sterilized milk than with a healthy child and several equally hearty cats?

Lait pur de la Vingeanne Stérilisé

Quillot frères
Montigny sur Vingeanne
Côte d'Or

Steinlen

Imp. CHARLES VERNEAU. 114 Rue Oberkampf. PARIS. (DÉPOSÉ.)

Jones

Seen here with his co-star Sigourney Weaver, Jones, an orange-striped cat, was one of the two survivors of the wrath of Geiger's fantastic, ravenous extraterrestrial in *Alien* (1979). *From* Alien, *courtesy of 20th Century-Fox.*

Pepper

Pepper, the very first movie-star cat, worked alongside such motion-picture greats as Charlie Chaplin, Fatty Arbuckle, and the Keystone Kops. Pepper was "discovered" when she climbed up from under a broken plank on director Mack Sennett's set. Sennett later said that Pepper was "as disarming as the lovely Lillian Gish."
Mack Sennett Comedies, photographed by George F. Cannons.

Not all cats are blue-collar workers, however. Although cats have a special talent for killing rodents, they occasionally have been put to work on less grueling assignments. Some have acted on the stage, while others have made names for themselves on television and in the movies. Despite the fact that cats are less prominent in motion-picture history than dogs are, a handful of exemplary felines have risen to superstar status over the years.

The first feline movie star ever was a stray kitten named Pepper who one day poked her head through the floorboards of a stage at Mack Sennett's famous movie studio in California. Eddie Cline, the director on the set, rescued the kitten and added her to the scene he was working on. The quickly improvised script called for actress Louise Fazenda to spill some cream while serving coffee to actor Sterling Ford. Pepper was placed back in the hole she had been lifted out of, which was near one of the legs of the table at which Ford was sitting. Film historian Raymond Lee describes what happened next: "Slowly the cream dripped down and cautiously Pepper stuck first her paw up and then her head; and sniffing the cream, she dipped her pinky into a tiny rivulet, and with aplomb even a professional might not have had, with one take she completed the scene, to loud applause."

Pepper was a great hit, and Sennett was so pleased he said that she was "as disarming as the lovely Lillian Gish." In several later movies she co starred with Frederick Wilhelm, a well-behaved white mouse. In one particularly memorable scene, the two drank milk from the same bowl; Pepper politely restrained herself from adding solid food to her diet. When Pepper finally wandered off, never again to be found, Sennett was so moved he said, "She had courage, that kitty. A lesson for all of us if a time like hers ever comes into our lives. She retired at the top. That's where her name will always shine. And I don't want no trainers hawking any other pussy around here! Pepper's our first and our last feline star!"

The second great cat star in movie history was Orangey, a placid orange tiger who won more awards than any other cat in show business. In his day, Orangey stole scenes from Ray Milland in *Rhubarb,* from Jackie Gleason in *Gigot,* and from Audrey Hepburn in *Breakfast at Tiffany's,* to mention only a few. He also appeared on television and was one of an elite group of animal stars to win more than one Patsy, the Oscar of the animal entertainment world (the first was for his title role in *Rhubarb,* the second for his portrayal of a cat named Cat in *Breakfast at Tiffany's*).

Like most cinematic cats, Orangey had to be trained before his first appearance on the screen. Frank Inn, a famous trainer in the fifties, once explained

his technique. "Cats are absolutely commercial," he said. "They won't work for a pet or an ear rub like other animals. They always have a paw out for a payoff after doing their stint. If the tidbit isn't there, you get a baleful stare, and you can be sure that all the coaxing in the world won't get that cat to do the trick again. You can fool a lot of people a lot of times, but you can fool a cat—just once."

Inn had a great deal of experience working with cats, and he strongly disagreed with the common notion that felines are impossible to train. "It's true that it's harder to train a cat than a dog," he said, "but a cat can still be taught to perform a number of tricks. You can teach it to come when you call it, and to perform a lot of tricks that most people tend to believe are the exclusive property of dogs. Tricks like fetching sticks and balls of string, or rolling over, or playing dead. I once had a cat who had been trained to go to the bathroom on a toilet, and to flush it after he was finished. All it takes is patience and, preferably, a young cat who hasn't had too much exposure to people who for some reason expect their cats to be independent and uncooperative."

Other cats have had important roles in movies. Pyewacket won a Patsy Award for his portrayal of a modern day witch's cat in the 1959 film *Bell, Book and Candle*. Pyewacket's co-stars in that film were James Stewart, Kim Novak, Jack Lemmon, and Ernie Kovacs. In the chilling 1979 movie *Alien*, an orange-striped cat named Jones played alongside Sigourney Weaver as one of two survivors of the destroyed ship *Nostromo*. A white longhair named Solomon added a feline touch to the forces of evil that pursued James Bond in *Diamonds Are Forever*. And a large ginger tabby played alongside Art Carney in *Harry and Tonto*. A few cats have even made it into television, the most notable being the prim Minerva on the series *Our Miss Brooks*. But the greatest strides towards stardom ever made by cats have been in the field of advertising. Cats have been used to peddle everything from shoe heels to cigars, and they have been associated with products as dissimilar as perfume and cat food.

The most successful advertising cat of all time was, of course, a fourteen-pound orange tiger named Morris. Like Pepper, Morris started out as a stray. He was discovered by noted animal trainer Bob Martwick in a Humane Society near Chicago, where he was due to be destroyed. Martwick thought the cat had star potential and so paid five dollars for his release. Because the cat had come within an inch of his life, Martwick named him Lucky. He also set about preparing him for an acting career, a job he found surprisingly easy. Unlike most cats, Morris was very easy to train. He would stay where he was put—an

Tonto

Tonto, a large ginger tabby "with eyes the color of marrons glacés," co-starred with Art Carney in Paul Mazursky's *Harry and Tonto* (1973). This intrepid feline was the fictional creation of Mazursky and Josh Greenfield.
From Harry and Tonto, courtesy of 20th Century-Fox.

Orangey

Although a real-life cat has never won an Oscar, Orangey, pictured here with Audrey Hepburn and George Peppard in *Breakfast at Tiffany's* (1961), won two Patsy awards for her cinematic achievements. Orangey, called "the world's meanest cat" by one movie executive, also appeared in *Rhubarb*, *Gigot*, and the TV series *Our Miss Brooks*.
From Breakfast at Tiffany's, *copyright © 1961 by Paramount Pictures Corporation and Jurow-Shepherd Production.*

enormous asset for work on television—and he was virtually impossible to distract. Martwick could even throw a bucket of water at Morris, and he would remain perfectly still.

Morris's television debut came in 1969, when he appeared in a commercial for the 9-Lives cat-food division of Star-Kist Foods, Inc. Called "9-Lives Presents Morris," the commercial was an immediate success, and Morris became a celebrity. He was even made an honorary director of Star-Kist and given the power to veto new cat-food flavors that didn't strike his fancy. In 1973 he won a Patsy for "outstanding performance in a TV commercial," a category that was created especially for him. During the final days of the Nixon administration, he was invited to the White House to "sign" an animal-protection bill by pressing an inky paw onto the paper.

When he wasn't jetting around the country or doing his bit before the cameras, Morris lived in a six-and-a-half-acre kennel near Chicago, where he lorded it over a houseful of dogs. The kennel was run by Morris's old friend Martwick along with Martwick's partner, Stuart Schroder. Morris didn't live in a cage, of course; he had the run of the place during the day, and at night he slept upstairs in Martwick's apartment. Morris died in 1978 of natural causes.

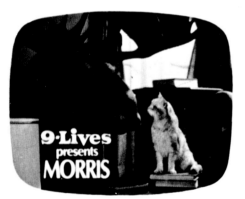

MORRIS: In the garage!

ANNCR: (VO) Nine-Lives presents Morris.

LADY: I found this in the attic!
MORRIS: It's not my side of the family.

LADY: Din din, Morris.

LADY: Where should I hang it?

MORRIS: I'll eat when the moose eats!

Morris's popularity did not diminish after his death, as executives at Star-Kist were surprised to discover. As a matter of fact, the extraordinary cat's grip on his fans actually seemed to increase. The executives quickly began what turned into an exhaustive two-and-a-half-year search for a suitable successor. The winner of the nationwide talent hunt was another stray, this one found in a Humane Society in California.

The new Morris looks and acts so much like the old one that even the most devoted fans have trouble telling them apart. And the new Morris has the same mysterious power to move his admirers. Barbara Burn, Morris II's "biographer," once described to me the magnitude of that power. "I've always allowed cats a certain kind of unique quality," she said, "but I certainly never thought of them as being stars of any sort. You know, they're just animals, for God's sake. And this cat seemed to just sit there. But then, at our first book signing at a B. Dalton, I looked at all the people who had stood in line on a rainy day to meet this cat, and I saw how their eyes lit up when they saw him. Then I realized that this cat really was special. There's something quite meaningful about him. Thirty-nine out of forty people on the street recognize him, and that, I think, is amazing."

Morris The Cat

One of the most famous individuals in modern feline history was Morris, the large, orange spokesman for 9 Lives cat food. Morris, called Lucky before his rise to fame, was found at the Humane Society of Hinsdale, Illinois, by his owner/trainer, Bob Martwick, in 1968. This feline superstar was so successful that he received a Patsy award in 1973 for being the best animal actor in TV commercials. He was also made an honorary director of Star Kist Foods, Inc., 9 Lives' parent company, where he was given the power to reject new cat-food flavors as suited his fancy. Morris was even the subject of a book, *Morris: An Intimate Biography*. In 1978, the nation mourned when Morris the Cat passed away.
Courtesy, Star Kist Foods, Inc.

LADY: Don't be finicky. There's Nine-Lives.

MORRIS: Maybe I'll start without him.

LADY: Super Supper? Beef and Liver!

MORRIS: Nine-Lives Beef and Liver! Yum yum!

ANNCR: (VO) Nine-Lives, nutritious foods cats really like.

Even Morris. MORRIS: They can stuff me with Nine-Lives anytime. (SFX: LIP SMACK)

ats have had more elevating assignments as well, most notably in the field of science. One of the earliest feline contributions to science came a century ago, when a cat served as one of Eadweard Muybridge's subjects in his monumental investigation of animal locomotion. The cat played only a passive role, of course, but its contribution was significant nonetheless. By walking, trotting, and galloping in front of Muybridge's specially designed lenses, the cat revealed the precise mechanics of how it got from one place to another. In our age of videotapes and laser holograms, this may not seem like much of a discovery, but in Muybridge's time it was important scientific news. Artists still use Muybridge's studies as models and references when they face the difficult task of depicting bodies in motion.

Muybridge's photographs reveal the cat to be every bit as graceful as it seems to the naked eye. The pictures prove that a cat has gaits similar to those of a horse, although the transitions between the cat's gaits are smoother and the motion is more refined. The photographs also underscore the domestic cat's relation to its cousins in the wild. Most of the pictures are quite beautiful. It is not for nothing that the cat has a reputation for being one of the most graceful animals in the world.

Eadweard Muybridge,
Animals in Locomotion,
The Cat

Neg. no. 329455, Courtesy of the American Museum of Natural History.

Displaying unusual musical
talents, this cat tickles the ivo-
ries with its paws.
*Copyright © Joe McNally/Cam-
era Five.*

Philippe Halsman, *Dali Atomicus*

In order to create a portrait of surrealist Salvador Dali in the air, photographer Philippe Halsman (1906–1979) hired three cats and worked with the help of four assistants. One assistant threw the water while the other three tossed the cats, who were very patient indeed. By the time he arrived at this final image, Halsman had shot the setup twenty-six times.
© 1968 by Philipe Halsman.

Cats played a significant role in the early days of space exploration. French scientists launched a thoroughly trained kitty ninety-eight miles into the sky aboard a rocket called the *Véronique*. The cat was prepared for its mission by being subjected to a bank of medical and physical tests and by being taught to remain absolutely motionless for extended periods of time. The cat's reactions to the journey gave scientists valuable information about a living creature's reactions to the rigors of space travel—information that would one day be applied to human beings embarking on lengthier trips away from earth.

Elsewhere in the scientific community, cats have served as invaluable test subjects for researchers working with new drugs and medical procedures that are too experimental to be used safely on human beings. This is a subject that depresses or angers many cat lovers, but the fact is that laboratory cats have enabled scientists to make great advances in their quests to conquer human suffering and disease. Cats have given researchers crucial insights into cancers, heart disease, nervous disorders, and many other ailments; they have even been used in experiments intended to plumb the depths of the human mind. Cats have been unwitting martyrs in these endeavors, but many of us can hope to live longer, and to pursue more fulfilling lives, as a direct result of their sacrifices.

Not all experiments with cats work out successfully. Certainly the most hilarious example of a failed experiment involved an attempt by the United States Army to train cats for use in military operations. Because cats have far more sensitive eyes than humans do, enabling them to see clearly even in near-total darkness, the Army thought they might be useful as guides for soldiers on night patrol. A number of specially trained cats were shipped to Vietnam in 1968, where they were to be tested in the jungle. The test, as most cat owners have probably already guessed, was a miserable failure. Here are some excerpts from the final Army report: "A squad, upon being ordered to move out, was led off in all different directions by the cats; on many occasions the animal led their troops racing through thick brush in pursuit of field mice and birds. Troops had to force the cats to follow the direction of the patrol; the practice often led to the animals stalking and attacking the dangling pack straps of the American soldiers marching directly in front of the animal. If the weather was inclement or even threatening inclemency, the cats were never anywhere to be found."

Unknown American Artist, *The Cat*

A very unusual piece of American naïve art, this bird-catching cat's head may be a tribute to someone's hunter cat or, perhaps, a family emblem. *National Gallery of Art, Washington, D.C., Collection of Edgar William and Bernice Chrysler Garbisch.*

Polly and Her Pals

Cicero's Cat

Comic-Strip Cats

If cats have not learned how to eat with a knife and fork in real life, they've at least learned to walk upright in comic strips. Dozens of cats have appeared in the funnies since the very first one in 1896. Many cats, in fact, have starred in their own strips: Krazy Kat, Garfield, Fritz, Pussycat Princess, and Heathcliff, to name a few.

Some comic-strip cats, like Garfield, are portrayed as real cats that run around on all fours and do the things that real cats do—like terrorize dogs, steal food, and oversleep. Others, like Krazy Kat, walk on two legs and use their front paws like human hands. They can answer the telephone, throw bricks, or fly an airplane, but they still think like cats. Finally, there are a number of feline comic-strip heroes who seem to be no more than humans wearing cat masks; Fritz the Cat is a good example. He is not really a cat but a little boy entering puberty. His chief concern is sex and his entire life revolves around its pursuit.

Cats make great comic-strip characters because they are physically versatile; they manage to find themselves in a variety of situations. Cats also seem to have a basically mischievous attitude toward the traditions and social taboos that humans take seriously. Or at least we assume they do, based on their aloofness in the face of life's major and minor events. Finally, we enjoy imagining what cats—which appear so mysterious—might be thinking. The comic-strip artist reveals that, as we suspected, Garfield feels no guilt and Felix is a charmer!

Felix the Cat

Unlike many other comic cats, Felix the Cat made his debut not in newspapers but on the silver screen. Credited with the creation of Felix, Pat Sullivan and his animation studio released their first silent Felix cartoons in 1917. However, Felix's inventor was probably Otto Messmer, one of Sullivan's artists. Felix was the star of the first "talkie" cartoon, a year before Disney's *Mickey Mouse*. He also appeared in one of the very first experimental television broadcasts in 1928 and remained NBC's official test pattern until the late 1930s. In 1927, Felix the Cat joined the other newspaper-comic cats when he received his own daily and Sunday strips.

E.W. Hammons
Presents

Felix the Cat
Cartoons by
Pat Sullivan

Produced by Bijou Films, Inc.

Educational Pictures
"THE SPICE OF THE PROGRAM"

PUT ME ON YOUR SCREEN AND SEE WHAT A BRIGHT LITTLE FELLOW I AM.
MY TRICKS WILL PUT YOUR AUDIENCES IN THE BEST OF HUMOR—AND I'LL MAKE 'EM LAUGH NINE TIMES AS MANY TIMES AS A CAT HAS LIVES.
I'M DOING IT NOW IN FIVE THOUSAND THEATRES FELIX

FELIX MEANS EXTRA PROFIT FOR THE SHOWMAN WHO EXPLOITS HIM.

EDUCATIONAL FILM EXCHANGES, Inc.
E.W. Hammons
President

MEMBER, MOTION PICTURE PRODUCERS AND DISTRIBUTORS OF AMERICA, INC.
WILL H. HAYS, PRESIDENT

George Herriman

George Joseph Herriman, the inspired creator of Krazy Kat, was born in New Orleans in 1880. A high-school dropout, he worked for his father, a baker, while he spent a great deal of time drawing. In 1901, Herriman married and moved to New York, where he earned a living as a political and sports cartoonist for *Judge*, *Life*, and the New York *News* and *World*. He also worked on several comic strips, including *Lariat Pete*, *Bud Smith*, and *Major Ozone*, before he began his association with William Randolph Hearst and his King Features Syndicate through the New York *Journal* in 1908. Even though *Krazy Kat* was never the popular phenomenon that *Peanuts* is today, Hearst, a devoted lover of Herriman's strip, kept *Krazy Kat* on—to the absolute delight of a select, almost fanatic, group of enthusiasts that included President Woodrow Wilson—until the artist's death in 1944.

I WAS CLEOPATRA ONCE SHE SAID.

archy and mehitabel

Originated by comic-verse writer, Don Marquis, archy and mehitabel is a collection of free verse, ostensibly composed by archy, a cockroach, in praise of mehitabel, his alley cat companion with a human soul. Mehitabel claimed to have passed through a number of reincarnations before assuming her feline form—certainly a come-down from such former identities as Cleopatra. George Herriman, the creator of *Krazy Kat*, provided the delightful drawings that accompanied all three volumes of lower-case, unpunctuated insect verse.

AND THEN, WHAT DID THE DUKE SAY TO YOU?

Krazy Kat

Many people consider George Herriman's *Krazy Kat* to be the greatest comic strip of all time. Originally a runner for another strip, *The Dingbat Family*, or *The Family Upstairs*, Krazy made his or her (its gender was of little importance and often changed) first appearance in the now-defunct New York *Journal* on June 20, 1910. Krazy and his/her brick-tossing paramour, Ignatz Mouse, gradually upstaged the Dingbats and were given their own strip on October 28, 1913.

King Features Syndicate, Inc.

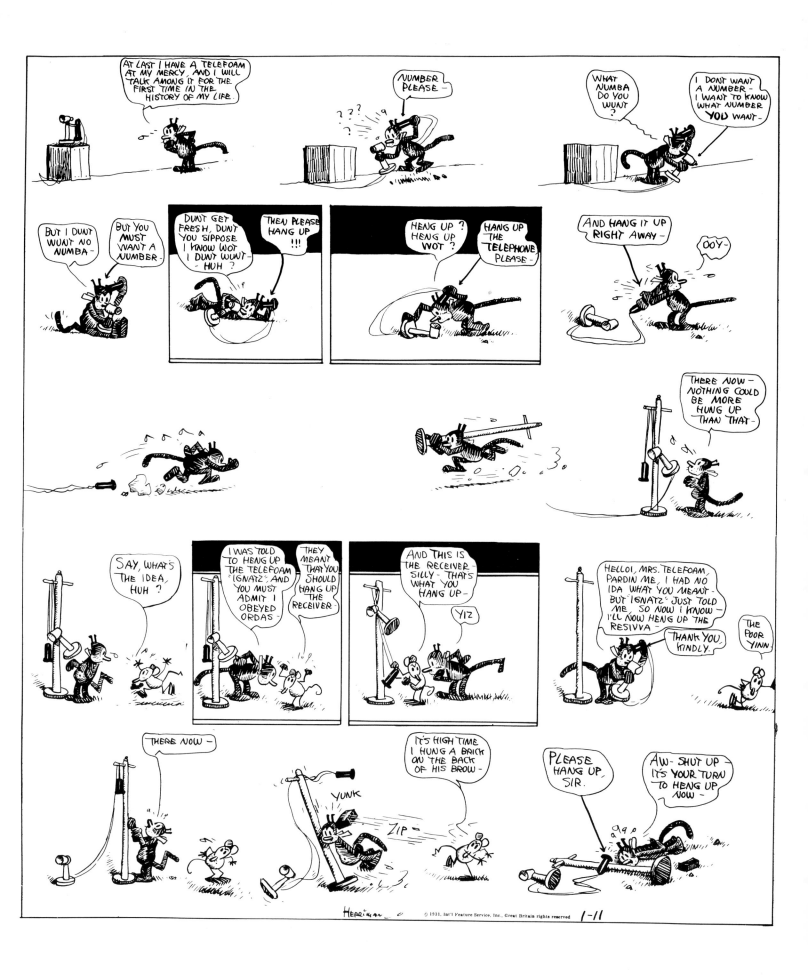

PART THREE

A DARK MIRROR

The Cat as Symbol

ne cherishes cats for what they are, but they are just as important for what they represent, or seem to represent. Much more than a mere house pet, the cat is a potent symbol whose influence on the course of human culture has been considerable. We may all think we know what cats *are*, but over the centuries we have never quite been able to arrive at an enduring definition of what they *mean*.

Cats, in their profound inscrutability, provide a very fertile ground for the human imagination. Their tantalizing aloofness and independence invite us to supply meanings, to flesh out the bare outline their behavior suggests. Much of man's relationship with cats has consisted precisely of this. We have reinvented the cat again and again through the course of our shared history, a fact that has sometimes brought our feline companions great prosperity and at other times subjected them to even greater suffering.

Michael Skott,
Black and White Cat
Copyright © Michael Skott.

Not only was the black cat a welcome guest at witches' sabbaths, it was often an essential ingredient in their brews.

The Cat that Walked by Himself

Rudyard Kipling provides a mythic explanation for several aspects of the house cat's personality in a wonderful story called "The Cat that Walked by Himself." Kipling traces the cat's legendary independence to a bargain its ancient ancestor struck with primitive man. The agreement they arrive at isn't entirely favorable to the cat—it calls for periodic doses of physical abuse—but it provides felines with a tentative place in human society without making them entirely dependent and servile in the way that dogs and other domesticated animals are.

Hear and attend and listen; for this befell and behappened and became and was, O my Best Beloved, when the Tame animals were wild. The Dog was wild, and the Horse was wild, and the Cow was wild, and the Sheep was wild, and the Pig was wild—as wild as wild could be—and they walked in the Wet Wild Woods by their wild lones. But the wildest of all the wild animals was the Cat. He walked by himself, and all places were alike to him.

Of course the Man was wild too. He was dreadfully wild. He didn't even begin to be tame till he met the Woman, and she told him that she did not like living in his wild ways. She picked out a nice dry Cave, instead of a heap of wet leaves, to lie down in; and she strewed clean sand on the floor; and she lit a nice fire of wood at the back of the Cave; and she hung a dried wild-horse skin, tail-down, across the opening of the Cave; and she said, "Wipe your feet, dear, when you come in, and now we'll keep house."

That night, Best Beloved, they ate wild sheep roasted on the hot stones, and flavoured with wild garlic and wild pepper; and wild duck stuffed with wild rice and wild fenugreek and wild coriander; and marrow-bones of wild oxen; and wild cherries, and wild grenadillas. Then the Man went to sleep in front of the fire ever so happy; but the Woman sat up, combing her hair. She took the bone of the shoulder of mutton—the big flat blade-bone—and she looked at the wonderful marks on it, and she threw more wood on the fire, and she made a Magic. She made the First Singing Magic in the world.

Out of the Wet Wild Woods all the wild animals gathered together where they could see the light of the fire a long way off, and they wondered what it meant.

Then Wild Horse stamped with his wild foot and said, "O my Friends and O my Enemies, why have the Man and the Woman made that great light in that great Cave, and what harm will it do us?"

Wild Dog lifted up his wild nose and smelled the smell of the roast mutton, and said, "I will go up and see and look, and say; for I think it is good. Cat, come with me."

"Nenni!" said the Cat. "I am the Cat who walks by himself, and all places are alike to me. I will not come."

"Then we can never be friends again," said Wild Dog, and he trotted off to the Cave. But when he had gone a little way the Cat said to himself, "All places are alike to me. Why should I not go too and see and look and come away at my own liking?" So he slipped after Wild Dog softly, very softly, and hid himself where he could hear everything.

When Wild Dog reached the mouth of the Cave he lifted up the dried horse-skin with his nose and sniffed the beautiful smell of the roast mutton, and the Woman, looking at the blade-bone, heard him, and laughed, and said, "Here comes the first. Wild Thing out of the Wild Woods, what do you want?"

Wild Dog said, "O my Enemy and Wife of my Enemy, what is this that smells so good in the Wild Woods?"

Then the Woman picked up a roasted mutton-bone and threw it to Wild Dog and said, "Wild Thing out of the Wild Woods, taste and try." Wild Dog gnawed the bone, and it was more delicious than anything he had ever tasted, and he said, "O my Enemy and Wife of my Enemy, give me another."

Rudyard Kipling produced a number of beautiful drawings to accompany his *Just So Stories*. This illustration for "The Cat that Walked by Himself" is as whimsical, and yet as logical, as the story itself.

The Woman said, "Wild Thing out of the Wild Woods, help my Man to hunt through the day and guard this Cave at night, and I will give you as many roast bones as you need."

"Ah!" said the Cat, listening. "This is a very wise Woman, but she is not so wise as I am."

Wild Dog crawled into the Cave and laid his head on the Woman's lap, and said, "O my Friend and Wife of my Friend, I will help your Man to hunt through the day, and at night I will guard your Cave."

"Ah!" said the Cat, listening. "That is a very foolish Dog." And he went back through the Wet Wild Woods waving his wild tail, and walking by his wild lone. But he never told anybody.

When the Man waked up he said, "What is Wild Dog doing here?" And the Woman said, "His name is not Wild Dog any more, but the First Friend, because he will be our friend for always and always and always. Take him with you when you go hunting."

Next night the Woman cut great green armfuls of fresh grass from the water-meadows, and dried it before the fire, so that it smelt like new-mown hay, and she sat at the mouth of the Cave and plaited a halter out of horse-hide, and she looked at the shoulder-of-mutton bone—at the big broad blade-bone—and she made a Magic. She made the Second Singing Magic in the world.

Out of the Wild Woods all the wild animals wondered what had happened to Wild Dog, and at last Wild Horse stamped with his foot and said, "I will go and see and say why Wild Dog has not returned. Cat, come with me."

"Nenni!" said the Cat. "I am the Cat who walks by himself, and all places are alike to me. I will not come." But all the same he followed Wild Horse softly, very softly, and hid himself where he could hear everything.

When the Woman heard Wild Horse tripping and stumbling on his long mane, she laughed and said, "Here comes the second. Wild Thing out of the Wild Woods, what do you want?"

Wild Horse said, "O my Enemy and Wife of my Enemy, where is Wild Dog?"

The Woman laughed, and picked up the blade-bone and looked at it, and said, "Wild Thing out of the Wild Woods, you did not come here for Wild Dog, but for the sake of this good grass."

And Wild Horse, tripping and stumbling on his long mane, said, "That is true; give it me to eat."

The Woman said, "Wild Thing out of the Wild Woods, bend your wild head and wear what I give you, and you shall eat the wonderful grass three times a day."

"Ah!" said the Cat, listening. "This is a clever Woman, but she is not so clever as I am."

Wild Horse bent his wild head, and the Woman slipped the plaited-hide halter over it, and Wild Horse breathed on the Woman's feet and said, "O my Mistress, and Wife of my Master, I will be your servant for the sake of the wonderful grass."

"Ah!" said the Cat, listening. "That is a very foolish Horse." And he went back through the Wet Wild Woods, waving his wild tail and walking by his wild lone. But he never told anybody.

When the Man and the Dog came back from hunting, the Man said, "What is Wild Horse doing here?" And the Woman said, "His name is not Wild Horse any more, but the First Servant, because he will carry us from place to place for always and always and always. Ride on his back when you go hunting."

Next day, holding her wild head high that her wild horns should not catch in the wild trees, Wild Cow came up to the Cave, and the Cat followed, and hid himself just the same as before; and everything happened just the same as before; and the Cat said the same things as before; and when Wild Cow had promised to give her milk to the Woman every day in exchange for the wonderful grass, the Cat went back through the Wet Wild Woods waving his wild tail and walking by his wild lone, just the same as before. But he never told anybody. And when the Man and the Horse and the Dog came home from hunting and asked the same questions same as before, the Woman said, "Her name is not Wild Cow any more, but the Giver of Good Food. She will give us the warm white milk for always and always and always, and I will take care of her while you and the First Friend and the First Servant go hunting."

Next day the Cat waited to see if any other Wild Thing would go up to the Cave, but no one moved in the Wet Wild Woods, so the Cat walked there by himself; and he saw the Woman milking the Cow, and he saw the light of the fire in the Cave, and he smelt the smell of the warm white milk.

Cat said, "O my Enemy and Wife of my Enemy, where did Wild Cow go?"

The Woman laughed and said, "Wild Thing out of the Wild Woods, go back to the Woods again, for I have braided up my hair, and I have put away the magic blade-bone and we have no more need of either friends or servants in our Cave."

Cat said, "I am not a friend, and I am not a servant. I am the Cat who walks by himself, and I wish to come into your Cave."

Woman said, "Then why did you not come with First Friend on the first night?"

Cat grew very angry and said, "Has Wild Dog told tales of me?"

Then the Woman laughed and said, "You are the Cat who walks by himself, and all places are alike to you. You are neither a friend nor a servant. You have said it yourself. Go away and walk by yourself in all places alike."

Then Cat pretended to be sorry and said, "Must I never come into the Cave? Must I never sit by the warm fire? Must I never drink the warm white milk? You are very wise and very beautiful. You should not be cruel even to a Cat."

Woman said, "I knew I was wise, but I did not know I was beautiful. So I will make a bargain with you. If ever I say one word in your praise, you may come into the Cave."

"And if you say two words in my praise?" said the Cat.

"I never shall," said the Woman, "but if I say two words in your praise, you may sit by the fire in the Cave."

"And if you say three words?" said the Cat.

"I never shall," said the Woman, "but if I say three words in your praise, you may drink the warm white milk three times a day for always and always and always."

Then the Cat arched his back and said, "Now let the Curtain at the mouth of the Cave, and the Fire at the back of the Cave, and the Milk-pots that stand beside the Fire, remember what my Enemy and the Wife of my Enemy has said." And he went away through the Wet Wild Woods waving his wild tail and walking by his wild lone.

That night when the Man and the Horse and the Dog came home from hunting, the Woman did not tell them of the bargain that she had made with the Cat, because she was afraid that they might not like it.

Cat went far and far away and hid himself in the Wet Wild Woods by his wild lone for a long time till the Woman forgot all about him. Only the Bat—the little upside-down Bat—that hung inside the Cave knew where Cat hid; and every evening Bat would fly to Cat with news of what was happening.

One evening Bat said, "There is a Baby in the Cave. He is new and pink and fat and small, and the Woman is very fond of him."

"Ah," said the Cat, listening. "But what is the Baby fond of?"

"He is fond of things that are soft and tickle," said the Bat. "He is fond of warm things to hold in his arms when he goes to sleep. He is fond of being played with. He is fond of all those things."

"Ah," said the Cat, listening. "Then my time has come."

Next night Cat walked through the Wet Wild Woods and hid very near the Cave till morning-time, and Man and Dog and Horse went hunting. The Woman was busy cooking that morning, and the Baby cried and interrupted. So she carried him outside the Cave and gave him a handful of pebbles to play with. But still the Baby cried.

Then the Cat put out his paddy paw and patted the Baby on the cheek, and it cooed; and the Cat rubbed against its fat knees and tickled it under its fat chin with his tail. And the Baby laughed; and the Woman heard him and smiled.

Then the Bat—the little upside-down Bat—that hung in the mouth of the Cave said, "O my Hostess and Wife of my Host and Mother of my Host's Son, a Wild Thing from the Wild Woods is most beautifully playing with your Baby."

"A blessing on that Wild Thing whoever he may be," said the Woman, straightening her back, "for I was a busy woman this morning and he has done me a service."

That very minute and second, Best Beloved, the dried horse-skin Curtain that was stretched tail-down at the mouth of the Cave fell down—*woosh!*—because it remembered the bargain she had made with the Cat; and when the Woman went to pick it up—lo and behold!—the Cat was sitting quite comfy inside the Cave.

"O my Enemy and Wife of my Enemy and Mother of my Enemy," said the Cat, "it is I: for you have spoken a word in my praise, and now I can sit within the Cave for always and always and always. But still I am the Cat who walks by himself, and all places are alike to me."

The Woman was very angry, and shut her lips tight and took up her spinning-wheel and began to spin.

But the Baby cried because the Cat had gone away, and the Woman could not hush it, for it struggled and kicked and grew black in the face.

"O my Enemy and Wife of my Enemy and Mother of my Enemy," said the Cat, "take a strand of the thread that you are spinning and tie it to your spindle-whorl and drag it along the floor, and I will show you a Magic that shall make your Baby laugh as loudly as he is now crying."

"I will do so," said the Woman, "because I am at my wits' end; but I will not thank you for it."

She tied the thread to the little clay spindle-whorl and drew it across the floor, and the Cat ran after it and patted it with his paws and rolled head over heels, and tossed it backward over his shoulder and chased it between his hind legs and pretended to lose it, and pounced down upon it again, till the Baby laughed as loudly as it had been crying, and scrambled after the Cat and frolicked all over the Cave till it grew tired and settled down to sleep with the Cat in its arms.

"Now," said Cat, "I will sing the Baby a song that shall keep him fast asleep for an hour." And he began to purr, loud and low, low and loud, till the Baby fell fast asleep. The Woman smiled as she looked down upon the two of them, and said, "That was wonderfully done. No question but you are very clever, O Cat."

That very minute and second, Best Beloved, the smoke of the Fire at the back of the Cave came down in clouds from the roof—*puff!*—because it remembered the bargain she had made with the Cat; and when it had cleared away—lo and behold!—the Cat was sitting quite comfy close to the fire.

"O my Enemy and Wife of my Enemy and Mother of my Enemy," said the Cat, "it is I: for you have spoken a second word in my praise, and now I can sit by the warm fire at the back of the Cave for always and always and always. But still I am the Cat who walks by himself, and all places are alike to me."

Then the Woman was very very angry, and let down her hair and put more wood on the fire and brought out the broad blade-bone of the shoulder of mutton and began to make a Magic that should prevent her from saying a third word in praise of the Cat. It was not a Singing magic, Best Beloved, it was a Still Magic; and by and by the Cave grew so still that little wee-wee mouse crept out of a corner and ran across the floor.

"O my Enemy and Wife of my Enemy and Mother of my Enemy," said the Cat, "is that little mouse part of your Magic?"

"Ouh! Chee! No indeed!" said the Woman, and she dropped the blade-bone and jumped upon the footstool in front of the fire and braided up her hair very quick for fear that the mouse should run up it.

"Ah," said the Cat, watching. "Then the mouse will do me no harm if I eat it?"

"No," said the Woman, braiding up her hair, "eat it quickly and I will ever be grateful to you."

Cat made one jump and caught the little mouse, and the Woman said, "A hundred thanks. Even the First Friend is not quick enough to catch little mice as you have done. You must be very wise."

That very minute and second, O Best Beloved, the Milk-pot that stood by the fire cracked in two pieces—*ffft!*—because it remembered the bargain she had made with the Cat; and when the Woman jumped down from the footstool—lo and behold!—the Cat was lapping up the warm white milk that lay in one of the broken pieces.

"O my Enemy and Wife of my Enemy and Mother of my Enemy," said the Cat, "it is I: for you have spoken three words in my praise, and now I can drink the warm white milk three times a day for always and always and always. But *still* I am the Cat who walks by himself, and all places are alike to me."

Then the Woman laughed and set the Cat a bowl of the warm white milk and said, "O Cat, you are as clever as a man, but remember that your bargain was not made with the Man or the Dog, and I do not know what they will do when they come home."

"What is that to me?" said the Cat. "If I have my place in the Cave by the fire and my warm white milk three times a day I do not care what the Man or the Dog can do."

That evening when the Man and the Dog came into the Cave, the Woman told them all the story of the bargain, while the Cat sat by the fire and smiled. Then the Man said, "Yes, but he has not made a bargain with *me* or with all proper Men after me." Then he took off his two leather boots and he took up his little stone axe (that makes three) and he fetched a piece of wood and a hatchet (that is five altogether), and he set them out in a row and he said, "Now we will make *our* bargain. If you do not catch mice when you are in the Cave for always and always and always, I will throw these five things at you whenever I see you, and so shall all proper Men do after me."

"Ah!" said the Woman, listening. "This is a very clever Cat, but he is not so clever as my Man."

The Cat counted the five things (and they looked very knobby) and he said, "I will catch mice when I am in the Cave for always and always and always; but *still* I am the Cat who walks by himself, and all places are alike to me."

"Not when I am near," said the Man. "If you had not said that last I would have put all these things away for always and always and always; but now I am going to throw my two boots and my little stone axe (that makes three) at you whenever I meet you. And so shall all proper Men do after me!"

Then the Dog said, "Wait a minute. He has not made a bargain with *me* or with all proper Dogs after me." And he showed his teeth and said, "If you are not kind to the Baby while I am in the Cave for always and always and always, I will hunt you till I catch you, and when I catch you I will bite you. And so shall all proper Dogs do after me."

"Ah!" said the Woman, listening. "This is a very clever Cat, but he is not so clever as the Dog."

Cat counted the Dog's teeth (and they looked very pointed) and he said, "I will be kind to the Baby while I am in the Cave, as long as he does not pull my tail too hard, for always and always and always. But *still* I am the Cat who walks by himself, and all places are alike to me."

"Not when I am near," said the Dog. "If you had not said that last I would have shut my mouth for always and always and always; but *now* I am going to hunt you up a tree whenever I meet you. And so shall all proper Dogs do after me."

Then the Man threw his two boots and his little stone axe (that makes three) at the Cat, and the Cat ran out of the Cave and the Dog chased him up a tree; and from that day to this, Best Beloved, three proper Men out of five will always throw things at a Cat whenever they meet him, and all proper Dogs will chase him up a tree. But the Cat keeps his side of the bargain too. He will kill mice, and he will be kind to Babies when he is in the house, just as long as they do not pull his tail too hard. But when he has done that, and between times, and when the moon gets up and night comes, he is the Cat that walks by himself, and all places are alike to him. Then he goes out to the Wet Wild Woods or up the Wet Wild Trees or on the Wet Wild Roofs, waving his wild tail and walking by his wild lone.

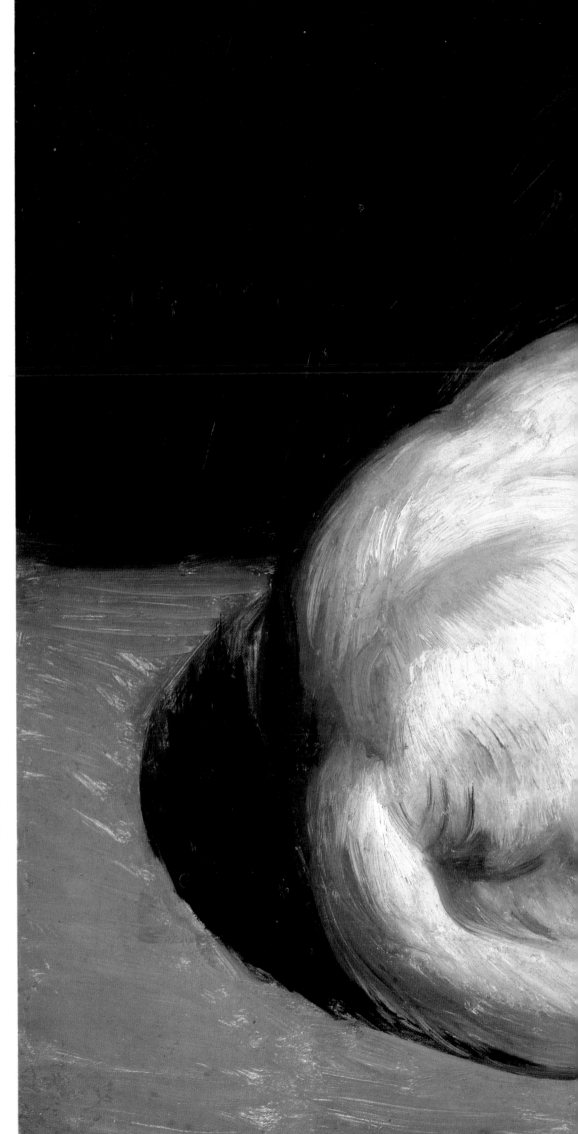

Théodore Géricault, *The White Cat*

Unlike the more violent and active animals portrayed by the painters of the French romantic school of the early nineteenth century, Géricault's (1791–1824) white cat is depicted in a rare moment of quiet repose. Yet, it is still represented with the broad, flamboyant brush strokes that characterize both the artist and the movement.
Ny Carlsberg Glyptok, Copenhagen, Denmark.

Bastet

In ancient Egypt, Bastet, represented in effigy sometimes as a woman with a cat's head and sometimes as a very graceful cat, was worshipped as the goddess of femininity and maternity. Centered in Busbastis, now a group of ruins called Tell Basta, the cult of Bastet began in the Eleventh Dynasty, nearly 4,000 years ago, and lasted well into the Roman period. Egyptian women envied Bastet for her beauty, her slanting eyes, and her noble, feline posture and sensuality. *Metropolitan Museum of Art, Purchase, 1958. Funds from various donors.*

Terry Gruber, *Buddha and Cat*

According to Buddhist legend, when it was time for the Buddha to enter Nirvana, all the animals in the world were called to bear witness. In its own independent way, the cat fell asleep and missed the ceremony. For this reason, the cat could not enter Nirvana, and it was the only animal that was not protected. Yet over the years the cat became so well loved that it was restored to the position of other animals. In fact, there are even temples dedicated to the cat in Japan. *Copyright © Terry Gruber.*

The Egyptians were the cat's first human companions. They were also his first venerators. As cats earned an important niche in the Egyptian economy— by combating the invasions of vermin that imperiled crops and food supplies— they gained a place in Egyptian spiritual life as well. In the very cradle of the cat/human relationship, cats began as servants and grew up to be gods.

Cat worship began gradually in Egypt. As cats came to occupy a larger and larger place in society, their spiritual significance increased. As time went by, they came to be identified with Bastet, the goddess of fertility and wife of the sun god, Ra. Statues of Bastet originally depicted the deity with a human body and the head of a cat, but later the human form was abandoned altogether. Thus did the first genuine cat goddess begin her reign.

The rules of conduct governing the Bastet cult were quite severe. Killing a cat was punishable by death, a fact that made most Egyptians careful not to be found even in the vicinity of a dead cat. Foreigners didn't always understand this prohibition; a Roman soldier who maliciously killed a cat during the reign of Ptolemy was immediately executed by a mortified populace. Bereaved Egyptians mourned dead cats by shaving off their eyebrows, weeping publicly, beating their breasts, and erecting monuments and memorials.

Furred Serpent

It is probable that no writer has done more to shape our ideas about cats than Carl Van Vechten. Here, in an excerpt from his classic, The Tiger in the House, *Van Vechten explains why cats sometimes bring out the very worst in their human companions.*

One is permitted to assume an attitude of placid indifference in the matter of elephants, cockatoos, H. G. Wells, Sweden, roast beef, Puccini, and even Mormonism, but in the matter of cats it seems necessary to take a firm stand. The cat himself insists upon this; he invariably inspires strong feelings. He is, indeed, the only animal who does. From his admirers he evokes an intense adoration which usually finds an outlet in exaggerated expression. It is practically impossible for a cat-lover to meet a stray feline on the street without stopping to pass the time of day with him. I can say for myself that it takes me considerably longer to traverse a street in which cats occur than it does a catless thoroughfare. But so magnetic an animal is bound to repel when he does not fascinate, and those who hate the cat hate him with a malignity which, I think, only snakes in the animal kingdom provoke to an equal degree. Puss has, indeed, been dubbed the "furred serpent." The association of the cat with witches and various superstitions is responsible for a good deal of this antipathy; there is also the aversion of those who love dogs and birds with unreasonable exclusions; finally it has pleased many small boys to make scientific investigation into the proverbial saying that a cat has nine lives. So the cat through the ages has been more cruelly and persistently mistreated than any other beast. This is, I suppose, natural, when we remember that in one epoch he was regarded as a god and in another as an adjunct of sorcery; accordingly he has suffered martyrdom along with other gnostics.

Cat burials often surpassed human burials in both grandeur and cost. Cats belonging to wealthy owners were usually mummified when they died and then buried in elaborate stone tombs. To keep the cats happy in the afterlife, mummified mice and saucers of milk were sometimes buried with them. A hundred years ago, farmers in Egypt stumbled upon an ancient cat cemetery containing 300,000 perfectly preserved mummies—weighing about twenty tons. Because the farmers didn't understand the archaeological value of the mummies, the entire find was ground up and sold as fertilizer.

Cat veneration was such a powerful force in Egypt that the nation's enemies were sometimes able to use it to their advantage. In 500 B.C. Persian soldiers laid siege to the Egyptian city of Pelusium but found themselves unable to achieve a final victory. They were on the verge of giving up the fight when their leader, Cambyses, had an idea. He sent his soldiers out into the countryside and told them to round up all the cats they could find. Eight days later, the Persian forces made a final march on Pelusium, with each soldier carrying one of the cats. When the Egyptians saw what was happening, they knew they had been defeated. Rather than fight back against the Persians, and in doing so risk killing or even injuring any of the cats, they quietly surrendered, and the final battle ended without a single casualty.

As always in relationships of this magnitude, a backlash was inevitable. Cats in Egypt simply became too powerful, a perilous state of affairs inviting resentment and, ultimately, reprisal. The Egyptians began to care less and less about the cat's actual contributions to their society, and Bastet slowly lost her hold on people's minds. Finally, four centuries after the birth of Christ, worship of Bastet was outlawed.

Arnold Genthe, *Boss of the Fish Dealer's Court*

Arnold Genthe (1869–1942) was a great American photographer whose studio techniques helped to elevate the art to its present status. Famed for his portraits of Isadora Duncan and her dancers as well as for his photographs of the San Francisco earthquake and fire of 1906, Genthe also produced several photo essays of American cities and their residents. *The Boss of the Fish Dealer's Court* was part of a study of New Orleans. *Reprinted from the collections of the Library of Congress.*

Cat deities did not disappear, however. Well before the cult died out in Egypt, the idea of Bastet was absorbed into other cultures and other religions. The Greeks assimilated elements of the Egyptian goddess into their Artemis (called Diana by the Romans), who was the sister of Apollo and the goddess of the moon. According to myth, Apollo created the lion in an attempt to frighten his sister, and Artemis responded sardonically by creating the cat, which was essentially a parody of the ferocious beast her brother has produced.

Another Greek, Aesop, found cats useful as characters in the fables for which we remember him today. He used cats to represent certain aspects of human nature, and each fable ends with a moral, or proverb, that is intended

Théophile Steinlen,
Chat et Chatte

Along with his marvelous volumes of cat drawings and elegant cat posters, Théophile Steinlen did a number of equally beautiful cat paintings. *Chat et Chatte* might be called a feline seduction scene.
Petit Palais Musée, Geneva, Switzerland.

These woodcuts illustrate the perennial favorites, Aesop's fable of the cat and the cock and La Fontaine's fable of the cat and the fox.

as a guide for behavior. Not all of these fables are flattering to cats. In one of them, a cat falls in love with a handsome young man and persuades the goddess Aphrodite to change her into a woman so she can marry him. Aphrodite agrees, the young man is smitten, and a wedding is arranged. All proceeds smoothly until, shortly after the ceremony, the new bride sees a mouse scampering across the floor and leaps from her husband's bed to chase it. Aphrodite, incensed, returns her to her feline form. The chastening moral is, "A bad man retains his character even if his outward appearance is altered."

Many centuries after Aesop, an Arabian storyteller created a much more charming story about cats. The tale is set aboard Noah's Ark, where the original pair of mice among the passengers have proved to be so prolific that the entire boat is overrun with their offspring. Noah takes command of the situation and passes his hand three times over the head of the lioness, who sneezes mightily and brings forth a pair of cats, one from each nostril. The cats control the rodent population for the rest of the voyage.

There are no cats in the Bible, but there are several in the Koran. Islam has always shown a high regard for felines. According to one story, Muhammed once cut off the sleeve of his robe rather than disturb his beloved cat, Muezza, who was sleeping on it. Another story says that Muhammed loved cats so dearly that he granted them the ability always to land on their feet. Even now, cats (but not dogs) are allowed inside mosques, where they are expected to control the rodent population. In Islam, as cat owners everywhere will be able to appreciate, cats are considered clean, dogs unclean.

Buddhists think rather less of the cat than Moslems do, although there is still a Buddhist temple in Tokyo dedicated exclusively to the spirits of departed felines. The Hindus, on the other hand, are positively worshipful. The so-called "law of Manu" states that "he who has killed a cat must withdraw to the middle of a forest and there dedicate himself to the life of the animals around him until he is purified." All the faithful, whether they have blood on their hands or not, are expected to open their own households to cats.

The cat had essentially no role in early Christianity, although in later centuries artists began to hint at a modest place for felines among more familiar icons. Saint Patrick and Saint Jerome were both associated with cats and sometimes painted in their company. An old English children's rhyme goes:

If I lost my little cat, I should be sad without it,
I should ask St. Jerome what to do about it,
I should ask St. Jerome, just because of that
He's the only Saint I know that kept a pussy-cat.

Saints Agatha, Gertrude, and Yves were all connected, to a greater or lesser degree, with cats. Dürer painted Adam and Eve in Eden with a very well-fed feline at their feet. Because of its habits, the cat in Christian art was taken as a symbol of betrayal. And for many years it was customary to place a cat at the feet of Judas in paintings of the Last Supper.

Al Frueh, *Log of the Ark*

In order to ensure the survival of the species, Noah, the first conservationist, puts a pair of lovebirds away for safekeeping in this 1915 comic drawing by Al Frueh.

The Vampire Cat of Nabeshima

Vampires, most often associated with Transylvania, appear in the folklore and legends of many countries, including Japan. According to an old Japanese folk tale, a demon vampire cat sucked the blood of a beautiful maiden and assumed her form in order to bewitch her lover, the prince. Ultimately, as in all vampire stories, the demon cat woman is hunted down and killed and the prince is released from her power.

Ando Hiroshige, *Cat at Window*

Ando Hiroshige (1797–1858) an artist of the Ukiyo-e school, was one of Japan's greatest printmakers. By making impressions of various carved-wood block on one sheet of paper, he created beautiful landscape· such as *Cat at Window*, from the series *Famous Sites of Edo: One Hundred Views*. In this print, a short-tailed cat, considered to be good luck in Japan, sits on a window sill in Asakusa and observes a large crowd returning from the Tori no Machi festival. This delicate landscape is dominated by Mount Fuji, which looms in the background.

Courtesy of the Freer Gallery of Art, Smithsonian Institution, Washington, D.C.

Ando Hiroshige, *Cat Bathing*

In Japanese folklore, cats were often cast as benevolent creatures. However, there are also a number of horror stories about them. Long-tailed cats were thought to be able to assume human form in order to bewitch innocent people. Although there is nothing really frightening about Hiroshige's seductive bathing cat, she, like her long-tailed relations, seems to take on human characteristics and might be considered quite bewitching.

Courtesy of the Freer Gallery of Art Smithsonian Institution, Washington, D.C.

THE INDISPENSABLE CAT

As is perhaps to be expected of an animal associated with the betrayer of Christ, the cat's only enduring place in Christianity was an entirely negative one. Because cats had long been connected with Pagan cults, they began to fall under official suspicion as the Church grew more and more powerful. In 962 hundreds of cats were burned to death in the French town of Metz as a part of the observance of Lent. The cats were thought to be witches, a belief that may have arisen not long before when a kindhearted official substituted a cat for a woman who had been sentenced to burn at the stake. As the flames leapt up, the cat jumped out of the bag in which it had been hidden, and the citizens standing nearby assumed that the convicted witch had merely changed her form in order to escape. Thenceforth, all cats were suspect.

Because of its supposed link with the devil, the cat played an important role in rites of black magic.

Photographer Unknown,
Cat in Kitty Sargent's Garden

In this turn-of-the-century photograph, Kitty Sargent and her kitty enjoy the outdoors. *Northampton Historical Society.*

The burnings at Metz were followed by several centuries of intermittent persecution. God-fearing Christians came to think of cats as messengers of the devil, or as the deadly collaborators of witches. In the thirteenth century Pope Gregory IX formally linked black cats with sorcery. This coincided with the beginnings of the notorious Inquisition, the Church's paranoid and bloody

attempt to rid itself of heretics. Because all cats were looked upon with suspi-cion, all cat owners were as well, and both fared badly in the courts. Church prosecutors searched the accused for birthmarks shaped like cat's paws, which were viewed as proof of complicity with the devil. Needless to say, the marks didn't have to be very clear to be damning. In the late fifteenth century the ill-named Pope Innocent VIII issued the bull "Against Sorcerers," a pronounce-ment that led to thousands of executions for heresy, often of people who were suspected only because they owned cats. Convicted witches were executed by any number of gruesome methods, sometimes by being drowned in sacks filled with cats. In many cases, cats alone were put on trial and executed.

Not even children were immune from the Church's wrath. In 1699 in the Swedish town of Mora, 300 children were tried for witchcraft after allegedly using cats to steal food for the devil. Fifteen of the children were executed, and thirty-six were publicly whipped every Sunday for a year.

At the coronation of Queen Elizabeth in 1558, live cats were stuffed into a wicker effigy of the Pope and then burned. In Picardy, Burgundy, Vosges, Alsace, and many other places, cats were ritually burned on special occasions, or for no occasion at all. Because the cat was believed to be the devil's represen-tative, killing him was a holy duty. On St. John's Eve all over France, in some cases well into the nineteenth century, cats were killed in celebratory bonfires. Bags or baskets full of live cats were suspended over the flames, while towns-people drowned out their cries of agony with hymns. Ashes from the fires were thought to bring good luck, and people greedily gathered them as soon as the coals had cooled. These rituals were even attended by the kings of France—Louis XIV, in fact, once danced around such a fire with a wreath of roses on his head. In the French national archives there still survives a receipt given to the man who earned pocket money by supplying the cats for these burnings: "Paid to Lucas Pommerieux, a guard on the embankment, 100 Paris sous, for supply-ing, over a period of years ending at Saint-Jean 1573, all the cats required for the customary fire and for supplying a large canvas sack to contain the said cats."

How to Fetch a Wart

Cats have long been the subjects (and often the victims) of human superstitions. In his novel Tom Sawyer, *Mark Twain describes a scene where Huckleberry Finn appears carrying a dead cat. When Tom asks him "what dead cats is good for" Huck answers, "cure warts with." "But say," asks Tom, "how do you cure them with dead cats?"*

"Why, you take your [dead] cat and go and get in the graveyard 'long about midnight when somebody that was wicked has been buried; and when it's midnight a devil will come, or maybe two or three, but you can't see 'em, you can only hear something like the wind, or maybe hear 'em talk; and when they're taking that feller away, you heave your cat after 'em and say, 'Devil follow corpse, cat follow devil, warts follow cat, I'm done with ye!' That'll fetch *any* wart."

The Black Cat

One of the most spine-tingling stories ever written about a cat is Edgar Allan Poe's tale, "The Black Cat." In this passage, the story's narrator describes the animal who eventually brings about his downfall.

Pluto—this was the cat's name—was my favorite pet and playmate. I alone fed him, and he attended me wherever I went about the house. It was even with difficulty that I could prevent him from following me through the streets.

Our friendship lasted, in this manner, for several years, during which my general temperament and character—through the instrumentality of the Fiend Intemperance—had (I blush to confess it) experienced a radical alteration for the worse. I grew, day by day, more moody, more irritable, more regardless of the feeling of others.... My pets, of course, were made to feel the change in my disposition. I not only neglected, but ill-used them. For Pluto, however, I still retained sufficient regard to restrain me from maltreating him, as I made no scruple of maltreating the rabbits, the monkey, or even the dog, when by accident, or through affection, they came in my way. But my disease grew upon me—for what disease is like Alcohol!—and at length even Pluto, who was now becoming old, and consequently somewhat peevish—even Pluto began to experience the effects of my ill temper.

One night, returning home, much intoxicated, from one of my haunts about town, I fancied that the cat avoided my presence. I seized him; when, in his fright at my violence, he inflicted a slight wound upon my hand with his teeth. The fury of a demon instantly possessed me. I knew myself no longer. My original soul seemed, at once, to take its flight from my body; and a more than fiendish malevolence, gin-nurtured, thrilled every fibre of my frame. I took from my waistcoat-pocket a pen-knife, opened it, grasped the poor beast by the throat, and deliberately cut one of its eyes from the socket! I blush, I burn, I shudder, while I pen the damnable atrocity.

Aubrey Beardsley, *The Black Cat*

English artist Aubrey Beardsley offered this version of *The Black Cat*, which accompanied the 1895 edition of Poe's classic horror tale.

"The Black Cat"

Since medieval times, black cats have been associated with witchcraft and the supernatural. Edgar Allan Poe's "The Black Cat" (1843) certainly belongs to this tradition. The narrator of this tale is obsessed and possessed by the demon alcohol, and he murders his black cat—not to mention his wife—under its influence. The spectre of his maimed and murdered pet returns in the form of another black cat, this one with a small white spot that gradually enlarges and takes on the shape of a gallows, foreshadowing the narrator's own demise.

Poe's story was translated into film in 1934, and starred Bela Lugosi as the ill-fated alcoholic.

From The Black Cat *(1934), courtesy of Universal Pictures.*

The tortures conceived for cats were appallingly various. One particularly fiendish device was the cat organ, or cat piano, which amused Europeans well into the nineteenth century. The cat organ looked very much like a regular organ, except that instead of pipes it had small cages filled with cats. When the keys of the organ were struck, the tails of particular cats were pulled, causing the animals to howl. Elsewhere in Europe, pranksters sealed cats in spiked barrels and rolled them down hills; archers used live cats as targets; and mischievous children set their pets on fire or threw them into rivers. In Denmark knights with lances tilted at cats in barrels—the very antithesis of chivalry.

In the Far East as in Europe, the cat fell out of favor after an initial period of grace and indeed of veneration. Stories of demon cats in Japan date from the thirteenth century, when a popular folktale told the story of an evil spirit who took the form of a cat in order to steal a magical sword from a holy man. One is led to wonder whether there is something inherent in the very nature of cats that makes them prone to victimization by their human companions, for nothing remotely similar (or at least nothing so nearly universal) has occurred in the history of the dog. The cat's fierce independence must taunt us in a way that awakens something ugly deep inside us. Cats can make us act in ways that most of us would prefer not to think about.

Fortunately for cats, and also for us, persecution on a wide scale eventually began to decline all over the world. In 1618 a law was passed in Ypres, France, that made it illegal to throw cats from the top of the local cathedral—until that time a popular activity during Lent. Tortures in one form or another continued, but as time went by official backing for them disappeared.

Given all of this, it's not too surprising that cats have been associated with thousands of superstitions over the centuries, many of which are still quite strong. Even an unquestionably rational citizen of the twentieth century may find that he is reluctant to cross the path of a black cat, or he may feel a pang of foreboding when a stray tom suddenly arches his back and spits. Because cats are so blasé about our daily comings and goings, we assume they're up to something sneaky. Where do cats go when they wander off in the middle of the night? What do they think about when they sit for hours at a time, gazing into space? Feline behavior invites a certain amount of human suspicion, which makes the cat a prime candidate as an object of superstition.

Cat superstitions abound in every corner of the world. Many of these superstitions involve cats' eyes, which are admittedly one of the most mysterious-looking creations in all of zoology. Plutarch thought that cats' eyes waxed and

This enigmatic nineteenth-century drawing by French illustrator, caricaturist, and political cartoonist Grandville depicts two cat spirits struggling for the soul of a cat woman against an industrial backdrop.

Beware of the Cat

Eleni Mylanos, *White Cat*
Copyright © Eleni Mylanos.

Cat in Basket

Cats go into drawers, boxes, shopping bags, cartons, baskets and countless other miniature hideaways.
Photograph by Nina Duran

Minnaloushe

The dark side of the cat's nature was well described by the Irish poet William Butler Yeats in a poem called "The Cat and the Moon."

The cat went here and there
And the moon spun round like a top,
And the nearest kin of the moon,
The creeping cat, looked up.
Black Minnaloushe stared at the moon,
For, wander and wail as he would,
The pure cold light in the sky
Troubled his animal blood.
Minnaloushe runs in the grass
Lifting his delicate feet.
Do you dance, Minnaloushe, do you dance?
When two close kindred meet,
What better than call a dance:
Maybe the moon may learn,

Tired of that courtly fashion,
A new dance turn.
Minnaloushe creeps through the grass
From moonlit place to place,
The sacred moon overhead
Has taken a new phase.
Does Minnaloushe know that his pupils
Will pass from change to change,
And that from round to crescent,
From crescent to round they range?
Minnaloushe creeps through the grass
Alone, important and wise,
And lifts to the changing moon
His changing eyes.

---

waned with the moon, and both the Greeks and Romans associated cats with their respective goddesses of the moon. In China some people still believe that you can tell the time of day by consulting the eye of a cat. Ancient Britons used the same method to foretell the future.

A cat's eye actually is a remarkable piece of equipment. The piercing glow we see at night when our headlights shine on the eyes of a cat is caused by light reflecting off the retina. This spectacular phenomenon was once thought to prove that cats were allied with the devil: to gaze into the eyes of a cat at night was to glimpse the fires of hell. The glow was also once thought to be a beacon enabling cats to see in pitch blackness, which is something only demons ought to be able to do. Some people still believe that cats can see in total darkness, although of course they can't; all vision requires at least a little light.

Cats have also been thought to have a supernatural ability to forecast and even influence the weather. In Japan and Scotland tortoiseshell cats were said to be able to predict storms. A cat that sneezes or chases its tail is sometimes said to be announcing a change in the weather. According to one authority, "Cats coveting the fire more than ordinary or licking their feet or trimming the hair of their heads and mustachios presages a storm." In certain parts of Kansas, a cat who washes his face before breakfast is said to be announcing that rain is on the way, while New Zealanders expect the same thing when a cat drowns in salt water.

Sailors, who may have a special affinity for superstitions, place great faith in the cat's weather-predicting abilities. Captain George H. Grant once wrote: "If a storm is approaching but hidden from the watchers on the bridge by the far rim of the horizon, cats become very active for a while; then, long before the barometer in the chart room has begun to drop, they will slink away into a comfortable corner and chock themselves off against the rolling of the vessel like a true blue-water man. . . . Not only do cats prognosticate the weather by their actions. Should disaster threaten during the passage of a storm, or danger beset the person who has been kind to them, they will endeavor to communicate a warning."

Cats are also said to be able to control or determine the weather. In Indonesia cats were once believed to be able to bring rain. When drought struck, cats were paraded around farm fields and then dunked in water or splashed. The farmers would then sit back to await the needed showers. In Sumatra a black cat is sometimes thrown into a river and splashed by women in order to bring about a storm. In Scotland it was once believed that throwing a cat into the sea would cause a shipwreck.

Cats have been used to bring about other changes in nature as well. Farmers in many cultures over the centuries believed that burying a cat in a newly sown field would ensure a bountiful harvest. Other peoples sought the same effect by throwing cats from towers. For a long time in Europe live cats were bricked up in new buildings in order to bring luck to the occupants. When a castle was restored in 1876, workers found the mummified body of a cat, excellently preserved, that had been walled up for 400 years. In Denmark in the last century, it was not unknown for peasants to bury live cats at their doorsteps in order to bring good luck.

Although many cat superstitions are still with us, the symbolic meaning of cats today is quite different from what it once was. We still read complex meanings into feline actions and inactions, but our interpretations tend to be more benign than they once were. Cats are still a potent symbol, though, even in a civilization such as ours. For good or ill, when we look into a cat's eyes, we see something very important to us—ourselves.

Arthur Rackham,
The Owl and the Pussycat

The renowned English book illustrator Arthur Rackham created this fluid drawing for Edward Lear's classic work of nonsense verse.

The contents of this bucket attract the undivided attention of two Highgate, Vermont, alley cats.
Copyright © Sonja Bullaty.

Among the thirty-three breeds of pedigree cats recognized by the Cat Fanciers' Association, there are approximately fifty possible variations in fur color, length, and texture. Purebreds also vary in other qualities such as size, origin, voice, and most important, personality. Not all pedigrees are acceptable for competition; some are either too new, too exotic, or just too peculiar. Here is a brief summary of the identifying characteristics of some of the more familiar as. well as some of the more unusual breeds.

Like the Russian Blue, the *Siamese* was a royal cat; it lived in and guarded palaces and temples in Siam. Although it is sometimes nervous and, like royalty, subject to disorders associated with inbreeding, the Siamese is still the most popular pedigree cat in the world.
Copyright © Neil Leifer/Camera 5.

The *Abbyssinian*, a playful, active cat, was first depicted in ancient Eqyptian art. Of all domestic felines, the ruddy-coated Abyssinian is the closest to the wild cat in disposition, yet it makes an excellent, outgoing pet.
Copyright © Neil Leifer/Camera 5.

Perhaps the most aristocratic pedigree feline is the often conceited *Persian* with its elegant, flowing coat. Although it requires daily brushing, the Persian is beloved by most cat fanciers.
Copyright © Michael Skott.

The "hypoallergenic" *Rex* might be described as having an avant-garde appearance. It is a small, often high-strung feline with a delicate frame and a kinky coat like a Persian lamb's.
Copyright © Creszentia Allen.

The *Manx* is a tailless, round, people-loving cat resembling a teddy bear. Although its missing appendage has been the subject of many a legend, the Manx simply comes from a different genetic strain than other breeds.
Copyright © Creszentia Allen.

Despite its exotic name, the *Tonkinese* is the first breed to originate in Canada. A cat with a "mink coat," the Tonkinese is a cross between a Siamese and a Burmese. It is friendly and outgoing, making it a perfect house pet.
Copyright © Creszentia Allen.

At one time, the magnificent *Turkish Angora* was near extinction, but zoo officials in Ankara came to its rescue and continued to breed it so that today we can still enjoy this long-haired, bushy-tailed feline.
Copyright © Creszentia Allen.

With its silky sable coat, the elegant *Burmese* is immensely popular for both its show potential and its friendly personality. Not a natural breed, the Burmese was produced by selective breeding in the United States, not, like the Birman, in Burma. *Copyright © Creszentia Allen.*

With a coat like shiny black patent leather and eyes like polished copper pennies, the *Bombay* is a recent addition to the rolls of pure-bred cats in the United States. This unique cat is a cross between the sable coated Burmese and the sturdy American Shorthair and looks like a miniature panther. *Copyright © Creszentia Allen.*

Dainty and elegant, the *Balinese* is a long-haired version of the ever-popular Siamese. The Balinese, a silken coated cat with a color-point pattern and a plume-like tail, was originally a coat length mutation of its shorthaired kin. *Copyright © Creszentia Allen.*

Esteemed by the czars, the *Russian Blue* is a truly regal cat with a coat as thick and lush as a beaver's. In fact, its coat is so luxuriant that, should you want to, you can trace designs in it with your finger. *Copyright © Creszentia Allen.*

A giant among cats, the huge *Maine Coon* is the long-haired version of the American Shorthair. Native to New England, this big, shaggy, and intelligent creature was once considered to be part raccoon. *Copyright © Neil Leifer/ Camera 5.*

For those cat fanciers who love the stocky bodies and sweet stubby faces of Persians but who have neither the time nor the inclination to care for their flowing coats, the *Exotic Shorthair* is the perfect feline. A cross between the Persian and the American Shorthair, the Exotic Shorthair is identical to its long-haired progenitor in every way but one: it has a soft, dense, medium coat. *Copyright © Neil Leifer/ Camera 5.*

B R E E D S

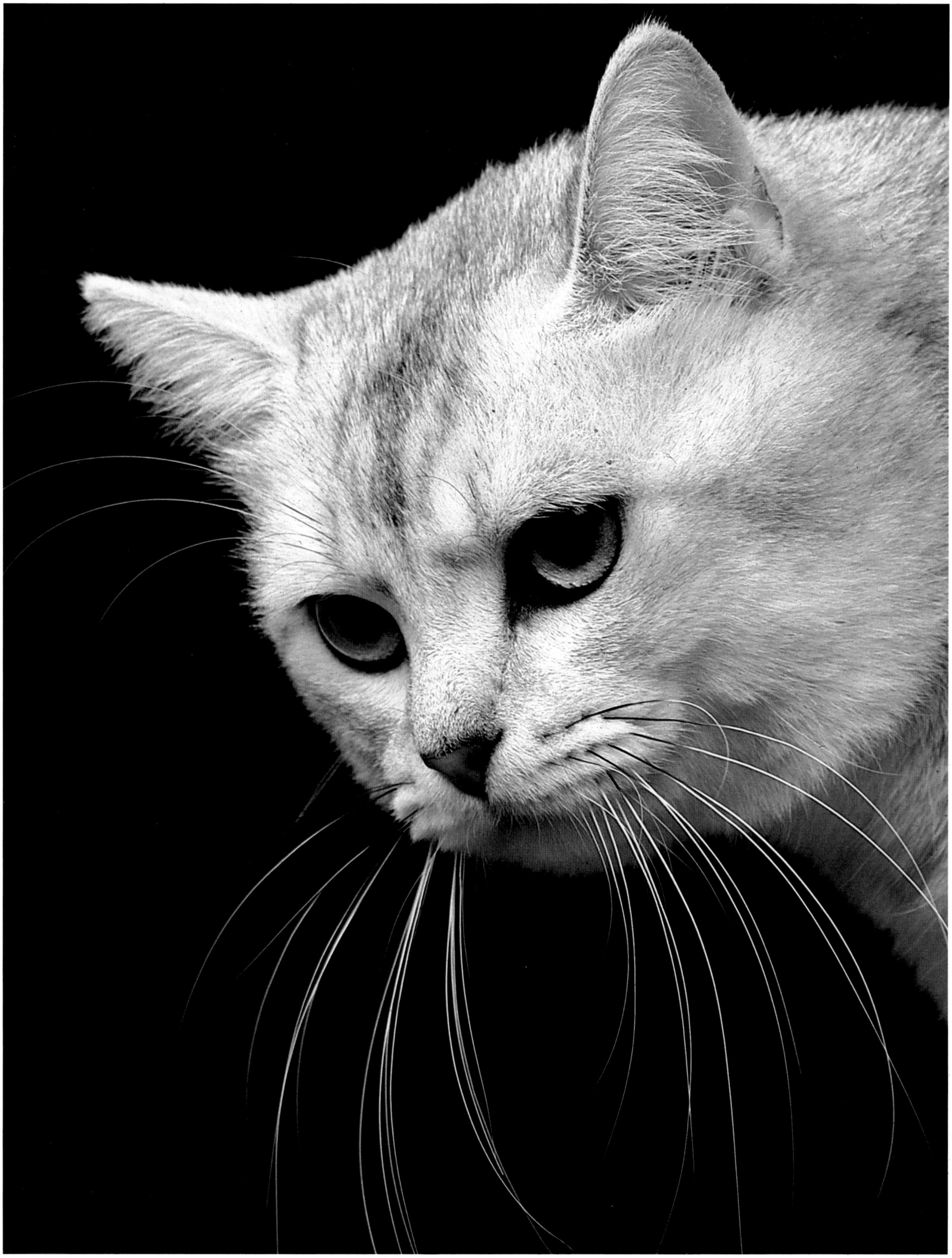

Alice in Wonderland, Lewis Carroll, excerpt from, 87

Alnaharwany, Ina Alalaf, "On a Cat That Was Killed as She Was Attempting to Rob a Dove House," 84

Anonymous, "Feline Affection," 36

archie and mehitabel, Don Marquis, 148

Bentham, Jeremy, 34

"The Black Cat," Edgar Allan Poe, excerpt from, 175

Boswell, James, on Samuel Johnson, 56

Bowring, John, on Jeremy Bentham, 34

"The Boy Who Drew Cats," Lafcadio Hearn, 88–89

"Calvin," Charles Dudley Warner, 76–82

Carroll, Lewis, *Alice in Wonderland*, excerpt from, 87

Carroll, Lewis, *Through the Looking Glass*, excerpt from, 71

"The Cat and the Moon," William Butler Yeats, 179

"The Cat That Walked by Himself," Rudyard Kipling, 152–157

de la Mare, Walter, "Five Eyes," 100

The Diary of a Young Girl, Anne Frank, excerpt from, 48

"Elegy," John Greenleaf Whittier, 83

"Elegy to Oscar, a Dead Cat," H. P. Lovecraft, 84

Epitaph, 83

"Feline Affection," Anonymous, 36

"Five Eyes," Walter de la Mare, 100

Frank, Anne, *The Diary of a Young Girl*, excerpt from, 48

Gray, Thomas, "Ode on the Death of a Favourite Cat Drowned in a Tub of Gold Fishes," 112

Hardy, Thomas, "Last Words to a Dumb Friend," 83

Hearn, Lafcadio, "The Boy Who Drew Cats," 88–89

Hoel Dha (Howell the Good), 96

"Huckleberry Finn," Mark Twain, excerpt from, 174

Huddesford, George, "Monody on the Death of Dick, an Academical Cat," 84

The Innocents Abroad, Mark Twain, excerpt from, 44

Johnson, Samuel, 56

"Jubilate Agno," Christopher Smart, 30

Kipling, Rudyard, "The Cat That Walked by Himself," 152–157

"Last Words to a Dumb Friend," Thomas Hardy, 83

Lear, Edward, "The Owl and the Pussycat," 90

Lovecraft, H. P., "Elegy to Oscar, a Dead Cat," 84

Marquis, Don, *archie and mehitabel*, 148

"Monody on the Death of Dick, an Academical Cat," George Huddesford, 84

Mother Goose, 86

"Ode on the Death of a Favourite Cat Drowned in a Tub of Goldfishes," Thomas Gray, 112

"On a Cat That Was Killed as She Was Attempting to Rob a Dove House," Ina Alalaf Alnaharwany, 84

"The Owl and the Pussycat," Edward Lear, 90

Perrault, Charles, "Puss in Boots," excerpt from, 86

Poe, Edgar Allan, "The Black Cat," excerpt from, 175

"Puss in Boots," Charles Perrault, excerpt from, 86

Roosevelt, Theodore, letter to his son Kermit, 32

Smart, Christopher, "Jubilate Agno," 30

Thoreau, Henry David, 104

Through the Looking Glass, Lewis Carroll, excerpt from, 71

The Tiger in the House, Carl Van Vechten, excerpt from, 160

Twain, Mark, *Huckleberry Finn*, excerpt from, 174

Twain, Mark, *The Innocents Abroad*, excerpt from, 44

Van Vechten, Carl, *The Tiger in the House*, excerpt from, 160

Warner, Charles Dudley, "Calvin," 76–82

Whittier, John Greenleaf, "Elegy," 83

Whittington, Dick, 102

Yeats, William Butler, "The Cat and the Moon," 179

Hokusai, *Girl and Cat*
Courtesy of the Freer Gallery of Art, Smithsonian Institution, Washington, D.C.

Mary Cassatt, *Girl Holding Cat*
Reproduced courtesy of the Library of Congress.

Abbyssinian, Neil Leifer, 182

Aborigine and Cat, William Coupon, 25

Advertisement for Cat's Paw Rubber Heels and Soles, Don Hamerman, 120

Allen, Creszentia, *Balinese*, 185; *Bombay*, 185; *Burmese*, 185; *Manx*, 184; *Rex*, 184; *Russian Blue*, 185; *Tonkinese*, 184; *Turkish Angora*, 184

Amelia C. Van Buren and Cat, Thomas Eakins, 46, 47

Animals in Locomotion, The Cat, Eadweard Muybridge, 140

Anonymous, *Children Playing Games on a Winter Day*, 89

Anonymous, *Girl with Grey Cat*, 60

Anonymous, *Man with Cat with Sunglasses*, 81

archie and mehitabel, George Herriman, 148

Artist Unknown, *Cat in Red Necklace*, 98-99

Artist Unknown, *Henry Wriothesely, Third Earl of Southhampton, in the Tower of London*, 22

Artist Unknown, *Tinkle, a Cat*, 77

Balinese, Creszentia Allen; 185

Brigitte Bardot, Culver Pictures, 20–21

Bartoll, William Thompson, *Girl and Cat*, 11

Bastet, 160

Beardsley, Aubrey, *The Black Cat*, 175

Beardsley Limner (attribution), *Child Posing with Cat*, 60

Beaux, Cecilia, *Man with a Cat (Henry Sturgis Drinker)*, 31

Benton, Thomas Hart, *Jessie, One Year Old*, 65

Black cat, 151

"The Black Cat," film still, 175

The Black Cat, Aubrey Beardsley, 175

Black and White Cat, Michael Skott, 150

Black Cat Cigarettes Advertisement, 121

Bombay, Creszentia Allen, 185

Bonnard, Pierre, *Children and Cat*, 62–63

Book illustration, Jules Pascin, 189

Boss of the Fish Dealer's Court, Arnold Genthe, 163

Botero, Fernando, *The Voyeur*, 49

Buckley, Peter, *Ernest Hemingway*, 41

Buddha and Cat, Terry Gruber, 161

Bullaty, Sonja, 181

Burmese, Creszentia Allen, 185

Calvin Coolidge and Timmie, 32

Caricature of Gautier, Nadar, 66

Cassatt, Mary, *Girl Holding Cat*, 188

The Cat, Unknown American Artist, 144

Cat, c. 1950, Ylla, 192

Cat at Window, Ando Hiroshige, 168

Cat in Basket, Nina Duran, 178

The Cat and the Cock, Arthur Rackham, 166

Cat Bathing, Ando Hiroshige, 169

Cat Crossing the Street in Traffic, Harry Warnecke, 16–17

The Cat in Eakins' Yard, Thomas Eakins, 75

Cat in Red Necklace, Artist Unknown, 98-99

Cat in Kitty Sargent's Garden, Photographer Unknown, 171

Cat Tombstone, 85

Charlie Chaplin, Culver Pictures, 43

Chat et Chatte, Théophile Steinlen, 164–165

The Cheshire Cat, Sir John Tenniel, 87

Child Posing with Cat, attributed to Beardsley Limner, 60

Children and Cat, Pierre Bonnard, 62–63

Children Playing Games on a Winter Day, Anonymous, 89

Cicero's Cat, 146

Des Chats, Théophile Steinlen, 105–109

Dick Whittington, Arthur Rackham, 103

A Dinner Scene in January, from a Flemish Book of Hours, 92

Doré, Gustave, *Puss in Boots*, 86

Drolling, Martin, *The Woman and the Mouse*, 114–115

Dufy, Raoul, *Woodcut*, 100

Duran, Nina, *Socks*, 6

Duran, Nina, *Cat in Basket*, 178

Eakins, Thomas, *Amelia C. Van Buren and Cat*, 46, 47

Eakins, Thomas, *The Cat in Eakins' Yard*, 75

Eakins, Thomas, *Self-Portrait*, 46

Engstead, John, *Raymond Chandler*, 40

Ernest Hemingway, Peter Buckley, 41

Exotic Shorthair, Neil Leifer, 187

Jules Pascin, *Book illustration*
Bibliothèque Nationale.

Colette, 38, 39

Coupon, William, *Aborigine and Cat*, 25

Culver Pictures, *Brigitte Bardot*, 20–21

Culver Pictures, *Charlie Chaplin*, 43

Culver Pictures, *Jeanette MacDonald*, 29 and back cover

Currier and Ives, *Three Little White Kittens (Their First Mouse)*, 118–119

Dali Atomicus, Philippe Halsman, 142–143

Davis, Joseph Hilliard, *Family Group with Cat, Child, and Vase*, 68–69

Family Group with Cat, Child and Vase, Joseph Hilliard Davis, 68–69

Fast Friends Passing Through the Gates of Sleepyland, 71

The Favorite Cat and De La-Tour, Painter, John Kay, 80

Feline Felicity, Charles Sheeler, 12

Felix the Cat, 147

Foujita, Tsugouharu, *Mrs. E.C. Chadbourne*, 54–55

Foujita, Tsugouharu, *Nude*, 50–51

Foujita, Tsugouharu, *Reclining Nude with Cat*, 52–53

French wallboard, 172–173

Frueh, Al, *Log of the Arc*, 167

Gaunnut, Gefferson, *Two Children*, 19

Genthe, Arnold, *Boss of the Fish Dealer's Court*, 163

Géricault, Théodore, *The White Cat*, 158–159

Girl and Cat, Hokusai, 188

Girl and Cat, William Thompson Bartoll, 11

Girl Holding Cat, Mary Cassatt, 188

Girl in Green Dress, attributed to Samuel Miller, 60

Girl with Cat, William Morris Hunt, 57

Girl with Grey Cat, Anonymous, 60

A Girl with a Kitten, J.B. Peronneau, 58

Grandville, 177

Greuze, J.B. *The Woolwinder*, 23

Paw Rubber Heels and Soles, 120

Hayward, Bill, *Hamlet*, 104

Henry Wriothesely, Third Earl of Southhampton, in the Tower of London, Artist Unknown, 22

Herriman, George, *archie and mehitabel*, 148

Hiroshige, Ando, *Cat at Window*, 168

Hiroshige, Ando, *Cat Bathing*, 169

Hirshfield, Morris, *Nude on Sofa with Three Pussies*, 26–27

The Histoire of Four-Footed Beasties, 76

Hockney David, *Mr. and Mrs. Clark and Percy*, 72–73

Hogarth, William, 116–117

Hokusai, *Girl and Cat*, 188

Hone, Nathaniel, *Kitty Fisher*, 113

Hunt, William Morris, *Girl with Cat*, 57

Ingres, J. A. D., *Madame Ingres' Kitten Asleep in Her Arms*, 82

Kipling, Rudyard, illustration for "The Cat That Walked by Himself," 1, 153

Kitty Fisher, Nathaniel Hone, 113

Krazy Kat, 148–149

Lady Chasing Cat with Parrot, Kangra, 101

La Fillette au Chat, Théophile Steinlen, 64

La Paresse, Félix Vallotton, 4

Lear, Edward, Drawings, 90, 91

Lear, Edward, "The Owl and the Pussycat," 90

Leatherdale, Marcus, *Self-Portrait/82*, 191

Le Chat du Concierge, Robert Sivard, 2

Leifer, Neil, *Abbyssinian*, 182; *Exotic Shorthair*, 187; *Maine Coon*, 186; *Siamese*, 182

Le Jeune Garçon au Chat, Pierre August Renoir, 62

Les Chats, Edouard Manet, 132

Little Miss Hone, Samuel F. B.Morse, 58

Log of the Arc, Al Frueh, 167

MacDonald, Jeanette, Culver Pictures, 29 and back cover

McNally, Joe, 141

Man with a Cat (Henry Sturgis Drinker), Cecilia Beaux, 31

Man with Cat with Sunglasses, Anonymous, 81

Madam Ingres' Kitten Asleep in Her Arms, J. A. D. Ingres, 82

Maine Coon, Neil Leifer, 186

Manet, Edouard, *Les Chats*, 132

Manx, Creszentia Allen, 184

Mary Jane Smith, Joseph Whiting Stock, 61

Mendoza, Tony, 94–95

Miller, Samuel (attributed), *Girl in a Green Dress*, 60

Mind, Gottfried, *Minette Washing*, 84

Minette Washing, Gottfried Mind, 84

Mr. and Mrs. Clark and Percy, David Hockney, 72–73

Mrs. E. C. Chadbourne, Tsugouharu Foujita, 54–55

Monument to a Cat, 102

Morris the Cat, 138–139

Morse, Samuel F. B., *Little Miss Hone*, 58

Muybridge, Eadweard, *Animals in Locomotion, The Cat*, 140

Mylanos, Eleni, *White Cat*, 176

Nadar, *Caricature of Gautier*, 66

Nelson, Janet, *Man With Cat*, 28

Nude, Tsugouharu Foujita, 50–51

Nude on Sofa with Three Pussies, Morris Hirshfield, 26–27

Orangey, 136

The Owl and the Pussycat, Arthur Rackham, 180

"The Owl and the Pussycat," Edward Lear, 90

Félix Vallotton, *Two Cats*

Gruber, Terry, *Buddha and Cat*, 161

Halsman, Philippe, *Dali Atomicus*, 142–143

Halsman, Philippe, *Wanda Landowska at the Harpsichord*, 37

Hamlet, Bill Hayward, 104

Hamerman, Don, Advertisement for Cat's

Jessie, One Year Old, Thomas Hart Benton, 65

Jones, 134

Kangra, *Lady Chasing Cat with Parrot*, 101

Kay, John, *The Favourate Cat and De La-tour, Painter*, 80

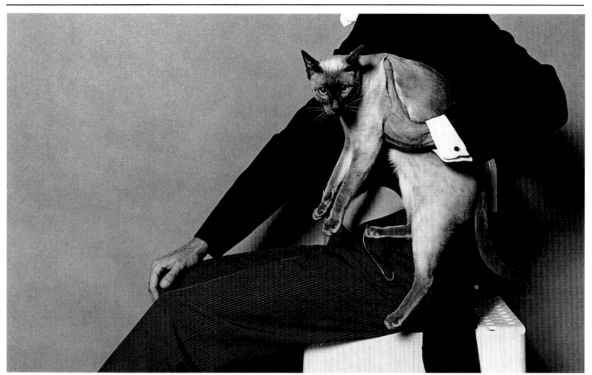

Marcus Leatherdale, *Self-Portrait/82*

Copyright © Marcus Leatherdale.

Pascin, Jules, Book illustration, 189
Penfield, Edward, Posters, 126, 127, 128, 129, 130, 131
Pepper, 135
Peronneau, J. B., *A Girl with a Kitten*, 58
Persian, Michael Skott, 183
Photographer Unknown, *Cat in Kitty Sargent's Garden*, 171
Picasso, Pablo, 42
Poster Advertising Sterilized Milk, Théophile Steinlen, 133
Puss in Boots, Gustave, Doré, 86

Rackham, Arthur, *The Cat and the Cock*, 166
Rackham, Arthur, *Dick Whittington*, 103
Rackham, Arthur, *The Owl and the Pussycat*, 180
Raymond Chandler, John Engstead, 40
Reclining Nude with Cat, Tsugouharu Foujita, 52–53
Renoir, Pierre August, *Le Jeune Garçon au Chat*, 62
Renoir, Pierre August, *Woman with a Cat*, 14
Rex, Creszentia Allen, 184
Russian Blue, Creszentia Allen, 185

Self-Portrait, Thomas Eakins, 46
Self-Portrait/82, Marcus Leatherdale, 191

Sheeler, Charles, *Feline Felicity*, 12
Siamese, Neil Leifer, 182
Sivard, Robert, *Le Chat du Concierge*, 2
Skott, Michael, *Black and White Cat*, 150
Skott, Michael, *Persian*, 183
Sloan, John, *Sunbathers on a Roof*, 35
Socks, Nina Duran, 6
Steinlen, Théophile, *Chat et Chatte*, 164–165
Steinlen, Théophile, *Des Chats*, 105–109
Steinlen, Théophile, Drawings by Steinlen, 5, 76, 83, 84
Steinlen, Théophile, *La Fillette au Chat*, 64
Steinlen, Théophile, Poster Advertising Sterilized Milk, 133
Stock, Joseph Whitting, *Mary Jane Smith*, 61
Sunbathers on a Roof, John Sloan, 35

Tenniel, Sir John, *The Cheshire Cat*, 87
Theodore Roosevelt and Slippers, 33
Three Little White Kittens (Their First Mouse), Currier and Ives, 118–119
Tinkle, A Cat, Artist Unknown, 77
Tonkinese, Creszentia Allen, 184
Tonto, 137
Tsuneyki, Razon (attribution), 8
Turkish Angora, Creszentia Allen, 184

Twain, Mark, Drawing by Mark Twain, 44
Twain, Mark, 44, 45
Two Cats, Félix Vallotton, 190
Two Children, Gefferson Gaunnut, 19
Unknown American Artist, *The Cat*, 144

Vallotton, Félix, *La Paresse*, 4
Vallotton, Félix, *Two Cats*, 190
The Vampire Cat of Nabeshima, 167
Van Mieris, Willem, *Woman and a Fish-Pedlar*, 97
The Voyeur, Fernando Botero, 49

Wanda Landowska at the Harpsichord, Philippe Halsman, 37
Warnecke, Harry, *Cat Crossing the Street in Traffic*, 16–17
White Cat, Eleni Mylanos, 176
The White Cat, Théodore Géricault, 158–159
Woman with a Cat, Pierre August Renoir, 14
Woman and a Fish-Peddlar, Willem van Mieris, 97
The Woman and the Mouse, Martin Drolling, 114–115
Woodcut, Raoul Dufy, 100
The Woolwinder, J. B. Greuze, 23

Ylla, *Cat*, c. 1950, 192

Ylla, *Cat, c. 1950*

The text was set in Goudy Old Style by U.S. Lithograph Inc., New York, New York.

SITUATIONAL
FUNCTIONAL
JAPANESE

VOLUME *1*: DRILLS
SECOND EDITION
TSUKUBA LANGUAGE GROUP

BONJINSHA CO.,LTD.

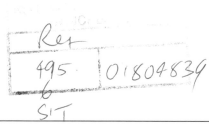
Published and distributed in Japan by BONJINSHA Co., Ltd.,
1F Ryōshin Hirakawachō Building, 1-3-13 Hirakawa-chō, Chiyoda-ku, Tokyo.
Telephone 03-3472-2240 Copyright © 1991, 1995 Tsukuba Language Group.
Printed in Japan.
First edition, 1991
Second edition, 1995   ISBN4-89358-314-X C3081

中部地方
ちゅうぶちほう

- 15 新潟（にいがた）
- 16 富山（とやま）
- 17 石川（いしかわ）
- 18 福井（ふくい）
- 19 山梨（やまなし）
- 20 長野（ながの）
- 21 岐阜（ぎふ）
- 22 静岡（しずおか）
- 23 愛知（あいち）

近畿地方
きんきちほう

- 24 三重（みえ）
- 25 滋賀（しが）
- 26 京都（きょうと）
- 27 大阪（おおさか）
- 28 兵庫（ひょうご）
- 29 奈良（なら）
- 30 和歌山（わかやま）

東北地方
とうほくちほう

- 2 青森（あおもり）
- 3 岩手（いわて）
- 4 宮城（みやぎ）
- 5 秋田（あきた）
- 6 山形（やまがた）
- 7 福島（ふくしま）

関東地方
かんとうちほう

- 8 茨城（いばらき）
- 9 栃木（とちぎ）
- 10 群馬（ぐんま）
- 11 埼玉（さいたま）
- 12 千葉（ちば）
- 13 東京（とうきょう）
- 14 神奈川（かながわ）

1 北海道（ほっかいどう）

CONTENTS

How to Use This Book ……………………………………………………… v

Abbreviations and Notations ………………………………………………… 1

LESSON 1 紹介する …………………………………………………… 2
しょうかい

LESSON 2 郵便局で …………………………………………………… 24
ゆうびんきょく

LESSON 3 レストランで ……………………………………………… 46

LESSON 4 場所を聞く ………………………………………………… 72
ばしょ き

LESSON 5 わからないことばを聞く ……………………………… 92

LESSON 6 事務室で ………………………………………………… 116
じ むしっ

LESSON 7 電話をかける（1）病院 …………………………… 136
でん わ びょういん

LESSON 8 許可を求める …………………………………………… 162
きょか もと

Appendix: Conversation Drills Check ………………………… 186

Index ………………………………………………………………… 199

How to Use This Book

Situational Functional Japanese is designed for complete beginners as well as those who have already studied a little Japanese.

This series consists of 3 volumes each of textbooks (Notes) and drillbooks. Each volume contains 8 lessons, making a total of 24 lessons.

Textbook (Notes):

> Vol.1　L 1 ~L 8

> Vol.2　L 9 ~L16

> Vol.3　L17~L24

Drillbooks:

| Vol.1　L 1 ~L 8 |
| Vol.2　L 9 ~L16 |
| Vol.3　L17~L24 |

Drillbooks:

The lessons in the drillbook are divided into the following four sections:

Ⅰ. New Words in Drills
Ⅱ. Structure Drills
Ⅲ. Conversation Drills
Ⅳ. Tasks and Activities

I. New Words in Drills

(1) The New Words are divided into Basic Words (inside the thick-lined boxes) and Additional Words (inside the thin-lined boxes). Basic words include basic vocabulary items which appear in the Structure Drills and in the Conversation Drills.

(2) Before beginning the Structure Drills, you should check through the vocabulary.

(3) You should memorize the Basic Words for each lesson.

(4) Verbs are shown with the structure particles for memorizing together. The elements shown with structure particles are roughly divided into groups ("thing," "person," etc.) on the basis of convenience.

II. Structure Drills

The Structure Drills (SD) are designed to accomplish the following:

(1) To consolidate the items covered in the Grammar Notes

(2) To give practice in using the correct forms

(3) To guide you beyond mechanical practice to become able to make your own sentences

(4) To make possible, enjoyable, easy-to-understand practice through the inclusion of pictures and illustrations

Types of Structure Drills:

1. Conjugation drill
2. Pattern drill
3. Drill explaining situations through illustrations and conversations
4. Sentence completion drill

Conjugation drills are drills of verb and adjective conjugations using illustrations, etc.

Pattern drills include simple substitution drills, but there are also drills with a twist involving not just a change in the position of words, but other words to be changed, too.

Drills explaining situations through illustrations and conversations are drills which involve looking at an illustration, making up sentences after reading about a certain situation, and reporting it to others.

Sentence completion drills include practice in making up sentences continuing from a previous or following sentence, and other drills in which you make up sentences using the structures you have learned.

How to use the Structure Drills:

(1) The examples or the first half of each SD for each lesson are recorded on the drill tapes. You should always practise SD while listening to the tapes, repeating aloud what you hear. It is all right to look at the pictures and illustrations in the textbook, but you should not read the text.

(2) Drills marked with ☆ are application drills, and may be omitted when time is short. These can also be used during the reviews. These are omitted from the tapes.

(3) Approximately ten exercises have been included in each lesson. Depending on the exercise, some are divided into **a** and **b** (groups) ; in principle, the a group consist of basic drills, while the **b** group are application drills.

(4) When a ○○, 〈 ? 〉, or _____ appear in the cue, you should make up sentences using information about yourself or the people or objects near you.

(5) Sections with straight underlining require the insertion of cue material, while wavy underlining indicates that particular attention should be paid to that section.

III. Conversation Drills

Conversation Drills (CD) are oral practices to be repeated several times so that the expressions in the strategies become habitual. It is also for practising in smaller units the functions used in the Model Conversation. And, in order to communicate well, accuracy and fluency are necessary. In order to achieve this, it is important for you to be able to express correctly the knowledge that you have gained from the Grammar Notes, Structure Drills and Conversation Notes, and to practise it until you can speak Japanese smoothly.

There are many variations for practising the CD but the main ones are the 4 following:

1. Substitution drill

   Practise until you can say it smoothly.

2. Response drill

   This is a form of practice to get you to reply to various questions without thinking.

3. Communication drill

   This is a form of practice using an information gap, to be practised in pairs or groups. Pictures and charts require you to think things through before practising.

4. Role play

   At the end of each lesson there is a "role play" practice using the strategies learned in that lesson in as natural a situation as possible. Practise with your friends and teachers.

How to use the Conversation Drills:

(1) Drills marked with ☆ are application drills, and may be omitted when time is short. These can also be used during the reviews.

(2) When you see 📼 in the CD, it means that the passage is recorded on a tape. Before practising in class, listen to the tape and practise by yourself. There is also a CD check list in the Appendix. This enables you to do a self check on how much you have understood of the tape.

(3) Approximately seven or eight exercises have been included in each lesson. Depending on the exercise, some are divided into a, b, c, etc.

(4) When there are no cue words or pictures and only the instruction is given for the communication drills, you should follow the teacher's instruction in the class.

(5) Sections with straight underlining require the insertion of cue material, while wavy underlining indicates that particular attention should be paid to that section.

IV. Tasks and Activities

The tasks are a central element of SFJ. The explanations in the Grammar and Conversation Notes, drills in SD and CD, are developed by the tasks, which are designed as real-life tasks.

The tasks are designed to achieve the following:

(1) To cover the four basic skills, in particular, reading and writing practice.

(2) To give information on life and culture in Japan.

(3) To improve learner motivation through the incorporation of games.

(4) Several of the listening and reading tasks include some new vocabulary and constructions, as preview material for later study.

The tasks can be divided into the following types according to content:

1. Tasks designed to be linked to language behaviour by focussing on the vocabulary used in certain situations.

2. Tasks focussing on checking grammatical items, and help you to actually use them.

3. Tasks designed to enable you to use the strategies studied in the conversational drills in a variety of different situations.

4. Tasks which serve to combine the material learned in the grammar and conversation sections.

The Tasks can be divided into the following according to the required skills:

1. Listening Tasks

2. Reading Tasks

3. Writing Tasks

4. Speaking Tasks

5. Tasks incorporating all of the above skills.

Use of Tasks and Activities:

(1) The Listening Tasks are recorded on the drill tapes. The scripts for these can be found at the back of the Teacher's Manual. Conversations are conducted at normal speed from the very beginning, so you may have some difficulty in understanding them at first. But the objective is to accustom you to natural conversation, so you should listen repeatedly until you get used to normal conversational speed.

(2) The answers to the task exercises are included in the Teacher's Manual. However, no answers are given for those tasks which can be answered in more than one way, and you are encouraged to answer these using information about yourself.

(3) In some reading tasks, all you need to do is to extract the information needed, without trying to understand every word and phrase.

（4）Practices marked with ☆ are those with a higher level of difficulty, and may be omitted when time is short.

（5）Tasks marked with a are meant to be practised by two or more learners together. Those learners studying on their own should try to find a teacher or friend with whom they can practise speaking.

Abbreviations and Notations

This is a list of main symbols used in this book:

⇨	refer
GN	Grammar Notes
CN	Conversation Notes
🅵	formal/polite speech
🅒	casual/plain speech
⬆	speaking to a Higher
⬇	speaking to a Lower
➡	speaking to an Equal
👨	spoken by male
👩	spoken by female
☆	complex, advanced drills
📼	recorded on the tape
👥	practice involving two or more people (Tasks)
♪	conversation after a chime (CD Check)
♫	conversation after chimes (CD Check)

Lesson 1

紹介する
しょう かい

Introducing (People)

● *New Words in Drills*

Countries:

日本	にほん	*Japan*
イギリス	Igirisu	*U.K.*
インド	Indo	*India*

Other words:

国	くに	*country*
専門	せんもん	*field of study, specialization*
先生	せんせい	*teacher, professor*
学生	がくせい	*student*
留学生	りゅうがくせい	*foreign student*
大学	だいがく	*university*
大学院	だいがくいん	*graduate school*
研究室	けんきゅうしつ	*seminar room*
うち		*(my) house/place*
私	わたし	*I*
友だち	ともだち	*friend*
日本人	にほんじん	*Japanese (people)*
日本語	にほんご	*Japanese language*
こちら		*here, this (person)*

Question words:

何	なん	*what?*
どこ		*where?*
どちら		*where? (polite)*

● *Additional New Words in Drills*

Places in Japan:

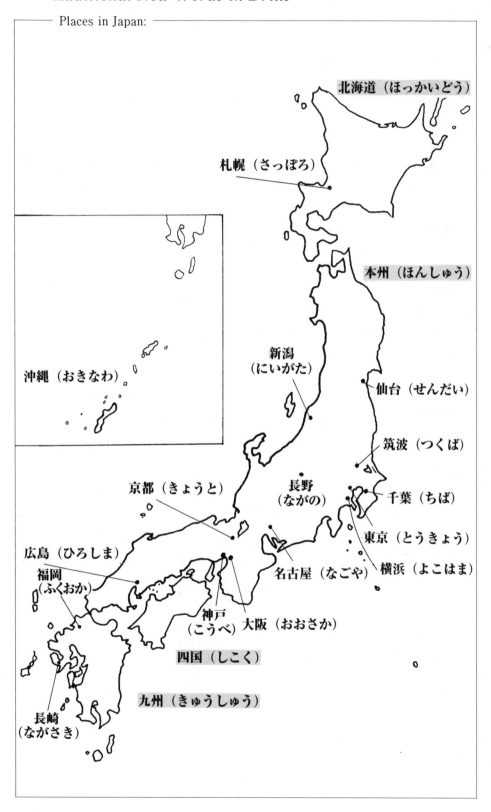

北海道（ほっかいどう）

札幌（さっぽろ）

本州（ほんしゅう）

沖縄（おきなわ）

新潟（にいがた）

仙台（せんだい）

筑波（つくば）

京都（きょうと）

長野（ながの）

千葉（ちば）

広島（ひろしま）

東京（とうきょう）

福岡（ふくおか）

名古屋（なごや）

横浜（よこはま）

神戸（こうべ）

大阪（おおさか）

四国（しこく）

九州（きゅうしゅう）

長崎（ながさき）

```
┌─── Fields of study: ──────────────────────────────┐
```

医学	いがく	medical science
音楽	おんがく	music
化学	かがく	chemistry
教育	きょういく	education
経営	けいえい	business administration
経済	けいざい	economics
コンピュータ	konpyuuta	computer science
生物	せいぶつ	biology
物理	ぶつり	physics
政治	せいじ	politics
法律	ほうりつ	law
社会学	しゃかいがく	sociology
歴史	れきし	history
地理	ちり	geography
哲学	てつがく	philosophy
宗教学	しゅうきょうがく	theology
心理学	しんりがく	psychology
文学	ぶんがく	literature
言語学	げんごがく	linguistics
国際関係	こくさいかんけい	international relations
数学	すうがく	mathematics
地学	ちがく	geology
工学	こうがく	engineering
電子工学	でんしこうがく	electronics
電気工学	でんきこうがく	electrical engineering
機械工学	きかいこうがく	mechanical engineering
遺伝子工学	いでんしこうがく	genetic engineering
土木工学	どぼくこうがく	civil engineering
建築	けんちく	architecture
農学	のうがく	agriculture
環境科学	かんきょうかがく	environmental science
生化学	せいかがく	biochemistry
薬学	やくがく	pharmacology
芸術	げいじゅつ	arts
美術	びじゅつ	fine arts
体育	たいいく	physical education

Structure Drills

1. Practise as in the example:

シャルマさん・留学生 → <u>シャルマさん</u>は<u>留学生</u>です。
りゅうがくせい

1. 山下さん・学生
   やました
3. リサさん・留学生

2. 山田さん・先生
   やまだ　　　せんせい
4. ○○さん・○○

2. Practise as in the example:

a. インド・留学生 → シャルマさんは<u>インド</u>の<u>留学生</u>です。

1. 大学院・学生
   だいがくいん
3. 私・友だち
   わたし　とも

2. 松見大学・学生
   まつみ
4. 木村先生・研究室・学生
   きむら　　けんきゅうしつ

b. インド・シャルマ → こちらは<u>インド</u>の<u>シャルマ</u>さんです。

1. 松見大学・山下

2. イギリス・リサ

3. 山田先生・研究室・田中

4. 私・友だち・リサ

5. 日本語・先生・○○
   にほんご

☆c. Now put in the proper order.

留学生・インド

→ ○○さんは<u>インド</u>の<u>留学生</u>です。

1. 物理・学生
   ぶつり
3. 私・先生・日本語

5. 先生・筑波大学・化学
   つくば　　かがく

2. 友だち・リサさん

4. 学生・研究室・山田先生

3．Make a negative sentence as in the examples:

      1) リサさん・先生　　　　→　リサさんは先生じゃありません。

      2) リサさん・インドの学生　→　リサさんはインドの学生じゃありません。

    1．田中さん・留学生　　　　　　　　2．シャルマさん・日本人

    3．山下さん・医学の学生　　　　　　4．山田先生・経済の先生

    5．リサさん・○○の学生　　　　　　6．○○さん・松見大学の学生

4．Practise the dialogue as in the example:

      1) リサさん・留学生　　　→　Q：リサさんは留学生ですか。

        <はい>　　　　　　　　　A：はい、そうです。

        <ええ>　　　　　　　　　A：ええ、そうです。

      2) リサさん・インドの学生　→　Q：リサさんはインドの学生ですか。

        <いいえ・イギリスの学生>　A：いいえ、インドの学生じゃありません。

                            イギリスの学生です。

    1．シャルマさん・学生　＜ええ＞

    2．サリーさん・インドの学生　＜いいえ・イギリスの学生＞

    3．山下さん・先生　＜いいえ・学生＞

    4．ピーターさん・大学院の学生　＜はい＞

    5．田中さん・筑波大学の学生　＜いいえ・松見大学の学生＞

    6．○○さん（Use your classmate's name）・○○の学生　＜？＞

    7．○○先生（Use your teacher's name）・教育の先生　＜？＞

5．Practise as in the example:

    a．シャルマ 　シャルマさんの国はインドです。

    1．リサ 　　　2．山下 　　　3．私

b. シャルマ → Q：<u>シャルマさん</u>の国はどこですか。
<ruby>国<rt>くに</rt></ruby>
A：インドです。

1. リサ
2. 山下<ruby><rt>やました</rt></ruby>
3. any name

6. Say these fields of study in Japanese.

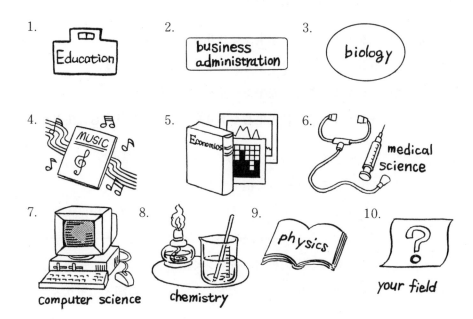

1. Education
2. business administration
3. biology
4. MUSIC
5. Economics
6. medical science
7. computer science
8. chemistry
9. physics
10. your field

7. Practise as in the example:

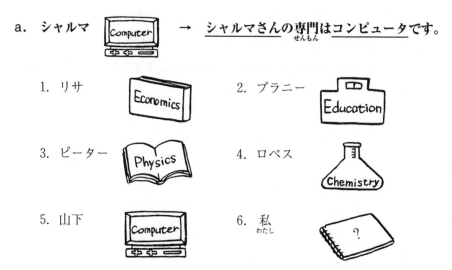

a. シャルマ [Computer] → <u>シャルマさんの専門はコンピュータです。</u>
<ruby>専門<rt>せんもん</rt></ruby>

1. リサ — Economics
2. プラニー — Education
3. ピーター — Physics
4. ロペス — Chemistry
5. 山下 — Computer
6. 私<ruby><rt>わたし</rt></ruby> — ?

b. シャルマ　　　　　→　Q：シャルマさんの専門は何ですか。
　　　　　　　　　　　　　　　　　せんもん　なん
　　　　　　　　　　　　　　A：コンピュータです。

1. 山下　　　　　2. ピーター　　　　3. ロペス
　 やました
4. プラニー　　　5. リサ　　　　　　6. any name

8. Practise as in the examples:

a. 1)　＜シャルマさん・学生＞＜リサさん・学生＞
　　　　　　　　　　　　がくせい
　　　　→シャルマさんは学生です。リサさんも学生です。

　　2)　＜シャルマさん・先生＞＜リサさん・先生＞
　　　　　　　　　　　　せんせい
　　　　→シャルマさんは先生じゃありません。リサさんも先生じゃありません。

1. ＜リサさん・留学生＞＜プラニーさん・留学生＞
　　　　　　　りゅうがくせい
2. ＜山下さん・先生＞＜田中さん・先生＞
　　 やました　　　　　 たなか
3. ＜シャルマさん・松見大学の学生＞＜田中さん・松見大学の学生＞
　　　　　　　　　まつみ だいがく
4. ＜プラニーさん・大学院の学生＞＜リサさん・大学院の学生＞
　　　　　　　　　　だいがくいん
5. ＜シャルマさんの専門・音楽＞＜山下さんの専門・音楽＞
　　　　　　　　　　　　おんがく
6. ＜リサさんの国・イギリス＞＜ジョンさんの国・イギリス＞
　　　　　　　くに

☆b. 1)　＜シャルマさん・学生＞＜リサさん・学生＞

　　　　→シャルマさんは学生です。リサさんも学生です。

　　2)　＜シャルマさん・留学生＞＜山下さん・留学生＞

　　　　→シャルマさんは留学生です。山下さんは留学生じゃありません。

1. ＜リサさん・学生＞＜山田さん・先生＞
　　　　　　　　　　　やまだ
2. ＜リサさん・松見大学の学生＞＜田中さん・松見大学の学生＞
3. ＜山下さんの先生・木村先生＞＜田中さんの先生・木村先生＞
4. ＜プラニーさん・大学院の学生＞＜ピーターさん・大学院の学生＞
5. ＜シャルマさんの専門・コンピュータ＞＜田中さんの専門・経営＞
　　　　　　　　　　　　　　　　　　　　　　　　　　けいえい
6. ＜シャルマさんの国・インド＞＜ロペスさんの国・インド＞

9．Get to know each other.

    a.   Introduce yourself to the other members of the class.

シャルマ：はじめまして。インドのシャルマです。

松見大学の留学生です。

専門はコンピュータです。

どうぞよろしくお願いします。

    b.   Introduce the student sitting next to you to the other members of the class.

こちらはシャルマさんです。

インドの留学生です。

シャルマさんの専門はコンピュータです。

    c.   Practise the following dialogue using your classmate's name.

Q：シャルマさんの国はどこですか。

A：インドです。

Q：シャルマさんの大学はどこですか。

A：松見大学です。

Q：シャルマさんの専門は何ですか。

A：コンピュータです。

☆10. Look at the picture and talk about each person as in the example:

シャルマさん → シャルマさんの国はインドです。

松見大学の留学生です。

シャルマさんの専門はコンピュータです。

インドのシャルマです。

大学は松見大学です。

専門はコンピュータです。

どうぞよろしく。

シャルマさん

松見大学の木村研究室の山下です。

専門はコンピュータです。

どうぞよろしく。

1. 山下さん

松見大学の田中です。

専門は経営です。

よろしくお願いします。

2. 田中さん

Conversation Drills

1. Introducing oneself （S-2a）

Look at the following situations and practise the example dialogues in pairs or three, as required. Next, try to practise without looking at the example, using your own names and countries.

a. Two students introduce themselves to each other.

A：Tanaka　　　　　　　　　　B：Yamashita

> A：はじめまして。＿＿＿＿＿です。どうぞよろしく。
> 　　　　　　　　　　(name)
> B：＿＿＿＿＿です。どうぞよろしく。

b. Two foreign students introduce themselves to each other.

A：Anil Sharma/India　　　　　B：Lisa Brown/United Kingdom

> A：＿＿＿＿＿の＿＿＿＿です。どうぞよろしく。
> 　　(country)　　(name)
> B：＿＿＿＿＿の＿＿＿＿です。
> 　こちらこそ、どうぞよろしく。

c. A student introduces himself to a professor.

A：Anil Sharma/India　　　B：Prof. Kimura

A：はじめまして。＿＿＿＿＿＿＿の＿＿＿＿＿＿ともうします。
　　　　　　　　　　（country）　　（name）
　　どうぞよろしくお願いします。
　　　　　　　　ねが
B：ああ、どうも。＿＿＿＿＿です。どうぞよろしく。

2. Introducing someone to someone else （S-2b）

a. A student introduces his friend to another student.

B：Lisa Brown/U.K.　　A：Yamashita　　C：Anil Sharma/India

A：シャルマさん、こちら、＿＿＿＿＿＿の＿＿＿＿さんです。

B：はじめまして。＿＿＿＿です。

C：どうも。

A：ブラウンさん、こちらは＿＿＿＿＿＿の＿＿＿＿さん。

C：＿＿＿＿です。どうぞよろしく。

B：どうぞよろしく。

b.   A student introduces his friend to a professor.

B：Anil Sharma/India   A：Yamashita   C：Prof. Tanaka/Tokyo University

A：田中先生、＿＿＿＿＿＿＿の＿＿＿＿＿ $\begin{cases}さん\\くん\end{cases}$ です。
　　た なかせんせい

B：はじめまして。＿＿＿＿＿ともうします。

C：どうも。

A：シャルマ $\begin{cases}さん\\くん\end{cases}$、こちらは＿＿＿＿＿＿の＿＿＿＿先生です。

C：＿＿＿＿＿です。

B：どうぞよろしくお願いします。
　　　　　　　　　　ねが

☆c.   A student introduces his friend to Yamanaka who is a company employee.

B：Anil Sharma   A：Yamashita   C：Yamanaka/I.B.M.

└── same seminar ──┘

A：山中さん、うちの研究室の＿＿＿＿＿さんです。
　　やまなか　　　　　けんきゅうしつ

B：はじめまして。＿＿＿＿＿ともうします。

C：どうも。

A：シャルマさん、こちらは＿＿＿＿＿＿の＿＿＿＿さん。
　　　　　　　　　　　　　　(company)　　　(name)

C：＿＿＿＿＿です。

B：よろしくお願いします。

13

☆d.　Introduction game

　　　　Form pairs and get a cue card on which someone's name, country（university, company, etc.）are written. Then introduce him/her to your partner in Japanese.

3．Saying what you want to be called　（S-2c）

A：a student　　　　B：Anil Sharma

A：ええと、<u>アニ</u>……

B：<u>アニル・シャルマ</u>です。　$\boxed{\begin{array}{c}\text{シャルマ}\\\hline\text{アニル}\end{array}}$ とよんでください。

A：あ、じゃ、<u>シャルマ</u>さん。

＊Use your own name.

4．Asking questions （G.I.3，4）

a.　One's country

＊Practise using a world map.

b.　One's specialization

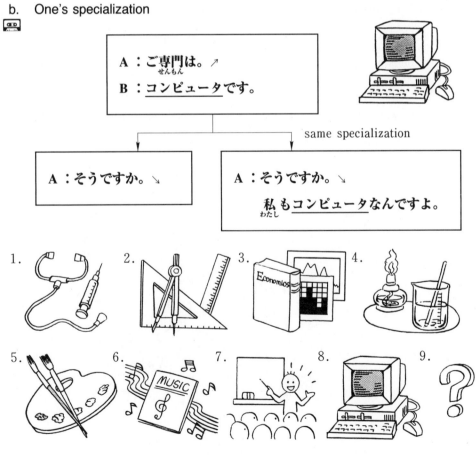

c. Various questions

Practise as shown in the example by using your own situation or the cue cards on which a name, country and specialization are written. (⇨CD 2.d)

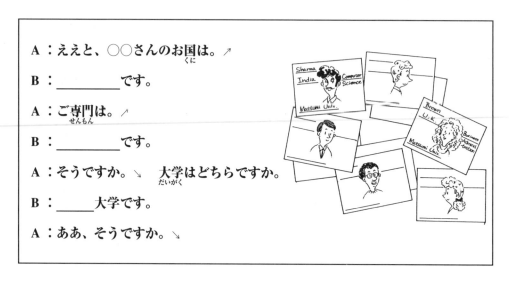

A：ええと、○○さんのお国は。↗
      くに

B：＿＿＿＿＿です。

A：ご専門は。↗
      せんもん

B：＿＿＿＿＿です。

A：そうですか。↘　大学はどちらですか。
                  だいがく

B：＿＿＿大学です。

A：ああ、そうですか。↘

☆d. Introduction chain

Students sit in a circle. One student introduces his/her imaginary friend A as 「Ａさんの国は〜です。」. Then, the next student repeats the first sentence and adds the introduction of a new friend B as 「Ａさんの国は〜です。Ｂさんの国は〜です。」. The third student repeats the previous two sentences and adds one more introduction. In the same way, continue to introduce as many people as can be remembered.

Students can also add 専門、大学、etc.

5. Giving a short answer

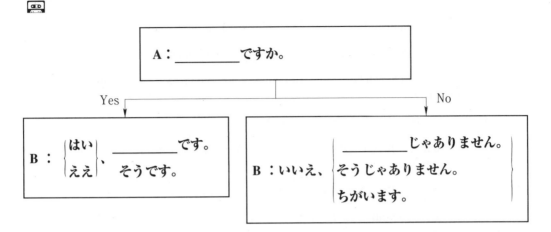

A：＿＿＿＿＿ですか。

Yes / No

B：｛はい／ええ｝、＿＿＿＿＿です。
そうです。

B：いいえ、｛＿＿＿＿＿じゃありません。
そうじゃありません。
ちがいます。｝

＊はい、ええ or いいえ alone can be used, too.　That is less formal, however.

1. シャルマさん
2. ～さん
3. 松見大学の学生
   まつみだいがく　がくせい
4. ～大学の学生
5. 留学生
   りゅうがくせい
6. インドの学生
7. ～の学生
8. 日本語の先生
   にほんご　せんせい
9. ～の先生
10. お国は～
    くに
11. ご専門は～
    せんもん
12. any question

6. Starting a conversation （S-1）

When you （＝A） meet Prof. Kimura （＝B） in the afternoon

A：あ、先生、こんにちは。

B：こんにちは。

12：00

6：00a.m.　6：00p.m.

12：00

1. When you meet Prof. Kimura in the morning

2. When you meet Prof. Tanaka in the evening

3. When you meet your friend Yamashita in the afternoon

4. When you meet your senior student Suzuki in the morning

5. Use your friend's name

6. Use your teacher's name

17

7. Saying "Goodbye" (S-3)

1. to Prof. Kimura after class （You will see him next week.）

2. to your close friend after class （You will see him/her later.）

3. to the office worker after finishing your business （You will see him/her tomorrow.）

4. to your friend before the long vacation

5. to your professor after a meeting （You are not sure when you will see him/her soon.）

6. Response to Prof. Kimura's 「それじゃ、また。」

7. Response to your friend's 「じゃ、またね。」

8. Response to the office worker's 「それじゃ、さようなら。」

8. Role play

1. You meet your academic advisor at a party and he introduces you to his students.

2. You meet your academic advisor at a party and you introduce your Japanese language teacher to him.

☆3. Use the cue cards and introduce each other.

| Meeting | → | Questions & Answers | → | Parting |

Tasks and Activities

1. Listen to the tape.

a. You will hear the self-introduction of six people （1～6）. Based on this, fill in the blanks below.

1. 名前：Jim Scott
　　なまえ
　　　　（ジム・スコット）

　　国　：アメリカ
　　くに
　　大学：東京大学
　　だいがく　とうきょう
　　専門：＿＿＿＿＿＿
　　せんもん

2. 名前：Toy

　　　　（トイ）

　　国　：＿＿＿＿＿＿

　　大学：千葉大学
　　　　　　ち　ば
　　専門：教育
　　　　　きょういく

3. 名前：村田　広
　　　　むら　た　　ひろし

　　国　：日本
　　　　　に　ほん
　　大学：＿＿＿＿＿＿

　　専門：コンピュータ

4. 名前：Ann Green

　　　　（アン・グリーン）

　　国　：＿＿＿＿＿＿

　　大学：筑波大学
　　　　　つく　ば
　　専門：経済
　　　　　けいざい

5. 名前：Herio Castro

　　　　（エリオ・カストロ）

　　国　：＿＿＿＿＿＿

　　大学：大阪大学
　　　　　おおさか
　　専門：医学
　　　　　い　がく

6. 名前：＿＿＿＿＿＿

　　国　：日本

　　大学：京都大学
　　　　　きょう　と
　　専門：化学
　　　　　か　がく

　　＊アメリカ　Amerika　U.S.A.　　～をべんきょうしています *(I am) studying* ～

b. You will hear a series of conversations between two people. Write which people （1～6）are talking.

　　1. ＿＿＿と＿＿＿　　2. ＿＿＿と＿＿＿　　3. ＿＿＿と＿＿＿

　　4. ＿＿＿と＿＿＿　　5. ＿＿＿と＿＿＿

19

2. The following strips make three sentences. Join the strips together to complete the sentences.

Example

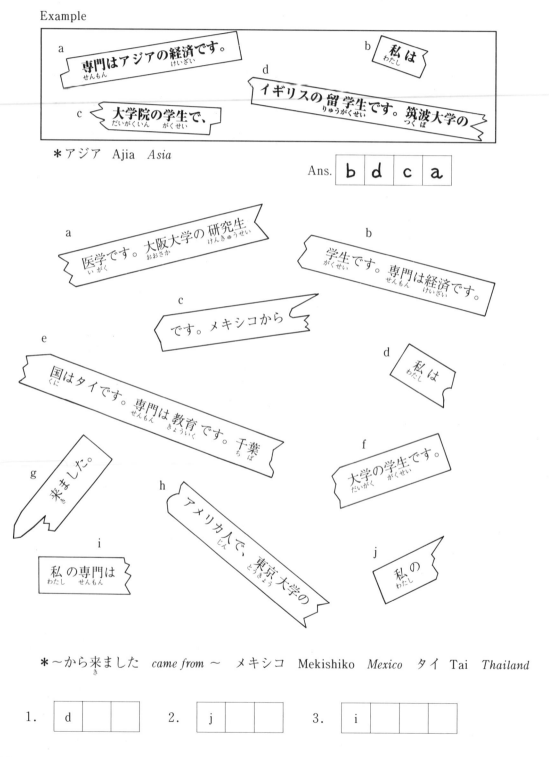

*アジア Ajia *Asia*

Ans. | b | d | c | a |

a 医学です。大阪大学の研究生
いがく　おおさか　けんきゅうせい

b 学生です。専門は経済です。
がくせい　せんもん　けいざい

c です。メキシコから

d 私は
わたし

e 国はタイです。専門は教育です。千葉
くに　　　　　せんもん　きょういく　　ちば

f 大学の学生です。
だいがく　がくせい

g 来ました。
き

h アメリカ人で、東京大学の
じん　とうきょう

i 私の専門は
わたし　せんもん

j 私の
わたし

*〜から来ました *came from* 〜　メキシコ Mekishiko *Mexico*　タイ Tai *Thailand*
き

1. | d | | | 2. | j | | | 3. | i | | |

☆3. You will hear a series of conversations between two people. Based on this, fill in the chart below.

国
くに

A	アメリカ	(U.S.A)
B	メキシコ	(Mexico)
C	ブラジル	(Brazil)
D	スペイン	(Spain)
E	日本 にほん	
F	中国 ちゅうごく	
G	オーストラリア	(Australia)
H	イラン	(Iran)

仕 事
し ごと

a	先生 せんせい	
b	エンジニア	(engineer)
c	ウェイトレス	(waitress)
d	デザイナー	(designer)
e	パイロット	(pilot)
f	医者 いしゃ	(medical doctor)
g	プログラマー	(programmer)
h	ピアニスト	(pianist)

名前 なまえ Name	国 くに Country	仕事 しごと Occupation	大学 だいがく University
ジョン John			ハワイ大学
リンダ Linda			京都大学 きょうと
山 田 やまだ	日本 に ほん		東京大学 とうきょう
マリオ Mario		学生 がくせい	名古屋大学 なごや

☆ 4. There are six people of different backgrounds. Each is standing hand in hand between two friends. Write in the space below, the letters corresponding to their names, countries, and fields of study.

名前 なまえ	国 くに	専門 せんもん
A） Ando	a） アルゼンチン (Argentine)	い） 医学 いがく
K） Ken	c） カナダ (Canada)	か） 化学 かがく
S） Sano	n） 日本 にほん	き） 教育 きょういく
N） Naomi	p） フィリピン (Philippines)	け） 経済 けいざい
M） Mina	t） チュニジア (Tunisia)	こ） コンピュータ
I） Irene	z） ザイール (Zaire)	せ） 生物学 せいぶつがく

1. Naomi のともだちは、チュニジア人とザイール人です。
2. Ando のともだちは、教育の学生です。
3. カナダ人のともだちは、ザイールの留学生です。
4. フィリピン人の名前は、Irene です。
5. Mina のともだちの専門は、化学です。
6. Sano はアルゼンチンから来ました。
7. Ken はカナダ人です。
8. Irene は、医学の学生です。
9. ザイール人の名前は、Ando です。
10. Ken の専門は、教育です。
11. Irene は、Sano と Ken のともだちです。
12. Naomi のともだちは、コンピュータの先生です。
13. チュニジア人は、生物学の学生です。
14. Irene のともだちは、教育の学生と経済の先生です。

① <u>N , n , か</u>　　　② <u>　, t ,　</u>　　　③ <u>　,　,　</u>
④ <u>I ,　,　</u>　　　⑤ <u>　,　,　</u>　　　⑥ <u>　,　, こ</u>

5. Fill in the blanks with the appropriate words, using the given information.

あなた　*You*	友だち　*Your friend*
名前：アニル	名前：マリア
国 ：インド	国 ：チリ *(Chili)*
大学：筑波大学	大学：東京大学
専門：コンピュータ	専門：教育

a. 1. あなた　*You*

わたしは、<u>アニル</u>です。つくば大学の＿＿＿＿＿で、国は＿＿＿＿です。
専門は、＿＿＿＿＿＿です。

2. 友だち　*Your friend*

わたしの友だちの＿＿＿＿さんです。＿＿＿＿から来ました。
＿＿＿＿さんの大学は＿＿＿＿＿です。専門は、＿＿＿＿＿＿。

b. Write about yourself and a friend in the same way.

Lesson 2

郵便局で
ゆう びん きょく

At the post office

● *New Words in Drills*

· is used only in Conversation Drills

— Verbs: —

<person>が
<place>に／へ

行きます	いきます	［いく］	*to go*
帰ります	かえります	［かえる］	*to return, to go home*
来ます	きます	［くる］	*to come*

<person>が
<thing>を

買います	かいます	［かう］	*to buy*
読みます	よみます	［よむ］	*to read*
書きます	かきます	［かく］	*to write*
聞きます	ききます	［きく］	*to listen, to hear*
見ます	みます	［みる］	*to see, to look at*
します		［する］	*to do*
勉強します	べんきょうします	［する］	*to study*

<person A>が
<person B/place>に／へ
<thing>を

出します	だします	［だす］	*to put out, to send*

— Facilities: —

郵便局	ゆうびんきょく	*post office*
銀行	ぎんこう	*bank*
駅	えき	*station*
図書館	としょかん	*library*
病院	びょういん	*hospital*
食堂	しょくどう	*cafeteria, refectory*
本屋	ほんや	*bookshop*

── Languages: ──

英語	えいご	*English*
〜語	〜ご	*〜 language*

── Other words: ──

テレビ	terebi	*television*
カメラ	kamera	*camera*
ラジオ	rajio	*radio*
ビデオ	bideo	*video*
ＣＤ	shiidii	*compact disc*
テープ	teepu	*tape*
時計	とけい	*watch, clock*
手紙	てがみ	*letter*
はがき		*postcard*
切手	きって	*stamp*
速達	そくたつ	*special delivery*
本	ほん	*book*
新聞	しんぶん	*newspaper*
映画	えいが	*movie*
漢字	かんじ	*kanji*
ひらがな		*hiragana*
・おかえし		*change* ＝ おつり

── Time words: ──

きょう		*today*
きのう		*yesterday*
あした		*tomorrow*
毎日	まいにち	*everyday*

── Other words: ──

・全部（で）	ぜんぶ（で）	*(in) total*
・それから		*and, also*
・ちょっと		*a little, for a while*
・〜円	〜えん	*〜 yen*
・〜まい		counter for flat objects

```
┌─ Question words: ──────────────────────────────────────────┐
│                                                            │
│   何              なに              what ?                  │
│   だれ                             who ?                   │
│ ・いくら                           how much ?              │
│                                                            │
└────────────────────────────────────────────────────────────┘
```

● *Additional New Words in Drills*

```
┌─ Mail service: ────────────────────────────────────────────┐
│                                                            │
│   エアログラム      earoguramu      aerogram               │
│   航空便           こうくうびん      airmail                │
│   船便            ふなびん          seamail                │
│   小包            こづつみ          parcel                 │
│                                                            │
└────────────────────────────────────────────────────────────┘
```

```
┌─ Numbers: ─────────────────────────────────────────────────┐
│                                                            │
│   0  れい／ゼロ    10  じゅう                               │
│   1  いち         11  じゅういち                            │
│   2  に          12  じゅうに        20  にじゅう           │
│   3  さん         13  じゅうさん      30  さんじゅう         │
│   4  よん／し      14  じゅうよん／し  40  よんじゅう         │
│   5  ご          15  じゅうご        50  ごじゅう           │
│   6  ろく         16  じゅうろく      60  ろくじゅう         │
│   7  なな／しち    17  じゅうなな／しち 70  ななじゅう        │
│   8  はち         18  じゅうはち      80  はちじゅう         │
│   9  きゅう／く    19  じゅうきゅう／く 90  きゅうじゅう       │
│  ────────────────────────────────────────────             │
│  100  ひゃく      1000  せん        10000  いちまん         │
│  200  にひゃく     2000  にせん                             │
│  300  さんびゃく   3000  さんぜん                           │
│  400  よんひゃく   4000  よんせん                           │
│  500  ごひゃく     5000  ごせん                             │
│  600  ろっぴゃく   6000  ろくせん                           │
│  700  ななひゃく   7000  ななせん                           │
│  800  はっぴゃく   8000  はっせん                           │
│  900  きゅうひゃく 9000  きゅうせん                          │
│                                                            │
└────────────────────────────────────────────────────────────┘
```

Structure Drills

1. Read aloud the following numbers.

3,	6,	8,	4,	2,	9,	5,	7,	1,
29,	83,	99,	37,	16,	75,	48,	50,	69,
420,	380,	940,	110,	625,	850,	501,	724,	208,
5000,	4800,	7600,	3900,	8800,	1550,	6050,	2700,	9300

2. Your instructor will read some numbers. Write them down.

3. Look at the picture and say an appropriate verb.

1.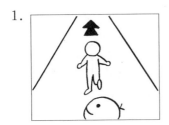

2.

3.

4.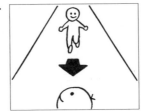

5.

6.

7.

8.

9.

10.

4. Say the names of places, then practice as in the example:

→ A：どこへ行きますか。

B：郵便局へ行きます。
ゆうびんきょく

post office

1.

bank

2.

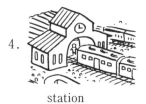

hospital

3.

library

4.

station

5.

cafeteria

6.

bookstore

5. Practise as in the examples:

読みます　　＜本＞　＜新聞＞　＜何＞
よ　　　　　　　ほん　　しんぶん　　なに

→ 本を読みます。

→ 新聞を読みます。

→ 何を読みますか。

1. 買います　　＜カメラ＞　＜時計＞　　　＜本＞　　＜何＞
   か　　　　　　　　　　とけい

2. 書きます　　＜手紙＞　　＜ひらがな＞　＜漢字＞　＜何＞
   か　　　　　てがみ　　　　　　　かんじ

3. 見ます　　　＜テレビ＞　＜ビデオ＞　　＜映画＞　＜何＞
   み　　　　　　　　　　　　　　えいが

4. 聞きます　　＜音楽＞　　＜テープ＞　　＜ＣＤ＞　＜何＞
   き　　　　　おんがく

5. 出します　　＜手紙＞　　＜はがき＞　　＜速達＞　＜何＞
   だ　　　　　　　　　　　　　　そくたつ

6. 勉強します　＜英語＞　　＜物理＞　　　＜生物＞　＜何＞
   べんきょう　えいご　　　ぶつり　　　　せいぶつ

6．Practise as in the example:

読みます ＜図書館・新聞＞
→ 図書館で新聞を読みます。

1. 買います ＜本屋・教育の本＞
2. 書きます ＜大学・手紙＞
3. 見ます ＜食堂・テレビ＞
4. 聞きます ＜うち・日本語のテープ＞
5. 出します ＜郵便局・手紙＞
6. 勉強します ＜筑波大学・医学＞
7. 買います ＜どこ・カメラ＞
8. 勉強します ＜どこ・日本語＞

7．Practise as in the examples:

見ます ＜友だち・ビデオ＞
→ 友だちとビデオを見ます。
→ 友だちといっしょにビデオを見ます。

1. 見ます ＜友だち・映画＞
2. 聞きました ＜リサさん・音楽＞
3. 勉強します ＜友だち・日本語＞
4. 行きます ＜先生・東京＞
5. 来ました ＜だれ・日本＞
6. 帰ります ＜だれ・うち＞

8．Answer as in the examples:

1) 東京へ行きますか。 ＜はい＞ → はい、行きます。
2) 研究室へ行きますか。 ＜いいえ＞ → いいえ、行きません。

1. 手紙を出しますか。 ＜はい＞
2. はがきを出しましたか。 ＜いいえ＞

3. 勉強しましたか。 ＜はい＞
4. 勉強しましたか。 ＜いいえ＞
5. ＣＤを聞きましたか。 ＜はい＞
6. ラジオを聞きましたか。 ＜いいえ＞
7. 帰りましたか。 ＜はい＞
8. 帰りますか。 ＜いいえ＞
9. 切手を買いますか。 ＜はい＞
10. 漢字の本を買いましたか。 ＜いいえ＞

9. Practise as in the examples:

日本語を勉強します ＜あした＞ ＜毎日＞ ＜きのう＞

→ あした日本語を勉強します。

→ 毎日、日本語を勉強します。

→ きのう日本語を勉強しました。

1. 手紙を書きます ＜毎日＞ ＜きのう＞
2. テレビを見ます ＜きのう＞ ＜あした＞
3. テープを聞きます ＜きょう＞ ＜毎日＞
4. 勉強しません ＜あした＞ ＜きのう＞
5. 新聞を読みます ＜あした＞ ＜きのう＞
6. 研究室へ行きます ＜毎日＞ ＜きのう＞
7. 大学へ来ません ＜きょう＞ ＜あした＞
8. 何をしますか ＜あした＞ ＜きのう＞ ＜毎日＞

10. Turn the word in ＜ ＞ into the topic of the sentence. Note some words cannot become a topic.

アリさんが本を買いました。

＜アリさんが＞ → アリさんは本を買いました。

＜本を＞ → 本はアリさんが買いました。

1. 山下さんが新聞を読みました。

   ＜山下さんが＞

   ＜新聞を＞

2. きょう田中さんがテレビを見ます。

   ＜田中さんが＞

   ＜テレビを＞

3. きのうプラニーさんがテープを聞きました。

   ＜テープを＞

   ＜プラニーさんが＞

4. だれが手紙を書きましたか。

   ＜手紙を＞

   ＜だれが＞

11. Interview the student next to you.

1. あしたどこへ行きますか。
2. 毎日、日本語を勉強しますか。
3. 国で日本語を勉強しましたか。
4. きのう日本語のテープを聞きましたか。

   どこで聞きましたか。
5. 毎日、新聞を読みますか。
6. どこで切手を買いますか。
7. きのうテレビを見ましたか。
8. どこで英語を勉強しましたか。

Conversation Drills

1. Greeting someone you meet on the street (S-1)

Look at the example dialogues and practise by using the cue words in the pictures below. If you are a female, use example dialogue a'.

a. Two friends

A：山下　　B：シャルマ
やました

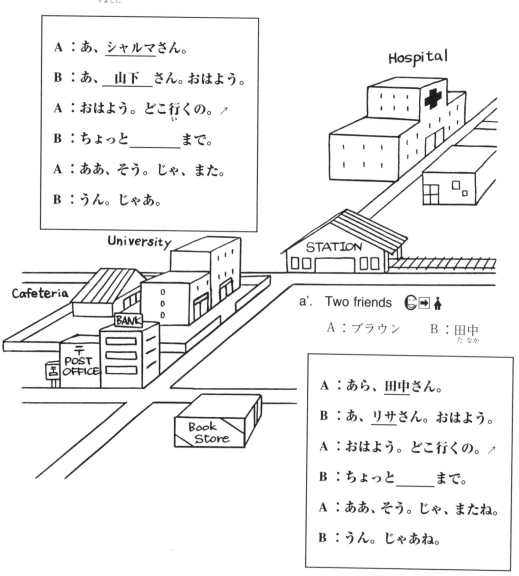

A：あ、シャルマさん。

B：あ、山下さん。おはよう。

A：おはよう。どこ行くの。↗
い

B：ちょっと＿＿＿＿まで。

A：ああ、そう。じゃ、また。

B：うん。じゃあ。

Hospital

University

Cafeteria

BANK

POST OFFICE

Book Store

STATION

a'. Two friends

A：ブラウン　　B：田中
たなか

A：あら、田中さん。

B：あ、リサさん。おはよう。

A：おはよう。どこ行くの。↗

B：ちょっと＿＿＿＿まで。

A：ああ、そう。じゃ、またね。

B：うん。じゃあね。

* Use そこまで if you don't want to specify your destination.

b. A teacher meeting a student

Use the cue cards showing the destination.

A：先生
せんせい

B：学生
がくせい

A：あ、＿＿＿＿＿ { さん。
　　　　　　　　　 くん。

B：あ、先生。おはようございます。

A：おはよう。どこ行くの。↗
　　　　　　　 い

B：ええ、ちょっと＿＿＿＿＿まで。

A：そう。それじゃ、また。

B：はい。じゃ、失礼します。
　　　　　　　　　 しつれい

c. A student meeting a teacher

A：学生　　B：先生

A：あ、先生。おはようございます。

B：ああ、＿＿＿＿＿ { さん。 } おはよう。
　　　　　　　　　　 くん。

A：どちらへ。↗

B：うん、ちょっと＿＿＿＿＿まで。

A：そうですか。それじゃ、失礼します。

B：うん。じゃ、また。

☆d.　Two neighbours 🔲

> A：あ、＿＿＿＿さん。
>
> B：ああ、＿＿＿＿さん。おはようございます。
>
> A：おはようございます。どちらへ。↗
>
> B：ええ、ちょっと＿＿＿＿まで。
>
> A：そうですか。じゃ、いってらっしゃい。
>
> B：はい。じゃ、失礼します。
> 　　　　　　　しつれい

2．Inviting someone to come with you（S-1）

If someone you are talking to happens to be going to the same place, you can invite him/her to come with you.

a.　Two friends 😊➡
🔳

> A：どこ行くの。↗
> 　　　い
> B：ちょっと＿＿＿＿まで。

> A：そう。じゃ、また。
> B：うん。じゃね。

> A：あ、｜私もよ。　👤
> 　　　　わたし
> 　　　　｜ぼくもだよ。👤
> B：じゃ、いっしょに行く。↗
> A：うん。

b. Find-a-partner game

A card similar to the one below (Q card) is given to a student. All other students are given a card showing a destination.

By asking the other students where they are going, the student with the Q card tries to find someone who is going to the same place and invite him/her to go together.

Q : You want to go to the _____, but you don't know

how to get there. Find a partner and go together.

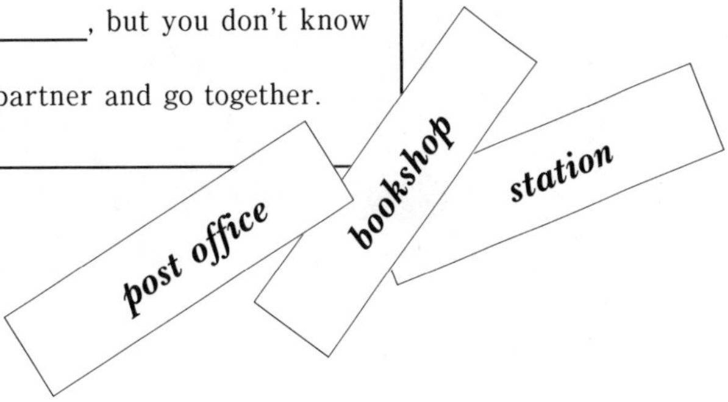

post office

bookshop

station

☆c. Where-to-go game

Divide the students into two groups. Each student in group A will be given a destination card and will take part in several dialogues. Students in group B will listen to the dialogues and fill in the blanks in the following chart.

名　前 な　まえ	行き先 い　さき	名　前	行き先
1.		5.	
2.		6.	
3.		7.	
4.		8.	

3. Sending a letter (S-2, S-3)

a. A customer asks to send an item of mail.

1. 船便
   ふなびん

2. 速達
   そくたつ

3. 小包
   こづつみ

4. 航空便
   こうくうびん

*   Use a letter similar to the one below.

b. Noting down the price

A：客（customer）   B：局員（office clerk）
　　きゃく　　　　　　　きょくいん

A：すみません。

B：はい。

A：これ、_____でお願いします。
　　　　　　　　　　ねが

B：ええと、これ、どこですか。

A：あ、_____です。

B：じゃ、280円です。
　　　　　　えん

A：はい。(Note down.)

*Use  ,

□ or and

name of the country

as you like.

☆c. Telling the price using the price list below (料金表)

航 空 便 こう くう びん	アジア	北アメリカ 中央アメリカ オセアニア	ヨーロッパ アフリカ 南アメリカ
手紙 （10gまで） てがみ （＋10gごとに） （for every 10 g）	90円 ＋60円	110円 ＋80円	130円 ＋100円
は が き	70円		

アジア	Ajia	*Asia*
北アメリカ	きた Amerika	*North America*
中央アメリカ	ちゅうおう Amerika	*Central America*
オセアニア	Oseania	*Oceania*
ヨーロッパ	Yooroppa	*Europe*
アフリカ	Afurika	*Africa*
南アメリカ	みなみ Amerika	*South America*

☆d. Asking how long it will take

A：客 (customer)　　B：局員 (office clerk)
　きゃく　　　　　　　　きょくいん

A ：すみません。

B ：はい。

A ：これ、_____でお願いします。
　　　　　　　　　　　　ねが

B ：ええと、これ、どこですか。

A ：あ、_____です。

　　どのぐらいかかりますか。

B ：そうですね。1 週間ぐらいでしょう。
　　　　　　　　　いっしゅうかん

A ：そうですか。じゃ、お願いします。

＊　Learn first the names of the days, weeks and months, etc.

　→ See L11 NW.

☆e.　When you can't catch what's being said:

A：客（customer）　　B：局員（office clerk）
　　きゃく　　　　　　　　　　きょくいん

A：すみません。

B：はい。

A：これ、_____でいくらですか。

B：インドですね。280円です。
　　　　　　　　　　えん

A：は。↗

B：280円です。

A：はい。じゃ、これで。（Pay）

4．Buying something at a post office（S-4）

a.　Buy

A：客（customer）　　B：局員（office clerk）

A：80円切手、3まいください。
　　きって

B：はい。240円です。

A：はい。（Pay）

B：ありがとうございました。

80円切手　　　　**3**

1. 50円切手	5	2. はがき	2
3. エアログラム	4	4. 80円切手	7
5. 10円切手	6	6. はがき	10
7. エアログラム	8	8. 80円切手	5
9. 50円切手	9	10. 100円切手	1

b. Buying various items

Use the example dialogue to buy what you want.

A：80円切手、3まい。
えんきって

B：はい。

A：ええと、それから、はがき、5まいください。

B：はい。ぜんぶで490円です。

A：はい。（Pay the money.）

B：ありがとうございました。

80円切手　　3　　　　はがき　　5

5. Receiving change （G.I. 3）

Listen for the price and pay the appropriate sum of money. Don't forget to check your change !

A：……

B：はい。ぜんぶで490円です。

A：じゃ、これでお願いします。
ねが

B：1000円ですね。510円のおかえしです。

A：どうも。

B：ありがとうございました。

6. Buying and paying (S-2, S-4)

Buy something you want and pay with a 500-yen coin, a 1000-yen or 5000-yen bill.

A：客（customer）　　B：局員（office clerk）

A：すみません。80円切手、3まい。

B：はい。

A：ええと、それから、はがき、5まいください。

B：はい。ぜんぶで490円です。

A：じゃ、これでお願いします。

B：1000円ですね。510円のおかえしです。

A：どうも。

B：ありがとうございました。

---

*　Use real money or paper money for the practice above.

7. Role play

1. In the afternoon, you go to the post office to send an airmail letter to your country ; you meet your friend on the way. Your friend also wants to buy some stamps, so you go together.

2. You send a parcel to your country, and buy five postcards and ten aerograms.

☆3. You buy ten postcards and three 80 yen stamps, and pay with a 1000 yen bill, but the clerk gives you only 200 yen change.

☆4. Observe what kind of conversation is actually done at the post office, and report that in the classroom.

Tasks and Activities

1. Listen to the tape and answer the following questions.

   a.   What is the time?   Choose from the following.

      1. morning · afternoon · evening

      2. morning · afternoon · evening

      3. morning · afternoon · evening

      4. morning · afternoon · evening

   b.   Where are they going ?

      1._____   2._____

      3._____   4._____

   c.   What is the social relationship between the two people. Are they on an equal or a different speech level?   Choose from the following.

      1. equal · different   2. equal · different

      3. equal · different   4. equal · different

2.  Listen to the tape, and choose the appropriate picture for the conversations.

1. _____   2. _____   3. _____   4. _____

a.

b.

c.

d.

e.

f.

保健センター　ほけん sentaa　*Health Center*
ほ けん

3. Listen to the tape. You will hear a conversation at a post office. Fill in the blanks.

	な　に	いくら
example	80円切手　　　　（ **3** ）まい	（ **240** ）円
1	はがき　　　　　（　　）まい 80円切手　　　　（　　）まい	ぜんぶで（　　　　）円
2	100円切手　　　　（　　）まい エアログラム　　（　　）まい	ぜんぶで（　　　　）円
3	手紙 （タイに航空便で）	（　　　　）円 ───────────── 200円でおつり（　　　　）円
☆4	手紙（速達で）	（　　　　）円 ───────────── 1000円でおつり（　　　　）円
☆5	本（フランスに船便で）	（　　　　）円 ───────────── 10000円でおつり（　　　　）円

タイ　Tai　*Thailand*　　フランス　Furansu　*France*

4．a． Fill in the appropriate words or numbers in the blanks.

1.

郵便局 ゆうびんきょく	
エアログラム	90円 えん
はがき	50円
切手 きって	80円

きのう、＿＿＿＿＿＿＿へ行きました。はがきを

＿＿＿＿まいと＿＿＿＿＿＿を＿＿＿＿まい買い

ました。ぜんぶで＿＿＿＿＿円でした。

2.

本屋 ほんや	
経済の本 けいざい	1800円
化学の本 かがく	1200円
医学の本 いがく	4600円
スペイン語の本 ご	950円
中国語の本 ちゅうごく	1800円
インドの音楽の本 おんがく	3980円

本屋で＿＿＿＿＿＿＿＿＿＿＿と

＿＿＿＿＿＿＿＿＿＿を買いました。

ぜんぶで＿＿＿＿＿円でした。

3.

デパート	
時計 とけい	3500円
	4200円
	7800円
テープ	380円
テレビ	32000円
カメラ	31000円
	42000円

＿＿＿＿＿＿で＿＿＿＿＿円の

時計と＿＿＿＿＿＿円のカメラを買

いました。ぜんぶで＿＿＿＿＿＿

円でした。

デパート depaato *department store*

☆b． Write a paragraph following any of the patterns above.

5．Read the following sentences and determine how much the person needs to pay.

1. まいにち駅でスポーツ新聞と英語の新聞を買います。スポーツ新聞は90円、英語の新聞は200円です。ぜんぶでいくらですか。

   スポーツ　supootsu *sports*

2. きょう、銀座で「ロッキーⅣ」を見ます。きっぷは１まい1600円です。インドの友だちといっしょに行きます。２まいでいくらですか。

   銀座　（a place name）　ロッキー　Rokkii *Rocky*（a movie title）

   きっぷ　*ticket*

☆3. きのう秋葉原へ行きました。ソニーのテレビは、４万８千円、東芝のテレビは４万５千円でした。セイコーの時計は１万８千円、キャノンのカメラは３万６千円、ニコンは４万２千円でした。ソニーのテレビと、セイコーの時計とニコンのカメラを買いました。ぜんぶでいくらですか。

   秋葉原　（a place name）　　　　ソニー　Sonii（a brand name）
   東芝　（a brand name）　　　　　セイコー　Seikoo（a brand name）
   キャノン　Kyanon（a brand name）　ニコン　Nikon（a brand name）

レストランで

At a restaurant

● *New Words in Drills*

• is used only in Conversation Drills

```
┌─ Verbs: ─────────────────────────────────────────────────
│
│  ┌─────────────────────┐
│  │ <person>が          │
│  │ <thing>を           │
│  └─────────────────────┘
│    食べます    たべます              ［たべる］      to eat
│    飲みます    のみます              ［のむ］        to drink
│
│  ┌─────────────────────┐
│  │ <person A>が        │
│  │ <person B/thing>を  │
│  └─────────────────────┘
│    待ちます    まちます              ［まつ］        to wait
│    呼びます    よびます              ［よぶ］        to call
│
│  ┌─────────────────────┐
│  │ <person A>が        │
│  │ <person B>に        │
│  │ <thing>を           │
│  └─────────────────────┘
│    教えます    おしえます            ［おしえる］    to teach
│    あげます                          ［あげる］      to give
│    貸します    かします              ［かす］        to lend, to rent
│    払います    はらいます            ［はらう］      to pay
│    注文します  ちゅうもんします      ［する］        to order
│
│  ┌─────────────────────┐
│  │ <person A>が        │
│  │ <person B>に/から   │
│  │ <thing>を           │
│  └─────────────────────┘
│    習います    ならいます            ［ならう］      to learn
│    もらいます                        ［もらう］      to receive
│    借ります    かります              ［かりる］      to borrow, to rent
│
└──────────────────────────────────────────────────────────
```

Food and drink:

コーヒー	koohii	*coffee*
紅茶	こうちゃ	*tea*
（お）茶	（お）ちゃ	*Japanese tea*
肉	にく	*meat*
魚	さかな	*fish*
たまご		*egg*
野菜	やさい	*vegetable*
くだもの		*fruit*
パン	pan	*bread*
ごはん		*rice*
朝ごはん	あさごはん	*breakfast*
昼ごはん	ひるごはん	*lunch*
晩ごはん	ばんごはん	*supper, dinner*

Other words:

辞書	じしょ	*dictionary*
かたかな		*katakana*
ペン	pen	*pen*
ノート	nooto	*note*
誕生日	たんじょうび	*birthday*
プレゼント	purezento	*present*
（お）金	（お）かね	*money*
レストラン	resutoran	*restaurant*
スーパー	suupaa	*supermarket*

Adverbs:

（ご）いっしょ（に）		*together*
べつべつ（に）		*separate(ly)*

Question words:

いつ		*when ?*
いくつ		*how many ? (things)*
何人	なんにん	*how many ? (persons)*
・何名（さま）	なんめい（さま）	*how many ? (persons)*

● *Additional New Words in Drills*

```
┌─ Food and drinks: ──────────────────────────────────────┐
```

（お）水	（お）みず	*water*
（お）酒	（お）さけ	*alcohol, sake*
日本酒	にほんしゅ	*sake*
ビール	biiru	*beer*
チーズ	chiizu	*cheese*
しお		*sull*
さとう		*sugar*
しょうゆ		*soy sauce*
ソース	soosu	*sauce*
定食	ていしょく	*set meal*

```
┌─ Other words: ──────────────────────────────────────────┐
```

（お）つり		*change*
はし		*chopsticks*
スプーン	supuun	*spoon*
タバコ/たばこ	tabako	*cigarettes*
マッチ	matchi	*matches*
はいざら		*ashtray*
メニュー	menyuu	*menu*

```
┌─ Counters: ─────────────────────────────────────────────┐
```

	〜つ（things）		〜人（persons）	
1 :	一つ	ひとつ	一人	ひとり
2 :	二つ	ふたつ	二人	ふたり
3 :	三つ	みっつ	三人	さんにん
4 :	四つ	よっつ	四人	よにん
5 :	五つ	いつつ	五人	ごにん
6 :	六つ	むっつ	六人	ろくにん
7 :	七つ	ななつ	七人	しちにん/ななにん
8 :	八つ	やっつ	八人	はちにん
9 :	九つ	ここのつ	九人	くにん/きゅうにん
10 :	十	とお	十人	じゅうにん

Menu in restaurants:

ホットコーヒー	hottokoohii	*hot coffee*
アイスコーヒー	aisukoohii	*iced coffee*
ミルクティー	mirukutii	*tea with milk*
レモンティー	remontii	*lemon tea*
コーラ	koora	*cola*
ミルク	miruku	*milk*
オレンジジュース	orenjijuusu	*orange juice*
トマトジュース	tomatojuusu	*tomato juice*
レモンジュース	remonjuusu	*lemon juice*
アイスクリーム	aisukuriimu	*ice cream*
サラダ	sarada	*salad*
ドレッシング	doresshingu	*dressing*
和風	わふう	*Japanese style*
～風	～ふう	*～ style*
ピザ	piza	*pizza*
サンドイッチ	sandoitchi	*sandwich*
ミックスサンドイッチ	mikkususandoitchi	*mixed sandwich*
チーズサンドイッチ	chiizusandoitchi	*cheese sandwich*
スパゲッティー	supagettii	*spaghetti*
ナポリタン	naporitan	*with tomato sauce*
ミートソース	miitosoosu	*with meat sauce*
カレーライス	kareeraisu	*rice curry*
チキンカレー	chikinkaree	*chicken curry*
ポークカレー	pookukaree	*pork curry*
ビーフカレー	biifukaree	*beef curry*
フライドチキン	furaidochikin	*fried chicken*
とりのからあげ		*fried chicken*
天ぷら	てんぷら	*tempura*
ライス	raisu	*boiled rice*

Structure Drills

1. Practise counting people and things.

   a. 何人ですか。
      なんにん

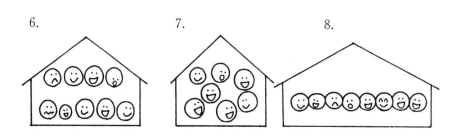

   b. いくつですか。

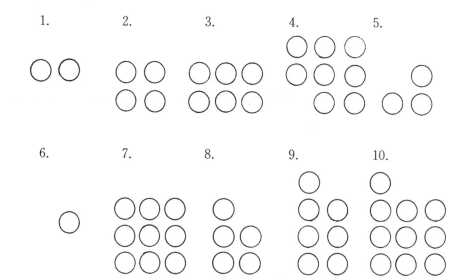

2. Look at the picture and give the appropriate verb.

1.(   )   2.(   )   3.(   ) 4.(   )

5.(   ) 6.(   )   7.(   )   8.(   )

9.(   ) 10.(   )   11.(   )   12.(   )

3. Practise as in the examples:

飲みます   ＜コーヒー＞   ＜レストラン＞
の
→　コーヒーを飲みます。

→　レストランでコーヒーを飲みます。

1. 飲みます   ＜ジュース＞   ＜食堂＞
                                              しょくどう
2. 注文しました   ＜紅茶＞   ＜レストラン＞
   ちゅうもん   こうちゃ
3. 見ます   ＜ビデオ＞   ＜研究室＞
   み   けんきゅうしつ

51

4. 食べました　　　　　＜昼ごはん＞　　　　＜食堂＞
　　　た　　　　　　　　　　ひる　　　　　　　　しょくどう
5. 待ちます　　　　　　＜友だち＞　　　　　＜駅＞
　　　ま　　　　　　　　　　とも　　　　　　　　えき
6. 買います　　　　　　＜魚と肉とやさい＞　＜スーパー＞
　　　か　　　　　　　　　さかな　にく
7. 借りました　　　　　＜本＞　　　　　　　＜図書館＞
　　　か　　　　　　　　　ほん　　　　　　　　と　しょかん
8. 毎日します　　　　　＜何＞　　　　　　　＜大学＞
　　まいにち　　　　　　　なに　　　　　　　　だいがく
9. きのう食べました　　＜何＞　　　　　　　＜うち＞

4. Look at the picture and complete the sentences.

1.

1) ブラウンさんはシャルマさんに

　＿＿＿＿＿＿＿＿＿＿＿＿＿＿＿＿＿。

2) シャルマさんはブラウンさんに

　＿＿＿＿＿＿＿＿＿＿＿＿＿＿＿＿＿。

2.

1) 先生は学生に
　せんせい　がくせい

　＿＿＿＿＿＿＿＿＿＿＿＿＿＿＿＿＿。

2) 学生は先生に

　＿＿＿＿＿＿＿＿＿＿＿＿＿＿＿＿＿。

3.

1) 先生はブラウンさんに

　＿＿＿＿＿＿＿＿＿＿＿＿＿＿＿＿＿。

2) ブラウンさんは先生に

　＿＿＿＿＿＿＿＿＿＿＿＿＿＿＿＿＿。

5．Practise as in the examples:

1）友だちにプレゼントをあげました。
とも

　＜ＣＤ＞

　→　友だちに<u>ＣＤ</u>をあげました。

2）友だちにプレゼントをあげました。

　＜山田さん＞
　　やまだ
　→　<u>山田さん</u>にプレゼントをあげました。

a.　1.

友だちにプレゼントをあげました。

＜リサさん＞

＜田中さん＞
　たなか

＜○○さん＞

2.

田中さんに英語を教えます。
　　　えいご　おし

＜生物＞
　せいぶつ

＜化学＞
　かがく

＜スペイン語＞
　　　　ご

3.

リサさんに手紙を書きました。
　　　てがみ　か

＜先生＞
　せんせい

＜友だち＞

＜○○さん＞

4.

リサさんに手紙を出しました。
　　　　　　だ

＜ジムさん＞

＜インド＞

＜国＞
　くに

5.

友だちにえんぴつを貸しました。
　　　　　　　　　か

＜山下さん・辞書＞
　やました　じしょ

＜リサさん・お金＞
　　　　　　かね

＜○○さん・ノート＞

b. 1.

友だちにプレゼントをもらいました。

＜手紙＞
てがみ

＜漢字の本＞
かんじ ほん

＜くだもの＞

2.

先生に日本語を習います。
せんせい にほんご なら

＜ひらがな＞

＜かたかな＞

＜フランス語＞
ご

3.

友だちにペンを借りました。
か

＜ジムさん＞

＜○○さん＞

☆6. Match A and B, and make sentences supplying appropriate particles.
Try making as many combinations as possible.

1) 本屋へ行きます。
ほんや い
2) 本屋で辞書を買います。
ほんや じしょ か

A.

本屋	辞書
テープ	英語
お金	うち
京都	友だち
先生	くだもの
ごはん	ジュース
プレゼント	図書館
水	やさい

B.

行きます	食べます
買います	あげます
飲みます	払います
帰ります	借ります
待ちます	教えます
呼びます	習います
もらいます	

7. Make questions about the underlined word, then answer them.

きのうスーパーへ行きました
→ Q：いつスーパーへ行きましたか。
　　 A：きのうです。

1. 800円 払いました
2. 木村先生が日本語を教えます
3. 留学生が7人来ました
4. たまごをみっつ食べました
5. 先生に辞書を借りました
6. インドに小包を出しました
7. 先週 (*last week*) かたかなを習いました
8. 食堂で昼ごはんを食べました

8. Practise the dialogue as in the example:

帰ります → A：いっしょに帰りませんか。
　　　　　 B：ええ、帰りましょう。

1. お茶を飲みます
2. 昼ごはんを食べます
3. 図書館へ行きます
4. 映画を見ます
5. テープを聞きます
6. 漢字を勉強します

B　　　A

9．Turn the word in ＜　＞ into the topic of the sentence.

きのうシャルマさんが研究室へ行きました。

＜シャルマさんが＞　→　シャルマさんはきのう研究室へ行きました。

＜研究室へ＞　　　　→　研究室へはきのうシャルマさんが行きました。

1. あしたリサさんが大学へ来ます。

   ＜あした＞

   ＜大学へ＞

2. 国の友だちに手紙を出します。

   ＜国の友だちに＞

   ＜手紙を＞

3. 国で日本語を勉強しました。

   ＜国で＞

   ＜日本語を＞

4. きのうの新聞を読みましたか。

   ＜きのうの新聞を＞

5. だれに英語を習いましたか。

   ＜英語を＞

6. いつ日本に来ましたか。

   ＜日本に＞

10. Practise the use of ［N］も as shown in the examples:

   1）アニルさんがチキンカレーを注文しました。　＜田中さん＞

   →　田中さんもチキンカレーを注文しました。

   2）アニルさんは魚を買いました。　＜肉＞

   →　アニルさんは肉も買いました。

   1. 先生に辞書を借りました。　　　　　＜テープ＞

   2. きのう銀行へ行きました。　　　　　＜郵便局＞

   3. 図書館で勉強します。　　　　　　　＜研究室＞

   4. 田中さんにプレゼントをあげます。　＜リサさん＞

5. きのう手紙を書きました。　　　　　　＜あした＞

11. Interview the student next to you.

1. 朝ごはんを食べましたか。

   何を食べましたか。

   そして、何を飲みましたか。

2. 晩ごはんはどこで食べますか。

3. いつ日本に来ましたか。

4. いつ国に帰りますか。

5. 国で日本語を習いましたか。

   ひらがなも習いましたか。

   かたかなは。

6. きょう手紙を書きますか。

   だれに書きますか。

   どこで書きますか。

7. きのう手紙が来ましたか。

8. きょうスーパーへ行きますか。

9. 誕生日 (birthday) に何をもらいましたか。

Conversation Drills

1. At the entrance (G.I. 1, 2)

Say how many of you there are.

1. 2. 3. 4. 5.

6. 7. 8. 9. 10.

2. Asking for something (S-1, S-2)

a.   A：客 (customer)　　B：ウェートレス (waitress)

> **A：すみません。コーヒー、ひとつ。**
>
> **B：はい。かしこまりました。**

coffee

1.

coffee

2.
ice cream

3.
salad

4.
soup

5.
Tempura set

6.
juice

7.
sandwich

8.
ice cream

9.
hamburger

10.
tea

b.

A：すみません。メニューありますか。

B：はい。どうぞ。

A：どうも。

1. soy sauce

2. spoon

3. chopsticks

4. sauce

5. sugar

6. salt

7. milk

8. water

9. bread

10. cigarette

11. matches

12. ashtray

1. しょうゆ　2. スプーン　3. はし　4. ソース　5. さとう　6. しお
7. ミルク　8. 水（みず）　9. パン　10. タバコ　11. マッチ　12. はいざら

3. Ordering (S-3a)

a. One customer

Practise the customer's part using the following cues:

A：客 (customer)　　B：ウェートレス (waitress)
　　きゃく

> **A：すみません。**
>
> **B：はい。ご注文は。**
> 　　　　ちゅうもん
>
> **A：ええと、天ぷら定食ください。**
> 　　　　てん　　ていしょく
>
> **B：はい。かしこまりました。**

1. beef curry

2. cheese sandwiches

3. fried chicken set

4. spaghetti with meat sauce

5. pizza

6. cola

7. black tea

8. coffee

9. beer

10. orange juice

11. vegetable salad

12. sake

---

1. ビーフカレー　2. チーズサンドイッチ　3. フライドチキンセット

4. スパゲッティーミートソース　5. ピザ　6. コーラ　7. 紅茶
　　　　　　　　　　　　　　　　　　　　　　　　　こうちゃ

8. コーヒー　9. ビール　10. オレンジジュース　11. サラダ　12. 酒
　　　　　　　　　　　　　　　　　　　　　　　　　　　　　さけ

☆b. Two customers

Practise the customers' parts using the following menu:

A：客　　B：ウェートレス　　C：別の客（another customer）
きゃく　　　　　　　　　　　　　べつ

A：すみません。

B：はい。ご注文は。
　　　　　ちゅうもん

A：ええと、{ 私
　　　　　　わたし
　　　　　　ぼく }は、天ぷら定食。
　　　　　　　　　　てん　ていしょく

B：はい。

C：{ 私
　　　ぼく }は、ビーフカレーとコーヒー。

B：天ぷら定食がおひとつ、ビーフカレーがおひとつ、

　　コーヒーがおひとつでございますね。

A：そう。

B：はい、かしこまりました。

〜〜〜〜〜〜〜　メニュー　〜〜〜〜〜〜〜

コーヒー	¥250	サンドイッチ（チーズ）	¥480
アイスコーヒー	¥250	（ミックス）	¥550
紅茶	¥250	スパゲッティー（ナポリタン）	¥500
コーラ（L）	¥300	（ミートソース）	¥550
（S）	¥200	ビーフカレー	¥750
ジュース（オレンジ）	¥380	チキンカレー	¥650
（トマト）	¥400	ピザ	¥680
（レモン）	¥400	サラダ	¥350
ビール	¥450	天ぷら定食	¥900
酒	¥550	とりのからあげ定食	¥850

＊You can ask for item not on the menu by using「ありますか。」.

4. At a restaurant (S-1, S-2, S-3)

Practise the customer's part using expressions learnt.

| Enter | → | Take a seat | → | Ask for the menu | → | Order |

5. Making a choice (S-3b)

Practise the customers' parts using the following cues:

A：客 (customer)　B：ウェートレス (waitress)　C：別の客 (another customer)
きゃく　　　　　　　　　　　　　　　　　　　　　　　べつ

A ：コーヒーください。

B ：コーヒーはアイスになさいますか、ホットになさいますか。

A ：ええと、ホットください。

C ：｛私／ぼく｝♂｛は／も｝｛アイス。／ホット。｝

B ：かしこまりました。

コーヒー	アイス	ホット
1. 紅茶 こうちゃ	レモンティー	ミルクティー
2. カレー	チキン	ビーフ
3. スパゲッティー	ナポリタン	ミートソース
4. ドレッシング	フレンチ	和風 (Japanese style) わふう
5. コーラ	S	L
6. サンドイッチ	チーズ	ミックス
7. 定食 ていしょく	ライス	パン
8. ジュース	オレンジ	レモン

<u>6</u>. Paying the cashier (S-5)

a. Paying together

Listen for the amount, then pay as in the example.

A：客　　B：会計（cash register）
　　きゃく　　　かいけい

A：お願いします。
　　ねが

B：はい、ごいっしょですか。

A：はい。

B：1800円になります。
　　　えん

A：はい。（paying money）

b. Receiving change

Pay with a large note and check your change.

A：はい。（pays）

B：はい、2000円おあずかりします。　（takes the money）

　200円のおかえしです。　（gives the change）

　ありがとうございました。

A：どうも。

☆c.　Paying separately

A：客　　　B：会計　　　C：別の客（another customer）
　　きゃく　　　　かいけい　　　　べつ

A　：お願いします。
　　　ねが

B　：はい、ごいっしょですか。

A　：いえ、べつべつにしてください。

$$\left\{\begin{array}{l}私\\ぼく\end{array}\right.$$ は、ビーフカレーとコーヒー。

B　：ええと、ちょうど1000円になります。
　　　　　　　　　　　　　　　　えん

A　：はい。（paying money）

C　：$$\left\{\begin{array}{l}私\\ぼく\end{array}\right.$$ は、天ぷら定食とコーヒー。
　　　　　　　　　　　　　てん　　　ていしょく

B　：1150円になります。

C　：はい。　　　　　　　　　　　　　　　（pays）

B　：はい。2000円おあずかりします。　（takes the money）

　　　850円のおつりです。　　　　　　（gives the change）

　　　ありがとうございました。

A・C：どうも。

☆ 7. Dealing-with-problems game （S-4）

START →

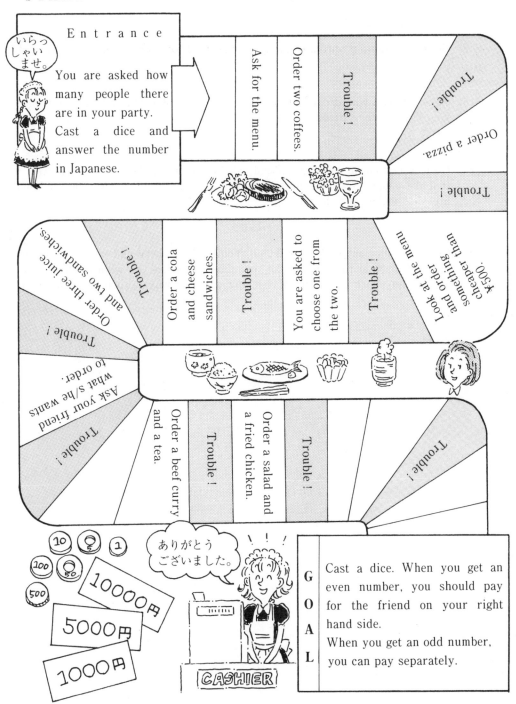

Entrance

いらっしゃいませ。

You are asked how many people there are in your party. Cast a dice and answer the number in Japanese.

Ask for the menu.

Order two coffees.

Trouble !

Trouble !

Order a pizza.

Trouble !

Look at the menu and order something cheaper than ¥500.

Trouble !

You are asked to choose one from the two.

Trouble !

Order a cola and cheese sandwiches.

Trouble !

Order three juice and two sandwiches.

Trouble !

Ask your friend what s/he wants to order.

Trouble !

Order a beef curry and a tea.

Trouble !

Order a fried chicken.

Order a salad and a fried chicken.

Trouble !

Trouble !

ありがとうございました。

CASHIER

GOAL

Cast a dice. When you get an even number, you should pay for the friend on your right hand side.

When you get an odd number, you can pay separately.

8 . Role play

1. Go to a restaurant by yourself, ask for the menu and order a cup of coffee and something to eat. (Use a real menu.)

2. Go to a restaurant with a friend and order food for both of you. Pay separately.

3. Take a friend who doesn't speak Japanese to a restaurant and order for both of you. Pay for your friend.

☆4. Go to a restaurant by yourself and ask for the menu. The waitress informs you that the choice is among the set lunches A, B and C. Ask what the set lunches are, then make your choice.

☆5. Go to a restaurant with your friend. You don't eat pork and your friend doesn't eat beef. Look at the menu, make sure that the dishes you want to choose do not contain any pork and beef by checking with the waiter, then order for both of you.

Tasks and Activities

1. Listen to the tape. You will hear a series of conversations at a restaurant.

~~~~ メニュー ~~~~

a.コーヒー	¥350	i.サンドイッチ（チーズ）	¥500
b.アイスコーヒー	¥350	j.　　　　　（ミックス）	¥550
c.紅茶	¥380	k.スパゲッティー（ナポリタン）	¥600
d.コーラ	¥350	l.　　　　　（ミートソース）	¥650
e.ジュース（トマト）	¥400	m.ビーフカレー	¥800
f.ジュース（オレンジ）	¥450	n.チキンカレー	¥750
g.アイスクリーム	¥480	o.ピザ	¥700
h.ビール	¥550	p.サラダ	¥450

---

a. Write the letters corresponding to what the person ordered.

1. _____
2. _____
3. _____
4. _____

b. Write how much the person will pay.

1. _____ 円
   えん
2. _____ 円
3. _____ 円
4. _____ 円

2. Listen to the tape. You will hear a series of conversations between a food shop staff and a customer. Match 1～4 with a～d below.

1. _____ 2. _____ 3. _____ 4. _____

a. すしや

sushi bar

b. ハンバーガーショップ

hamburger restaurant

とろ　*fatty part of tuna*
たまご　*egg*

c. たちぐいそば

soba stand

d. レストラン

天ぷらそば　*buckwheat noodle soup topped with tempura*
てん

3. Listen to the tape. You will hear a series of conversations about groups of people who would like to order sandwiches. Note down the orders and fill in the chart below.

サンドイッチの店
みせ

		example	1	2	3	4
やさいサンド	vegetable	**1**				
ツナサンド	tuna					
たまごサンド	egg					
ハムサンド	ham	**1**				
ミックスサンド	mix	**1**				
ハンバーグサンド	hamburger					
ぜんぶで	total	**3**				

サンド　sando *sandwich*　　ツナ　tsuna *tuna*　　ハム　hamu *ham*

ミックス　mikkusu *mix*　　ハンバーグ　hanbaagu *hamburger*

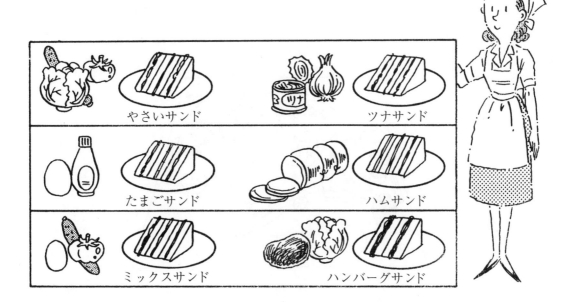

やさいサンド　　ツナサンド

たまごサンド　　ハムサンド

ミックスサンド　　ハンバーグサンド

☆4. The picture below shows a table after lunch. Read the report and determine who sat where.

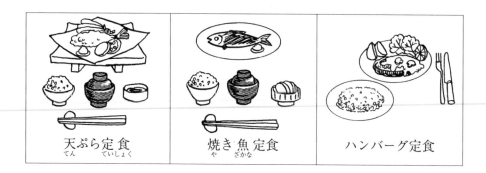

天ぷら定食
てん　　　ていしょく

焼き魚定食
や　ざかな

ハンバーグ定食

私とAさんは天ぷら定食を注文しました。
わたし　　　　　　　　　　　　　　　ちゅうもん

Bさんは焼き魚定食を食べました。
た

Cさんはハンバーグ定食を注文しました。

私はCさんにえびの天ぷらをあげました。

それから、Aさんはコーヒーを飲みました。
の

焼き魚　grilled fish　　えび　prawn

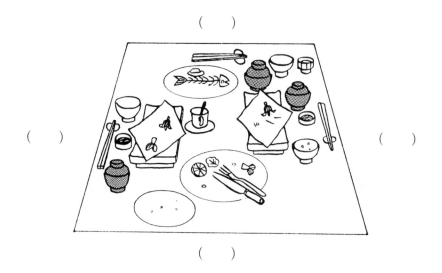

5．a．　Look at the picture and fill in the blanks in the following report.

きのう、山下さんと田中さんは、喫茶店へ＿＿＿＿＿＿＿＿＿＿。
　　　　やました　　たなか　　　　　きっさてん

山下さんはホットコーヒーを＿＿＿＿＿＿＿＿＿＿＿＿＿。田中

さんはオレンジジュースを＿＿＿＿＿＿＿＿＿＿＿＿。ぜんぶ

で630円でした。山下さんは1000円＿＿＿＿＿＿＿＿＿＿＿＿。
　　　えん

おつりを370円＿＿＿＿＿＿＿＿＿＿＿＿＿＿＿。

☆　b．　Make a report about the meal you had.

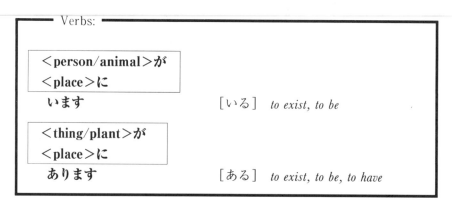

Lesson 4

場所を聞く
ば しょ き
Asking the whereabouts

● *New Words in Drills*

・ is used only in Conversation Drills

— Verbs:

<person/animal>が <place>に		
います	［いる］	*to exist, to be*

<thing/plant>が <place>に		
あります	［ある］	*to exist, to be, to have*

— Locational words:

上	うえ	*on, above*
下	した	*under, below*
前	まえ	*front*
後ろ	うしろ	*behind*
中	なか	*inside*
となり		*next to*
近く	ちかく	*close to*
右	みぎ	*right*
左	ひだり	*left*

— Things:

えんぴつ		*pencil*
かばん		*bag*
かさ		*umbrella*
電話	でんわ	*telephone*
つくえ		*desk*
いす		*chair*

ドア	doa	*door*
まど		*window*
・せんたく機	せんたくき	*washing machine*
自動販売機	じどうはんばいき	*vending machine*
コピー機	kopii き	*copy machine, photocopier*
ラジカセ	rajikase	*radio cassette tape recorder*
・ポスト	posuto	*mailbox, postbox*
花	はな	*flower*

Places:

部屋	へや	*room*
教室	きょうしつ	*classroom*
事務室	じむしつ	*general office*
コンピュータ室	konpyuuta しつ	*computer room*
(お) 手洗い	おてあらい	*toilet*
階段	かいだん	*stairs*
デパート	depaato	*department store*
アパート	apaato	*apartment, flat*
喫茶店	きっさてん	*coffee shop*
バス停	basu てい	*bus stop*
～階	～かい	counter for floors (storeys)

People and animals:

男の人	おとこのひと	*man*
女の人	おんなのひと	*woman*
男の子	おとこのこ	*boy*
女の子	おんなのこ	*girl*
子ども	こども	*child*
犬	いぬ	*dog*
ねこ		*cat*

Time words:

けさ		*this morning*
こんばん		*this evening, tonight*

---- Question words: ----

何語	なにご	*what language ?*
どなた		*who ?*

---- Other words: ----

・ゆっくり		*slowly*
・〜側	〜がわ	*〜 side*

● *Additional New Words in Drills*

---- Things and places: ----

たな		*shelf*
ふとん		*futon, quilt*
テープレコーダー	teepurekoodaa	*tape recorder*
カレンダー	karendaa	*calendar*
ロッカー	rokkaa	*locker*
宿舎	しゅくしゃ	*dormitory, hall*
駐車場	ちゅうしゃじょう	*parking lot*
映画館	えいがかん	*cinema*
このへん		*around here*

---- ko/so/a/do system: ----

これ	この〜	ここ	こっち
それ	その〜	そこ	そっち
あれ	あの〜	あそこ	あっち
どれ	どの〜	どこ	どっち

Structure Drills

1. Look at the picture, and make sentences as in the example:

ふとんがあります。

グーグー

2. Make sentences as in the example:

テレビ・上・電話
　　うえ　でんわ
→　テレビの上に電話があります。

1. ふとん・下・新聞
　　　　した　しんぶん
2. いす・近く・テープレコーダー
　　　　ちか
3. テレビ・前・本
　　　　まえ　ほん
4. テレビ・となり・時計
　　　　　　　と けい
5. まど・近く・カレンダー
　　　　ちか
6. ふとん・上・ねこ
7. テレビ・後ろ・かさ
　　　　うし
8. ふとん・中・男 の子
　　　　なか　おとこ　こ

75

3. Look at the picture and practise the dialogues.

a. いすの<u>上</u>_{うえ} → Q：<u>いすの上</u>に何_{なに}がありますか。

A：かばんがあります。

1. かばんの中_{なか}　　2. たなの上　　3. ドアの近_{ちか}く

4. いすの下_{した}　　5. ねこの前_{まえ}　　6. テレビの左_{ひだり}

7. たなの右_{みぎ}

b. まどの近く → Q：<u>まどの近く</u>にだれがいますか。

A：<u>男</u>_{おとこ}の<u>子</u>_こがいます。

1. ドアの前　　2. 女_{おんな}の人_{ひと}の後_{うし}ろ　　3. 女の子の前

c. かばん → Q：かばんはどこにありますか。

A：｛ いすの上にあります。

いすの上です。

1. えんぴつ　　2. 時計_{とけい}　　3. ラジカセ　　4. 男の子

5. 女の子　　6. ねこ　　7. 花_{はな}　　8. たな

4．Look at the picture and practise the dialogue as in the examples:

1）お手洗い　　→　Q：お手洗いはどこにありますか。

　　　て あら　　　　　A：階段の近くにあります。
　　　　　　　　　　　　　　かいだん ちか

2）ピーターさん　→　Q：ピーターさんはどこにいますか。

　　　　　　　　　　　　A：コンピュータ室にいます。
　　　　　　　　　　　　　　　　　　　しつ

1. ロペスさん	2. 自動販売機 じ どうはんばい き	3. シャルマさん
4. リサさん	5. 木村先生の研究室 き むらせんせい けんきゅうしつ	6. コピー機 き
7. 電話 でん わ	8. テレビ	9. リーさん
10. 食堂 しょくどう		

5．Practise the dialogue with your partner using the given words.

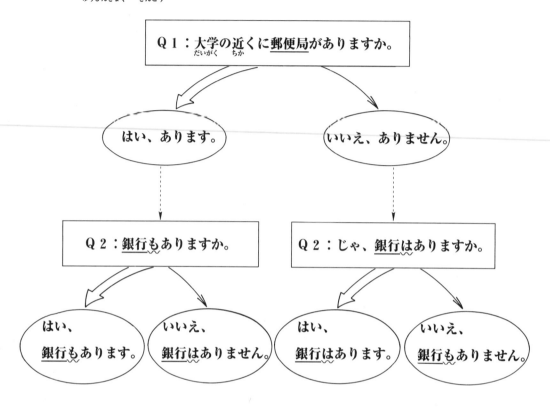

郵便局・銀行
ゆうびんきょく　ぎんこう

Q１：大学の近くに郵便局がありますか。
　　　だいがく　ちか

はい、あります。　　　　いいえ、ありません。

Q２：銀行もありますか。　　　Q２：じゃ、銀行はありますか。

はい、銀行もあります。　いいえ、銀行はありません。　はい、銀行はあります。　いいえ、銀行もありません。

1．デパート・スーパー　　　2．銀行・本屋
　　　　　　　　　　　　　　　　　　ほん や
3．レストラン・喫茶店　　　4．本屋・バス停
　　　　　　　きっさ てん　　　　　　　　　　てい

☆ 6．Practise the dialogue with your partner, using real-life information.

1）Q：教室の中に電話がありますか。　A：｛ええ、あります。
　　　きょうしつ なか でんわ　　　　　　　いえ、ありません。

2）Q：つくえの上に何がありますか。　A：本があります。
　　　　　　うえ　なに　　　　　　　　　　ほん

78

7. Answer the questions as in the examples:

1) Q：つくえの上に何がありますか。
　　＜本＋えんぴつ＞
A：本とえんぴつがあります。

2) Q：つくえの上に何がありますか。
　　＜本＋えんぴつ……＞
A：本やえんぴつがあります。

1. こんばん何を食べますか。 　　＜パン＋たまご……＞
2. けさ何を飲みましたか。 　　＜ジュース＋コーヒー＞
3. スーパーで何を買いましたか。 　　＜肉＋やさい……＞
4. あしたどこへ行きますか。 　　＜郵便局＋スーパー＞
5. だれといっしょに行きますか。 　　＜和田先生＋山下さん……＞

8. Practise the dialogue, using real-life information.

a.　Q：これ
　　　　それ　は何ですか。
　　　　あれ

　　A：○○です。

b.　だれの本　→　Q：これ
　　　　　　　　　　それ　はだれの本ですか。
　　　　　　　　　　あれ

　　　A：○○さんの本です。

1. だれのかさ 　　2. どこの時計 　　3. 何の本
4. 何語の辞書 　　5. どなたのかばん

c.　これ　→　これは○○さんの本です。

1. それ 　　2. あれ 　　3. どれ

d. **Q**：この
　　　その ｝ ○○はどこで買いましたか。
　　　あの

　　A：○○で買いました。

e. **Q**：○○さんの○○はどれですか。

　　A：これ
　　　それ ｝ です。
　　　あれ

f. Look at the picture and practise the dialogue with your partner.

シャルマ　→　**Q**：<u>シャルマさん</u>はどの人ですか。

　　　　　　　A：(pointing) この人です。

1. 田中　　　　　　　2. リサ　　　　　　3. ピーター　　　　4. 鈴木
　たなか　　　　　　　　　　　　　　　　　　　　　　　　　　すずき
5. プラニー

Conversation Drills

1. Confirming information (S-4)

a. Repeating, just confirming information

> **A**：<u>あそこ</u>ですよ。
>
> **B**：<u>あそこ</u>ですか。↗
>
> **A**：ええ。↘

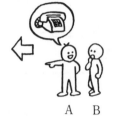

b. Repeating, showing that you are convinced

> **A**：<u>つくえの上</u>ですよ。
> <small>うえ</small>
>
> **B**：<u>つくえの上</u>ですね。↗
>
> **A**：ええ。↘

つくえの……

1. ドアの……

2.

3.

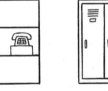

4. 宿舎の……
   <small>しゅくしゃ</small>

5. 2階の……
   <small>かい</small>

6. ロッカーの……

7. 階段の……
   <small>かいだん</small>

8. 事務室の……
   <small>じむしつ</small>

9. 郵便局の……
   <small>ゆうびんきょく</small>

上
下 <small>した</small>
前 <small>まえ</small>
後ろ <small>うし</small>
中 <small>なか</small>
となり
近く <small>ちか</small>
ここ
そこ
あそこ
こっち側 <small>がわ</small>
あっち側
1 階
2 階
3 階

2. Asking the whereabouts of something (S-2, S-5)

a. A is certain that what s/he is looking for is nearby.

> A：せんたく機は｜どこですか。↗
> ｜どこでしょうか。↘
>
> B：せんたく機ですか。↗
>
> A：ええ。

事務室
じむしつ

せんたく機

図書館
としょかん

食堂
しょくどう

お手洗い
てあら

電話
でんわ

コピー機

1.

2.

3.

4.

5.

6.

b. A is not certain that what s/he is looking for is nearby.

> A：このへんに、電話｜ありますか。↗
> ｜ありませんか。↗
>
> B：電話ですか。↗
>
> A：ええ。

ポスト

バス停
てい

郵便局
ゆうびんきょく

銀行
ぎんこう

スーパー

本屋
ほんや

喫茶店
きっさてん

1.

2.

3.

4.

5.

3. Asking/showing the whereabouts of something (S-2, S-4, S-5)

a. A is looking for a washing machine at the dormitory.

> A：せんたく機はどこでしょうか。↘
>
> B：せんたく機。↗
>
> A：ええ。
>
> B：せんたく機なら、**1階** { にあります / です } よ。
>
> A：**1階**ですか。↗
>
> B：ええ。

1階

1. 階段の近く
2. お手洗いのとなり
3. 3階のあっち側
4. 4階のこっち側

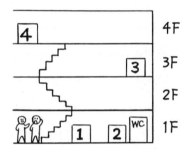

b. A is looking for a telephone on the street.

> A：このへんに、電話ありませんか。↗
>
> B：電話ね。↘
>
> A：ええ。
>
> B：ああ、**郵便局の前** { にあります / です } よ。
>
> A：**郵便局の前**ですね。↗
>
> B：ええ。

郵便局の前

1. 喫茶店の前
2. スーパーの中
3. バス停の近く
4. ポストのとなり

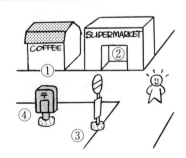

4. Starting and ending a conversation: asking for information (S-1, S-2, S-6)

Have a dialogue with a classmate and fill in the map. If necessary, A confirms the information received.

> A：すみません。
>
> B：はい。
>
> A：あの、［Asking where］
>
> B： ［Telling where］
>
> A：どうもありがとうございました。
>
> B：いいえ。

a. In the university building, you are looking for the following:

電話 でんわ	日本語の教室 にほんご きょうしつ
お手洗い てあらい	コンピュータ室 しつ
事務室 じむしつ	木村先生の研究室 きむらせんせい けんきゅうしつ

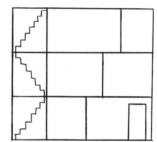

b. In the street, you are looking for the following:

電話	銀行 ぎんこう
バス停 てい	映画館 えいがかん
ポスト	スーパー

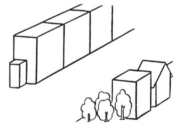

5. Asking the whereabouts of a person (S-1, S-2, S-6)

a.

a-1. You are looking for your friend Yamashita.

Ask the following people:

1. your friend
2. a senior student
3. Yamashita's adviser

山下さんは。↗

山下さん（は） { どこですか。↗ / どこでしょうか。↘

a-2. You are looking for Kimura-sensee.

Ask the following people:

1. a senior student

2. your adviser

3. your friend

木村先生は。↗   Ⓖ
き むらせんせい

木村先生は { どちらですか。↗   📄

どちらでしょうか。↘   📄⬆

b. Looking for someone

Ask where they are and fill in the chart.

A：すみません。あの、[Asking where]

B knows ─────────────────── B doesn't know

B：＜place＞です。

A：あ、そうですか。↘

どうもありがとう

ございました。

B：いいえ。

B：すみません。ちょっと

わからないんですけど。

A：あ、そうですか。↘

どうもすみませんでした。

B：いいえ。

	コンピュー タ室 しつ	研究室 けんきゅうしつ	教室 きょうしつ
2F		研究室	教室
1F	研究室	教室	事務室 じ む しつ

1. 木村先生

2. 山下 やました

3. シャルマ

4. 山田先生 やま だ せんせい

5. 田中 た なか

6. ブラウン

☆c. Asking whereabouts game

Practise b with the entire class and fill in the chart.

6. Getting someone to repeat something you didn't catch (S-1, S-3, S-6)

　a. Catching the key word and repeating it for confirmation

> B：**自動販売機のとなりにありますよ。**
>
> A：**じどう……。**
>
> B：**じどうはんばいき。**
>
> A：**じどうはんばいき。**

☆b. Asking where a telephone is, and asking for repetition more slowly

> A：**あの、すみません。このへんに、電話ありませんか。**↗
> でんわ
>
> B：[Telling where]
>
> A： { **あの、すみません。ゆっくりお願いします。**（polite）
> ねが
> 　　{ **え。**↗（less polite）
>
> B：[Repeating the key phrase]
>
> A：[Catching the key word]
>
> B：[Explaining the key word in Japanese]

A understands ↓　　　　　　　　　　　　　A cannot understand ↓

> A：**ああ、わかりました。**
> 　　**どうもありがとう**
> 　　**ございました。**

> A：**あのう……。**
> 　　**どうもすみませんでした。**

☆7. Asking/showing the whereabouts

Practise with the entire class and fill in the maps. Play both parts by taking turns according to the flow-chart.

A: Ask B where something or someone is, and mark it on the map.

B: Tell A where it is, looking at the map on which it is marked.

```
┌─────────────────────────────┐
│    Start a conversation      │
└─────────────────────────────┘
               │
┌─────────────────────────────┐
│ Ask where something/someone is │
└─────────────────────────────┘
               │
┌─────────────────────────────┐
│  Confirm the information     │
└─────────────────────────────┘
               │
┌─────────────────────────────┐
│    End the conversation      │
└─────────────────────────────┘
```

＊When B can't answer the question or A can't understand what A is being told, A ends the conversation politely.

a. In the students' room, you are looking for the following:

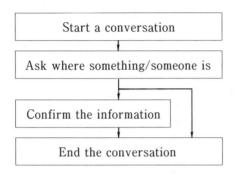

山下さん やました	テープレコーダー
田中さん たなか	コピー機 き
木村先生 きむらせんせい	山下さんのかばん

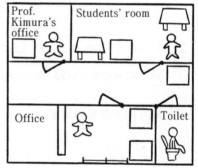

b. On the street, you are looking for the following:

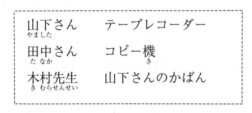

電話 でんわ	スーパー
バス停 てい	本屋 ほんや
郵便局 ゆうびんきょく	喫茶店 きっさてん

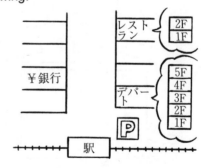

8. Role play

1. Ask your teacher where something/someone is.

☆2. Ask your classmate where something/someone is.

☆3. On campus, ask someone where is the nearest telephone.

Tasks and Activities

1. Look at the table and listen to the tape. Answer the questions by writing the corresponding numbers in the blanks below.

1	5	10	6
8	12	14	3
15	2	9	16
11	7	13	4

example   __**16**__

1. _____

2. _____

3. _____

4. _____

2. Look at the picture. Listen to the tape and write down the numbers to show where you think each item should be in the picture.

a. 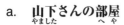 山下さんの部屋

①ラジカセ

②ペン

③手紙

④ねこ

b. 大学
だいがく

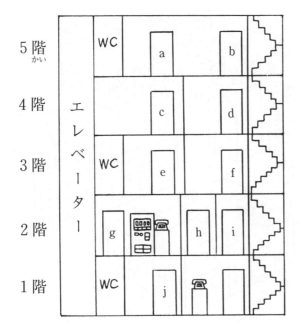

①山田先生
やまだせんせい

②山下くん
やました

③木村先生
きむらせんせい

④テープレコーダー

3. Read the following sentences and identify the person by filling in the blanks （ ）.

私の右にDさんがいます。Dさんの前はCさんです。CさんのとなりにB
わたし みぎ まえ
さんとEさんがいます。AさんはBさんの前にいます。Aさんのとなりは
Eさんと私です。

☆4. Look at the following picture.

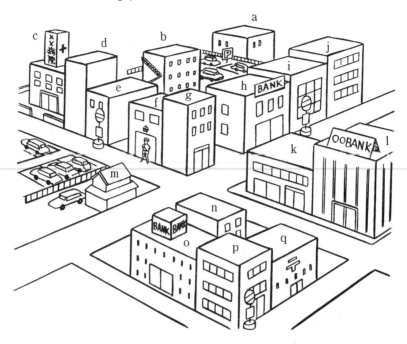

a. Read the following message and determine where the person is.

1.

> いま、XX アパートにいます。病院のとなりです。
>
> アパートの前に駐車場があります。　　　　　　　川田
>　　　　　まえ　ちゅうしゃじょう　　　　　　　　　かわだ

　　　いま *now*

2.

> いま、ABC ビルにいます。銀行のとなりです。
>　　　　　　　　　　　ぎんこう
> ビルの前にバス停があります。
>　　　　　　てい
> ビルのうしろは駐車場です。　　　　　　　　　　中山
>　　　　　　　　　　　　　　　　　　　　　なかやま

☆b. Practise using the above patterns with other students.

90

5. a. Look at the pictures and describe the changes you can find between them.

[20年前]
ねんまえ
20 years ago

[今]
いま
now

木　*tree*　　車　*car*
き　　　　　くるま

example　20年前は犬がいました。今はいません。
　　　　　　　　いぬ

1. _____

2. _____

3. _____

4. _____

☆b. Talk about similar changes back home.

● **New Words in Drills**

・ is used only in Conversation Drills

Verbs:

＜person＞が

起きます（Ⅱ）	おきます	[おきる]	*to get up, to wake up*
寝ます（Ⅱ）	ねます	[ねる]	*to go to bed, to lie down*
立ちます（Ⅰ）	たちます	[たつ]	*to stand up*
泳ぎます（Ⅰ）	およぎます	[およぐ]	*to swim*
・困ります（Ⅰ）	こまります	[こまる]	*to be at a loss*

＜person＞が
＜thing＞を

使います（Ⅰ）	つかいます	[つかう]	*to use*
取ります（Ⅰ）	とります	[とる]	*to take*
開けます（Ⅱ）	あけます	[あける]	*to open*
閉めます（Ⅱ）	しめます	[しめる]	*to close*
つけます（Ⅱ）		[つける]	*to turn on*
消します（Ⅰ）	けします	[けす]	*to turn off*

＜person＞が
＜thing／place＞に

すわります（Ⅰ）		[すわる]	*to sit down*
乗ります（Ⅰ）	のります	[のる]	*to ride, to get on*
入ります（Ⅰ）	はいります	[はいる]	*to go / come in*

＜person＞に／が
＜thing＞が

わかります（Ⅰ）		[わかる]	*to understand*

＜person＞が
＜place＞に
＜thing＞を

・はります（Ⅰ）		[はる]	*to put, to stick*

<person A>が
<person B>に
<matter>を

話します（Ⅰ）	はなします ［はなす］	*to talk, to speak*
・聞きます（Ⅰ）	ききます ［きく］	*to ask*

<person A>が
<person B>に

・言います（Ⅰ）	いいます ［いう］	*to say, to tell*

─── Other words: ───

ことば		*word*
・字	じ	*letter, character*
意味	いみ	*meaning*
住所	じゅうしょ	*address*
名前	なまえ	*name*
電話番号	でんわばんごう	*telephone number*
パーティー	paatii	*party*
（お）ふろ		*bath, bath room*
プール	puuru	*swimming pool*
電気	でんき	*light, electricity*
荷物	にもつ	*package*
・自転車	じてんしゃ	*bicycle*
タクシー	takushii	*taxi*
バス	basu	*bus*
空港	くうこう	*airport*
テスト	tesuto	*test*
・宿題	しゅくだい	*homework*
休み	やすみ	*holiday*
～本	ほん/ぼん/ぽん	counter for long objects
・ほかの～		*other ～*

─── Question words: ───

どうして	*why ?*
・どんな	*what sort ?*

● *Additional New Words in Drills*

```
┌─── Other words: ──────────────────────────────────────┐
│                                                        │
│   掲示板        けいじばん            bulletin / notice board │
│   宅急便        たっきゅうびん          delivery service      │
│   ワープロ      waapuro              word processor       │
│                                                        │
└────────────────────────────────────────────────────────┘
```

```
┌─── Time words: ───────────────────────────────────────┐
│                                                        │
│   今週        こんしゅう            this week           │
│   先週        せんしゅう            last week           │
│   来週        らいしゅう            next week           │
│   毎週        まいしゅう            every week          │
│   今月        こんげつ             this month          │
│   先月        せんげつ             last month          │
│   来月        らいげつ             next month          │
│   毎月        まいつき/まいげつ      every month         │
│   日曜日       にちようび            Sunday             │
│   月曜日       げつようび            Monday             │
│   火曜日       かようび             Tuesday            │
│   水曜日       すいようび            Wednesday          │
│   木曜日       もくようび            Thursday           │
│   金曜日       きんようび            Friday             │
│   土曜日       どようび             Saturday           │
│                                                        │
└────────────────────────────────────────────────────────┘
```

Structure Drills

1. Look at the picture and say an appropriate verb. You can find the
answer on the next page.

行きます

Answers:

1. 行きます
2. 来ます
3. 帰ります
4. 出します
5. 買います
6. 勉強します
7. 読みます
8. 書きます
9. 見ます
10. 聞きます
11. 注文します
12. 飲みます
13. a. あげます b. もらいます
14. 食べます
15. a. 教えます b. 習います
16. a. 借ります b. 貸します
17. 取ります
18. 使います
19. 話します
20. 言います
21. 起きます
22. 寝ます
23. 乗ります
24. 入ります
25. 待ちます
26. 呼びます
27. 立ちます
28. すわります
29. わかります
30. 泳ぎます
31. つけます
32. 消します
33. 開けます
34. 閉めます

2. Put the appropriate particle in the parentheses:

てがみ（　を　）出します。

1. 国（　　　　）帰ります。
2. コンピュータ（　　　）使います。
3. プール（　　　）泳ぎます。
4. 部屋（　　　）電気（　　　）消しました。
5. 友だち（　　　）本（　　　）借ります。
6. 友だち（　　　）図書館（　　　）勉強します。
7. 国（　　　）手紙（　　　）書きます。
8. 友だち（　　　）日本語（　　　）話しました。
9. シャルマさん（　　　）リサさん（　　　）花（　　　）あげました。
10. ここに住所（　　　）名前（　　　）書いてください。

3. Answer the questions.

   a.   1. 来月 東京へ行きますか。
             らいげつ とうきょう い
       2. 先週 手紙をもらいましたか。
           せんしゅう てがみ
       3. 今月 国に帰りますか。
          こんげつ くに かえ
       4. 毎月 図書館で本を借りますか。
         まいつき としょかん ほん か
       5. 先月 何語の本を読みましたか。
         せんげつ なにご よ
       6. 来週 プールで泳ぎますか。
         らいしゅう およ
       7. 毎週 どこでコンピュータを使いますか。
         まいしゅう つか
       8. 先週の土曜日に何をしましたか。
          どようび なに

☆b.   Look at Sharma-san's schedule and answer the following questions.

25	MON	山下さんにテレビをもらう
26	TUE	リサさんと図書館で勉強する
27	WED	東京へ行く
28	THU	↓
29	FRI	木村先生に 本をかりる
30	SAT	リサさんと えいがを見る
31	SUN	プールで 泳ぐ

1. 火曜日は何をしますか。
   かようび

2. 何曜日にテレビをもらいますか。
   なんようび

3. 何曜日に東京へ行きますか。

4. 何曜日にプールで泳ぎますか。

5. 金曜日は何をしますか。
   きんようび

4. Practise as in the example:

   a. 聞きます → 聞く ― 聞いて ― 聞いた
     き

       Ⅰ. 書きます   泳ぎます   行きます   飲みます
         か   の
         読みます   呼びます   話します   貸します
                        よ   はな   か

出します だ	買います か	立ちます た	待ちます ま
言います い	使います つか	取ります と	すわります
乗ります の	入ります はい	払います はら	もらいます
帰ります かえ	習います なら	消します け	

Ⅱ.

食べます た	教えます おし	あげます	寝ます ね
起きます お	見ます み	つけます	開けます あ
閉めます し			

Ⅲ.

来ます き	します	勉強します べんきょう	注文します ちゅうもん

b. Your instructor will say some verbs. Point at the pictures on p95.

5. Practise as in the example:

京都へ行く・国へ帰る
きょうと　い　　くに

A：京都へ行きますか。
B：いいえ、行きません。
A：どうしてですか。
B：国へ帰るんです。

1. パーティーに行く・国から友だちが来る
とも　　　　く
2. あした大学へ来る・東京へ行く
だいがく　　とうきょう
3. シャルマさんもうちに来る・病院へ行く
びょういん
4. 事務室へ行った・木村先生の研究室に行った
じむしつ　　　きむらせんせい　　けんきゅうしつ
5. 田中さんもリサさんのうちに行った・国に帰った
たなか
6. この本を買った・友だちに借りた
ほん　か　　　　　　　か

6. Practise as in the examples:

1) どこで食べますか。　→　どこで食べるんですか。

2) 何を買いましたか。　→　何を買ったんですか。
なに

1. だれと勉強しますか。　→

2. どこへ行きましたか。　→

3. 何を飲みましたか。　→

4. どこで泳ぎますか。　→

5. 何に乗りますか。　→

6. だれに手紙を書きましたか。　→

7. Practise making a request as in the example:

この漢字を教えます　→　この漢字を教えてください。

1. あした、私のうちへ来ます

2. テープをよく（carefully）聞きます

3. 電気をつけます

4. テレビを消します

5. こっちを見ます

6. あしたの朝、事務室へ行きます

7. お金はあそこで払います

8. ほかの人（some other person）に聞きます

9. タクシーを呼びます

10. まどを開けます

11. ドアを閉めます

12. ここに住所と電話番号を書きます

13. このコピー機を使います

14. 教室では日本語を話します

15. 毎日、漢字を勉強します

8. Complete the sentences using ～から.

ペンがありません　＋　貸してください

→　ペンがありませんから、貸してください。

1. 来週、国に帰ります　＋　大学に来ません

2. バスがありません　＋　タクシーに乗ってください

3. 電話番号がわかりません　＋　教えてください

4. 国の友だちが来ます　＋　あした空港へ行きます

5. きょうは日曜日です　＋　郵便局は休みです。

6. このことばの意味がわかりません　＋　教えてください

9. Complete the sentence using the appropriate form of verb.

私はわかりませんから、ほかの人に＿＿＿＿＿＿＿＿。

→　私はわかりませんから、ほかの人に聞いてください。

1. バスがありませんから、タクシーを＿＿＿＿＿＿＿＿＿＿＿＿＿＿＿＿。

2. お金がありませんから、＿＿＿＿＿＿＿＿＿＿＿＿＿＿＿＿＿＿＿＿。

3. 日本語がわかりませんから、英語で＿＿＿＿＿＿＿＿＿＿＿＿＿＿。

4. この漢字がわかりませんから、＿＿＿＿＿＿＿＿＿＿＿＿＿＿＿＿。

5. あしたテストですから、こんばん＿＿＿＿＿＿＿＿＿＿＿＿＿＿＿。

10. Combine the sentences in the proper order.

本を買いません。
お金がありません。

→　お金がありませんから、本を買いません。

1. このことばの意味がわかりません。
ほかの人に聞きます。

2. きょう大学に行きません。
東京に行きます。

3. 手紙を出しました。
手紙を書きました。

4. 手紙をもらいました。
手紙を書きました。

5. 貸してください。
お金がありません。

Conversation Drills

1. Introducing a question (S-1)

Practise A's part by looking at the picture, supplying the appropriate question words.

A：外国人 *(foreigner)* 　　B：日本人 *(Japanese)*
　　がいこくじん　　　　　　　　　にほんじん

> **A：ちょっと、すみません。**
>
> **B：はい。**
>
> **A：掲示板にこれがあったんですけど。**
> 　　けいじばん
>
> **B：ええ。**
>
> **A：これ、何でしょうか。**
> 　　　　なん

掲示板にこれがあった

1. ドアにあった

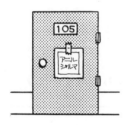

2. 銀行から来た
　　ぎんこう　き

3. 事務室でもらった
　　じむしつ

4. 図書館からきた
　　としょかん

2．Asking how something is read（S-2）

a. While one student practises A's part, the others fill in one blank below with key words from the conversation.

A：外国人（foreigner） B：日本人（Japanese）
　　がいこくじん　　　　　　　　にほんじん

A：ちょっと、すみません。
B：はい。
A：これ、何て読むんですか。
　　　　なん　よ
B：ああ、たっきゅうびんですよ。

Yes ↓

A：たっきゅうびんですか。↗
B：ええ。そうです。
A：どうも。
　　ありがとうございました。

No →

A：たきゅうびんですか。↗
B：いいえ。
　　たっきゅうびんです。
A：たっきゅびん。↗
B：いいえ。
A：Long sound
　　Small「っ」　　がありますか。
　　　　「ん」
B：ええ。
A：たっきゅうびん。↗
B：ええ、そうです。
A：どうも、ありがとう。

	key word	1	2	3	4	5
eg.	たっきゅうびん	✗	✗	○		
1						
2						
3						

1.

2.

3.

b. Asking how something is read and its meaning（S-2a）

A：あの字、何て読むんですか。
B：こ・しょ・う。
A：こしょうですか。
B：ええ、そうですよ。
A：どんな意味ですか。
B："Out of order" ですよ。
A：そうですか。

1. 営業中

2. 準備中

3.

在　室	
授業中	●
会議中	
自　宅	

4. 非常口

5. 使用中

3. Asking for the equivalent Japanese or English word (S-2c)

a.　A、B：学生
　　　　　　がくせい

> A：あのう。これ、日本語で何ていうんですか。
> 　　　　　　　　　にほんご　なん
> B：ああ、じどうはんばいきですよ。
> A：じどうはんばいきですね。↗
> B：ええ、そう。
> A：どうもありがとう。

1.

2.

3.

4.

5.

6.

b.

> A：あのう、"homework" って日本語で何ていうんですか。
> 　　　　　　　　　　　　　　にほんご　なん
> B：ええと……　しゅくだい。
> A：しゅくだいですね。↗
> B：ええ、そう。↘

homework

1. graduate school　　　2. Goodnight.

3. medical science　　　4. Congratulations.

5. economics　　　　　6. Say it again, please.

7. engineering　　　　　8. Speak more slowly, please.

c.

> A：あのう、宿舎って英語でどんな意味ですか。↗
> しゅくしゃ　えいご　　　　　　　　　い み
>
> B：ああ、"dormitory" ですよ。
>
> A：そうですか。ありがとうございます。
>
> B：いいえ。

宿舎

1．新聞 　　　　　2．時計 　　　　　3．辞書 　　　　　4．忘れる
　しんぶん　　　　　　　　と けい　　　　　　　　じ しょ　　　　　　　　わす

5．遊ぶ 　　　　　6．教科書を見ないでください
　あそ　　　　　　　　きょう か しょ　み

7. Other words of which you want to know the meaning.

4. Finishing the conversation when B can't answer (S-4)

a.

> A：これ、英語で何ていうんですか。
> 　　えい ご　なん
>
> B：ううん。困ったな。わかんないな。↘
> 　　　　　こま
>
> A：じゃ、{ いいです。 / けっこうです。 } ありがとうございました。

b.

> A：保健センターは、どこでしょうか。
> 　ほ けん
>
> B：さあ。ちょっと……。
>
> A：ああ、そうですか。
>
> B：あの、ほかの人に聞いてください。
> 　　　　　　ひと　き
>
> A：はい。どうも、すみませんでした。

保健センター

1．お手洗い 　　　　2．事務室 　　　　3．学生食堂
　て あら　　　　　　　　じ む しつ　　　　　　がくせいしょくどう

4．木村先生の研究室 　　5．留学生センター
　き むらせんせい　けんきゅうしつ　　りゅうがくせい

☆5. Asking the meaning of an announcement you couldn't understand
(S-2)

Practise with a teacher by using the patterns below.

３０５号室のシャルマさん。
ごうしつ

電話がありましたから、事務室に来てください。
でんわ   じむしつ   き

Pattern 1

> A：あのう、すみません。
>
> B：はい。
>
> A：今、何て言ったんですか。
>   いま なん い
>
> B：［Repeating the message］
>
> A：どうもありがとうございました。

Pattern 2

> A：あのう、＜word＞ってどんな意味ですか。
>   いみ
>
> B：ええと。＜the meaning of the word＞ですね。
>
> A：＜the meaning of the word＞ですか。↘
>
> B：ええ、そうです。

☆6．Asking the meaning （S-2)

You will find three memos below. Have a conversation with your teacher, following the chart:

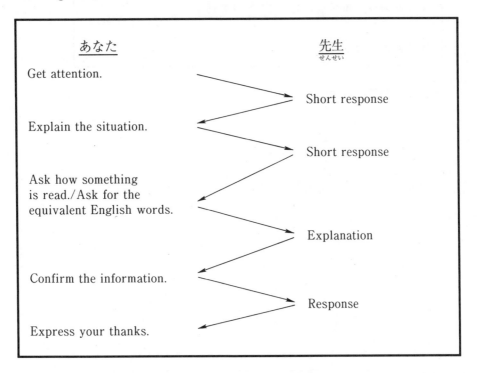

あなた　　　　　　　　　　先生
せんせい

Get attention.

　　　　　　　　　　Short response

Explain the situation.

　　　　　　　　　　Short response

Ask how something
is read./Ask for the
equivalent English words.

　　　　　　　　　　Explanation

Confirm the information.

　　　　　　　　　　Response

Express your thanks.

1．ドアにあった

> リサ・ブラウンさん
>
> 　指導教官に至急
> 　電話してください。
> 　　　　　2月26日　10：15
> 　　　　　　　　　　関

2．掲示板にあった
けい じ ばん

> 　　　　　　　平成7年2月15日
> 国費留学生のみなさんへ
>
> 　平成7年度の奨学金の書類を
> わたします。
> 　2月20日(火)から、留学生係り
> に取りに来て下さい。

3．事務室にあった
じ む しつ

> 　　　　　　　平成7年1月3日
> 　　　学生宿舎料金改定について
> 平成7年度4月から下記のとおり改定されますのでお知らせします。

7. Confirming the information (S-3)

a.

> A：あのう、<u>事務室</u>って、<u>宿舎の事務室</u> ｛ですか。
> じむしつ　　　　しゅくしゃ　　　でしょうか。
>
> B：ええ、そうです。

事務室　宿舎の事務室

1. センター　　　留学生センター
　　　　　　　　りゅうがくせい
2. スーパー　　　東友
　　　　　　　　とうゆう
3. 本屋　　　　　大学会館の本屋
　ほんや　　　　だいがくかいかん
4. 郵便局　　　　大学の郵便局
　ゆうびんきょく
5. 先生　　　　　日本語の先生
　せんせい　　　にほんご
6. 鈴木さん　　　女の鈴木さん
　すずき　　　　おんな
7. 山田さん　　　事務室の山田さん
　やまだ　　　　じむしつ
8. 研究室　　　　木村先生の研究室
　けんきゅうしつ　きむら

b.

> A：あのう、<u>事務室</u>って、<u>宿舎の事務室</u>ですか。
>
> B：いいえ。<u>大学の事務室</u>です。

事務室　宿舎の事務室　大学の事務室

1. 郵便局　　　大学の郵便局　　　駅前の郵便局
　　　　　　　　　　　　　　　えきまえ
2. 先生　　　　日本語の先生　　　英語の先生
　　　　　　　　　　　　　　　えいご
3. 鈴木さん　　女の鈴木さん　　　男の鈴木さん
　　　　　　　　　　　　　　　おとこ
4. 山田さん　　事務室の山田さん　日本語の先生の山田さん
5. 研究室　　　木村先生の研究室　田中先生の研究室
　　　　　　　　　　　　　　　たなか

8. Role play

1. You are introduced to a Japanese businessman. He gives you his name card but you cannot read his name. Ask him how to read his name.

2. You are on a bus. You hear an announcement but you cannot understand it. Ask someone sitting nearby what was said.

Tasks and Activities

1. Listen to the tape. You will hear a series of conversations where a person requests or orders somebody to do something. Choose the picture corresponding to what the person said.

example __a__   1.___   2.___   3.___   4.___   5.___

a.

b.

c.

d.

e.

f.

2. Listen to the recorded messages and fill in the missing words in the blanks.

1.

田中さんから電話がありました。

_____

あした漢字の本を
（　　　）ください。

2.

山下さんから電話がありました。

_____

あした木村先生の
研究室に（　　　）
ください。

3.

橋本さんから電話がありました。

_____

こんばん うちに
（　　　）ください。

4.

渡辺さんから電話がありました。

_____

日曜日に（　　　）を
（　　　）ください。

5.

高橋さんから電話がありました。

_____

本のお金を
（　　　）円
（　　　）ください。

3. The following is an exercise for two people. Choose a page and let your partner have the other. Take turns to ask each other the reading and meaning of the Japanese signs, or the Japanese equivalent of the English words.

[A]

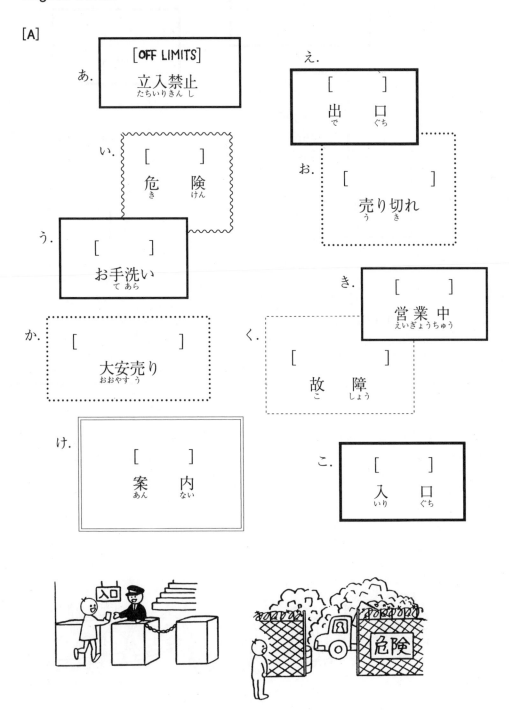

あ. [OFF LIMITS] 立入禁止
たちいりきんし

い. [　　] 危　険
き　　けん

う. [　　] お手洗い
て あら

え. [　　] 出　口
で　　ぐち

お. [　　　] 売り切れ
う　き

か. [　　　　] 大安売り
おおやす う

き. [　　　] 営業中
えいぎょうちゅう

く. [　　　] 故　障
こ　　しょう

け. [　　] 案　内
あん　　ない

こ. [　　] 入　口
いり　　ぐち

[B]

あ.
（たちいりきんし　）
立入禁止
OFF LIMITS

え.
（　　　　　　）
出口
EXIT

い.
（　　　　　　）
危険
DANGER

お.
（　　　　　　）
売り切れ
SOLD OUT

う.
（　　　）
お手洗い
TOILET

か.
（　　　　　　）
大安売り
BARGAIN SALE

き.
（　　　　　　）
営業中
OPEN

く.
（　　　　　）
故障
OUT OF ORDER

け.
（　　　　　）
案　内
INFORMATION

こ.
（　　　　）
入口
ENTRANCE

4. Listen to the tape. You will hear a telephone conversation between Yamashita-san and Tanaka-san. Fill in Yamashita-san's schedule.

山下さんのスケジュール
やました

月 MON	B. テスト	
火 TUE		
水 WED		
木 THU		
金 FRI		
土 SAT		
日 SUN		

A.テニス（田中さんと）
 たなか
B.テスト
C.プール（ジョンさんと）
D.映画（リサさんと）
 えいが

5. Crossword puzzle

Read the following clues and fill in the puzzle with ひらがな.

よこ（Clues across）

a. 山下さんは松見□□□□の学生です。

b. □□□を届けます。

c. 「お願いします。」「ちょっと□□□ください。」

d. 自転車で宿舎へ□□□ます。

e. homework は、日本語で何ですか。

たて（Clues down）

1. 事務室へ□□□ください。

2. リサさんの□□はイギリスです。

3. 日曜日は宿舎でカレーライスを□□□ます。

4. 毎日、□□□□□、毎月

5. スーパーで肉と野菜を□□ます。

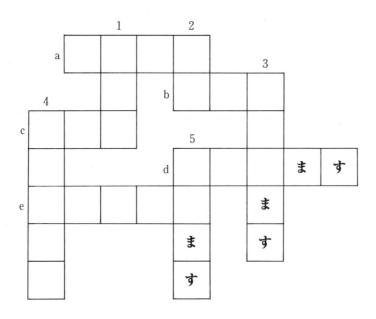

6. Play *SUGOROKU*

How to play : Throw the dice. Take as many steps as indicated by the dice. The teacher will ask a question or give an instruction. If you can answer the question or follow the instruction correctly, you may stay on that space. If you can not, go back two spaces.

Below are some examples of the teacher's questions / instructions.

あした、何をしますか。

ドアをあけてください。

"Good morning" は日本語で何て言うんですか。

9	10	11
8		12
7		13
6		14
5		15
4		16
3		17
2		18	19	20
1

↑
スタート（START）

26	27	28	29
25			30
24			31
23		33	32
22		34
21		ゴール (GOAL)

▨ : やすみ

▦ : instruction

事務室で
じ　む　しつ

At the office

● *New Words in Drills*

· is used only in Conversation Drills

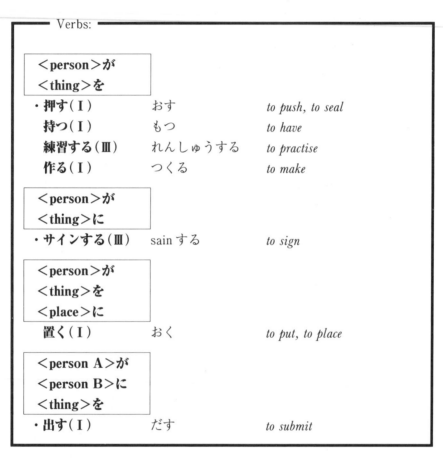

Verbs:

<person>が
<thing>を

· 押す（Ⅰ）	おす	*to push, to seal*
持つ（Ⅰ）	もつ	*to have*
練習する（Ⅲ）	れんしゅうする	*to practise*
作る（Ⅰ）	つくる	*to make*

<person>が
<thing>に

· サインする（Ⅲ）	sain する	*to sign*

<person>が
<thing>を
<place>に

置く（Ⅰ）	おく	*to put, to place*

<person A>が
<person B>に
<thing>を

· 出す（Ⅰ）	だす	*to submit*

Adjectives:

大きい	おおきい	*large, big*
小さい	ちいさい	*small, little*
新しい	あたらしい	*new*
古い	ふるい	*old*
かんたん（な）		*easy, simple*
難しい	むずかしい	*difficult*
いい		*good*

重い	おもい	*heavy*
軽い	かるい	*light*
高い	たかい	*expensive*
安い	やすい	*cheap*
長い	ながい	*long*
短い	みじかい	*short*
おもしろい		*interesting*
静か(な)	しずか(な)	*quiet*
うるさい		*noisy*
きれい(な)		*beautiful, clean*
便利(な)	べんり(な)	*convenient*
おいしい		*delicious*
悪い	わるい	*bad*

Adverbs and question words:

とても	*very*
あまり	*not so~* （＋*neg.*）
どう	*how ?*

Other words:

パスポート	pasupooto	*passport*
IDカード	aidiikaado	*ID card*
・はんこ／印鑑	／いんかん	*seal*
授業	じゅぎょう	*class, lesson*
・ボールペン	boorupen	*ball-point pen*
電車	でんしゃ	（*electric*）*train*
物価	ぶっか	*prices*
・文法	ぶんぽう	*grammar*
・忘れ物	わすれもの	*something left behind*
・～号室	～ごうしつ	counter for room no.
～ページ	～peeji	counter for pages
・～方	～かた	*how to~*

● *Additional New Words in Drills*

┌─── Adjectives and adverb: ───────────────────────────────┐

けっこう（な）	*fine*
にぎやか（な）	*lively, crowded*
ずいぶん	*quite, very*

└──┘

┌─── Time words: ──┐

いま	*now*
あさって	*the day after tomorrow*

└──┘

┌─── Words for official papers: ───────────────────────────┐

学生証	がくせいしょう	*student card*
奨学金	しょうがくきん	*scholarship*
受講届け	じゅこうとどけ	*course registration form*
申し込み書類	もうしこみしょるい	*application form*
～研究科	～けんきゅうか	*postgraduate course in* ～
専攻	せんこう	*one's major, field of study*
コース名	koosu めい	*course title*
学籍番号	がくせきばんごう	*student number*
国籍	こくせき	*nationality*
年齢	ねんれい	*age*
年	とし	*age*
（満）～歳	（まん）～さい	～*years old*
生年月日	せいねんがっぴ	*date of birth*
性別	せいべつ	*sex*
写真	しゃしん	*photograph*

└──┘

Structure Drills

1. Look at the following pictures and make a sentence as in the example:

このかさは安いです。

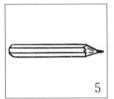 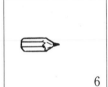  

2．Practise as in the examples:

大きい <small>おお</small>	大きいです	大きくありません 大きくないです	大きかったです	大きくありません でした 大きくなかったです
新しい <small>あたら</small>				
おもしろい				
難しい <small>むずか</small>				
長い <small>なが</small>				
高い <small>たか</small>				
いい				
きれいだ	きれいです	きれいじゃありません きれいじゃないです	きれいでした	きれいじゃありません でした きれいじゃなかったです
静かだ <small>しず</small>				
便利だ <small>べんり</small>				
かんたんだ				
テストだ	テストです	テストじゃありません テストじゃないです	テストでした	テストじゃありません でした テストじゃなかったです
先生だ <small>せんせい</small>				
土曜日だ <small>どようび</small>				
男の人だ <small>おとこ ひと</small>				

3. Practise as in the examples using the pictures on the preceding page.

    1) Q：安いですか。 → A：はい、安いです。

    2) Q：高いですか。 → A：いいえ、｜高くありません。
                                      高くないです。

4. Practise the dialogue with your partner.

    ○○さんの部屋　　＜新しい／静かだ＞

    →　Q：○○さんの部屋は新しいですか。

       A：ええ、新しいです。　／　いいえ、｜新しくありません。
                                          新しくないです。

       Q：静かですか。

       A：ええ、静かです。　／　いいえ、｜静かじゃありません。
                                        静かじゃないです。

    1. ○○さんの辞書　　　　　＜新しい／便利だ＞
    2. ○○さんのカメラ　　　　＜小さい／重い＞
    3. ○○さんの国の家　　　　＜大きい／きれいだ＞
    4. 大学の食堂　　　　　　　＜おいしい／静かだ＞
    5. 日本の映画　　　　　　　＜おもしろい／高い＞

5. Practise as in the example. Give your own answer.

    宿題　→　Q：宿題はどうですか。
            A：むずかしいです。

    1. 日本のテレビ　　　　　2. 食堂のごはん

    3. ○○さんのアパート　　4. 大学の図書館

    5. 漢字の勉強

6．Practise as in the examples:

1）きのうのテレビ・おもしろい　　＜はい＞

→　Q：きのうのテレビはおもしろかったですか。

A：はい、とてもおもしろかったです。

2）きのうの晩ごはん・おいしい　　＜いいえ＞

→　Q：きのうの晩ごはんはおいしかったですか。

A：いいえ、│あまりおいしくありませんでした。
　　　　　　│あまりおいしくなかったです。

1．きのうのテスト・難しい　　　　　＜いいえ＞

2．京都・きれいだ　　　　　　　　　＜はい＞

3．きのうの映画・いい　　　　　　　＜いいえ＞

4．日本の物価・高い　　　　　　　　＜？＞

5．日本の食べ物・おいしい　　　　　＜？＞

☆7．For each topic, make as many sentences as you can using the adjectives in the box.

私の家　→　私の家は古いです／新しいです／大きいです／

小さいです／静かです　etc.

1．○○大学

2．大学の郵便局

3．私のかばん

4．漢字

5．漢字の辞書

6．コンピュータ

7．○○先生

8．私の部屋

9．○○の定食

10．日本のデパート

大きい　小さい　新しい　古い
難しい　かんたんだ　いい
悪い　重い　軽い　高い　安い
長い　短い　静かだ　便利だ
きれいだ　おいしい　おもしろい

8. Practise as in the example:

a. 名前を書く＋はんこを押す
   → 名前を書いて、はんこを押してください。

   1. IDカードを持つ ＋ 事務室へ行く
   2. テープを聞く ＋ 答える
   3. うちに帰る ＋ 勉強する
   4. 郵便局へ行く ＋ エアログラムを買う
   5. ここに来る ＋ 説明する
   6. 本を読む ＋ 練習する

b. 友だちを呼ぶ＋パーティーをする
   → 友だちを呼んで、パーティーをしました。

   1. シャルマさんのうちに行く ＋ いっしょにテレビを見る
   2. うちに帰る ＋ （お）ふろに入る
   3. 肉とやさいを買う ＋ カレーを作る
   4. カレーを作る ＋ リサさんと食べる
   5. タクシーを呼ぶ ＋ 病院に行く

9. Practise Q and A with your partner. Give factual answers.

   けさ・起きた → Q：けさ起きて、何をしましたか。
                  A：新聞を読みました。

   1. けさ・大学へ来た
   2. きのう・うちへ帰った
   3. 来週○○へ行く

10. Make sentences as in the example, choosing between に and で.

教室・勉強する
きょうしつ　べんきょう

→　教室で勉強します。

1. プール・泳ぐ
   およ

2. 電車・乗る
   でんしゃ　の

3. このいす・すわる

4. このノート・書く
   か

5. 喫茶店・待つ
   きっさてん　ま

6. 電車の中・本を読む
   なか　ほん　よ

7. 図書館・勉強する
   としょかん

8. つくえの上・置く
   うえ　お

9. 部屋・入る
   へや　はい

10. 事務室・ペンを借りる
    じむしつ　か

11. 東京・英語を教える
    とうきょう　えいご　おし

12. リサさんのアパート・ビデオを見る
    み

Conversation Drills

1. Informing the office of the purpose of your visit（S-1）

a. You have received a message.

If necessary, ask your teacher about the words you don't know.

A：学生（student）　　B：事務員（office clerk）

> A：あの、402号室のシャルマですけど、
> 　　　　　　ごうしつ
> 　　これ、お願いします。（Showing the note）
> 　　　　　　ねが
> B：ああ、宅急便ですね。
> 　　　　　たっきゅうびん
> A：ええ。

> 402号室のシャルマさん
>
> 宅急便をあずかっています。
>
> 　　　　　　　事務室
> 　　　　　　　じむしつ

☆b. You have found an item that has been left behind.

A：学生（student）　　B：事務員（office clerk）

> A：あの、教室にこれがあったんですけど。
> 　　　　　きょうしつ
> B：ああ、わすれものですね。どうも。
> A：いいえ。

教室

1. 食堂　　　　2. コンピュータ室　　　3. 電話の近く　　　4. コピー機の上
　しょくどう　　　　　　　　　　しつ　　　　　でんわ　ちか　　　　　き　うえ

2. Asking for instructions（G.I. 1，S-2）

Choose a suitable word for each illustration.

> すみません。書き方　｛がわからないんですけど。
> 　　　　　か　かた　　｛を教えてください。
> 　　　　　　　　　　　　　　おし

1.
2.
3.
4.

5.
6.
7.

書き方　読み方　使い方　やり方　作り方
か　かた　　よ　　　　つか　　　　　　　　　つく

3. Receiving instructions（G.I. 1）

Listen to each instruction and choose a suitable illustration.

ここにはんこ押してください。
　　　　　　　お

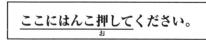

1.
2.
3.
4.

5.
6.
7.
8.

4. Having your mistake corrected （S-3）

Confirm your teacher's instructions by using the words listed below to elicit the correct information.

A：学生 （student）　　B：事務員／先生 （office clerk / teacher）
　　がくせい　　　　　　　じ む いん　せんせい

> B：**名前書いてください。**
> 　　な まえ か
> A：**ここ**ですか。↗
> B：いや、**そこ**じゃなくて**こっち**。
> A：ああ、**こっち**ですか。↘
> B：そうです。

ここ？

---

1. 国の 住所？
　 くに　じゅうしょ

2. ここ？

3. 部屋の 番号？
　 へ や　ばんごう

4. これ？

5. かさ？

6. 9 ページ？

7. 文法？
　 ぶんぽう

8. あした？

5．Correcting others' mistakes （S-3）

The information about yourself is correct, but the information about the other person might be wrong except his/her name. Check the information with the other person.

> A：シャルマさん、お国はタイですね。
>
> B：いいえ、タイじゃなくてインドです。
>
> A：あ、インドですか。失礼しました。
>
> 　　ええと、お部屋は402号室ですね。
>
> B：ええ、そうです。
>
> （＊Continue like this.）

A（Brown）has the information below:

名前	：ブラウン
国	：イギリス
部屋	：210号室
専門	：経済
指導教官	：山田

名前	：シャルマ
国	：タイ　インド
部屋	：402号室
専門	：教育
指導教官	：中村

6. Indicating that you can't comply (S-4, S-5)

a. Asking for advice implicitly

Choose a suitable excuse for each instruction.

A：学生（student）　B：事務員（office clerk）

> B：ここにはんこ押してください。
>
> A：ええと、はんこは持ってないんですけど。
>
> B：じゃ、サインでいいですよ。
>
> A：はい。

はんこは持ってない

> 電話がない　　　　　　日本語がわからない
>
> 〜は持っていない　　　漢字がわからない
>
> いま、持っていない

b. Giving an alternative

Choose a suitable alternative to each instruction.

A：学生（student）　　B：事務員（office clerk）

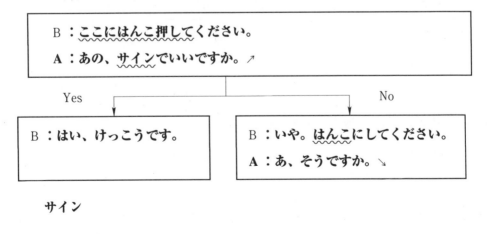

サイン

> 英語　　来週　　ひらがな　　えんぴつ

7. Asking for instructions and receiving them （G.I. 1，S-2，S-4）

Ask how to fill in the form using the data given or your own. If necessary, indicate that you can't comply.

A：学生（student）　　B：事務員（office clerk）

A：すみません。書き方がわからないんですけど。

B：はい。

A：あの、ここは何を書くんですか。

B：［Giving instructions］

A：（After filling in the form）これでいいですか。

B：はい、けっこうです。

---

name	：プラニー（女）	student number	：01823
nationality	：タイ	field of study	：教育学
date of birth	：1968年3月3日	course	：修士課程
		adviser	：中村たかし
address（Japan）	：松見市緑町6-1-3 あかね荘306号		TEL：(0123)51-2904

名前：	性別：（男・女）	国籍：
生年月日：　　　年　　月　　日	年齢：　満　　　才	
住所：　　　　　　　　　　　　　　　TEL：（　　　　　）		
専攻コース：（博士・修士）課程　　　　　　　　　　　　研究科		
学籍番号：　　　　　　　　　　指導教官：		

☆8. Expressing surprise

Choose a suitable adjective and practise in pairs.

大きい／小さい？
おお　ちい

```
A：わあ、↗ ずいぶん大きいですね。↘

B：そうですね。↘
```

1. 長い／短い？
   なが　みじか

2. 高い／安い？
   たか　やす

3. 重い／軽い？
   おも　かる

4. 新しい／古い？
   あたら　ふる

5. しずか／うるさい？

9. Role play

1. Explain the purpose of your visit to the office:

   a. You have received a message that your parcel is in the dormitory office.

   b. You have received a message that the bag you left behind is in the office.

   c. You have found an item that has been left behind.

2. Fill in a form, asking an office clerk for instructions.

☆3. Ask a Japanese friend how to make a paper crane.

Tasks and Activities

1. Listen to the tape and choose the picture which matches the conversation.

1. _____ 2. _____ 3. _____ 4. _____

1.

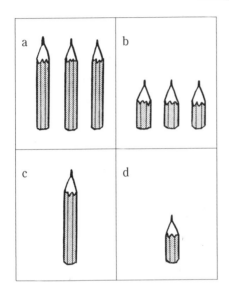

2.

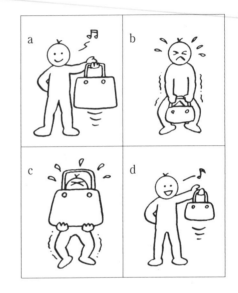

3.

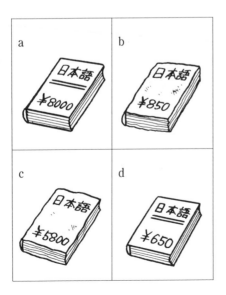

4.

2. a. The following are descriptions of animals, places and objects.
Listen to the tape and identify them.

1. _____ 2. _____

3. _____ 4. _____

ぞう　　　きりん

ライオン

図書館　　喫茶店　　電話　　とけい
としょかん　きっさてん　でんわ
　　　　　　　　　　　　　　　ゆびわ　　めがね

☆b. Practise by describing objects in your classroom.

3. Fill in the blanks with appropriate words to make a story.

1. _____に_____を_____ました。
むずかしかったです。

example　犬に日本語を教えました。むずかしかったです。
　　　　いぬ　にほんご　おし

2. _____と_____に_____ました。うるさかったです。

example　犬とおふろに入りました。うるさかったです。
　　　　　　　　　　はい

3. _____で_____を_____ました。安かったです。
　　　　　　　　　　　　　　　　　　　　　　　やす

4. _____と_____を_____ました。おもしろかったです。

5. _____で_____を_____ました。おいしかったです。

133

4. a. You have received a letter and some photos from Smith-san. Read the letter and arrange the photos by letter, according to the time sequence.

> 先週 山下さんといっしょに海へ行きました。
> 山下さんは、たくさん写真をとりました。
> 電車に乗って行きました。海にはたくさん
> 人がいました。海で泳いで、喫茶店で
> 昼ごはんを食べました。貝のペンダントを
> 買って帰りました。とても楽しかったです。
>
> 8月1日　　　　ジェーン スミス

先週 せんしゅう　　山下 やました　　海 sea うみ　　行く い　　写真 photo しゃしん　　電車 でんしゃ　　乗る の　　人 ひと

泳ぐ およ　　喫茶店 きっさてん　　昼ごはん ひる　　食べる た　　貝 a seashell かい

ペンダント pendant　　買う か　　帰る かえ　　楽しい be pleasant たの

8月1日 がつついたち

(　　) → (　　) → (　　) → (　　)

a.

b.

c.

d.

e.

f.

b. Look at the following photos. Based on the photos, fill in the blanks in the letter below.

＿＿＿＿＿＿、＿＿＿＿＿＿といっしょに
スキーへ行きました。＿＿＿＿＿＿に乗って行き
ました。スキー場にはたくさん人がいました。
山小屋で＿＿＿＿＿＿を飲みました。
それから、＿＿＿＿＿＿を買って帰りま
した。とても楽しかったです。
＿＿月＿＿日　　　　＿＿＿＿＿＿

スキー　*ski*　　スキー場　*ski slope*　　　山小屋　*cottage*　　絵はがき　*picture postcard*

☆c. Write your friend a letter about your trip.

Lesson 7

電話をかける（１）病院
でん　わ　　　　　　　　　　　　　　　びょう　いん

Phoning（１）：A hospital

● *New Words in Drills*

・ is used only in Conversation Drills

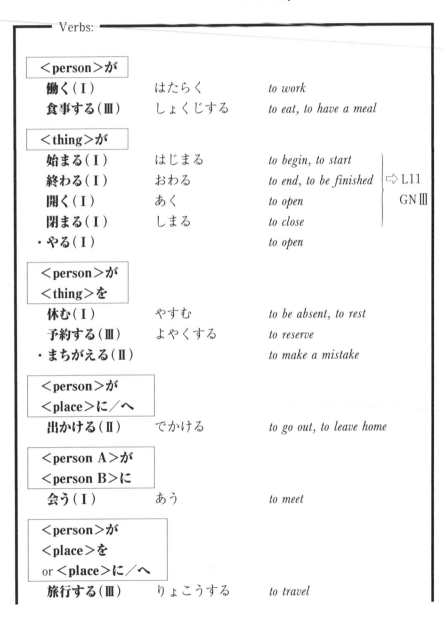

Verbs:

＜person＞が

働く（I）	はたらく	*to work*
食事する（Ⅲ）	しょくじする	*to eat, to have a meal*

＜thing＞が

始まる（I）	はじまる	*to begin, to start*
終わる（I）	おわる	*to end, to be finished*
開く（I）	あく	*to open*
閉まる（I）	しまる	*to close*
・やる（I）		*to open*

⇨ L11 GN Ⅲ

**＜person＞が
＜thing＞を**

休む（I）	やすむ	*to be absent, to rest*
予約する（Ⅲ）	よやくする	*to reserve*
・まちがえる（Ⅱ）		*to make a mistake*

**＜person＞が
＜place＞に／へ**

出かける（Ⅱ）	でかける	*to go out, to leave home*

**＜person A＞が
＜person B＞に**

会う（I）	あう	*to meet*

**＜person＞が
＜place＞を
or ＜place＞に／へ**

旅行する（Ⅲ）	りょこうする	*to travel*

136

＜person A/thing A＞が **＜person B/thing B＞と**		
ちがう（Ⅰ）	ちがう	*to differ*
＜person A＞が **＜person B＞に** **＜thing＞を**		
返す（Ⅰ）	かえす	*to return, to give back*
お願いする（Ⅲ）	おねがいする	*to request*
・**相談する（Ⅲ）**	そうだんする	*to consult (with)*
・**うかがう（Ⅰ）**		*to ask*

─── Adjectives and adverbs: ───

忙しい	いそがしい	*busy*
ひま（な）		*to have time, to be free*
元気（な）	げんき（な）	*fine, healthy*
だいじょうぶ（な）		*all right*
痛い	いたい	*painful*
たくさん		*many, much*
よく		*well*

─── Other words: ───

昼休み	ひるやすみ	*lunchtime, lunchhour*
家族	かぞく	*family*
母	はは	*(my) mother*
病気	びょうき	*sickness, illness*
気分	きぶん	*feeling*
頭	あたま	*head*
料理	りょうり	*dish, food*
試験	しけん	*examination*
レポート	repooto	*report*
・**論文**	ろんぶん	*thesis*
コンパ	konpa	*students' party*
会社	かいしゃ	*company*
・**内線**	ないせん	*extension*

```
┌─ Time words: ────────────────────────────────────┐
│                                                    │
│   午前        ごぜん           a.m., morning        │
│   午後        ごご            p.m., afternoon       │
│   〜中        〜ちゅう         during 〜            │
│   夕方        ゆうがた         evening              │
│   〜月〜日     〜がつ〜にち     〜 th (day) of 〜 (month) │
│   〜時〜分     〜じ〜ふん       〜 minutes past 〜   │
│   〜時半       〜じはん         half past 〜         │
│   〜ごろ                       about 〜             │
│   何時        なんじ           what time ?          │
│   最近        さいきん         recently             │
│                                                    │
└────────────────────────────────────────────────────┘
```

● *Additional New Words in Drills*

```
┌─ Places: ──────────────────────────────────────────┐
│                                                      │
│  スポーツセンター  supootsusentaa   sports center     │
│  駅前            えきまえ          area near the station │
│                                                      │
└──────────────────────────────────────────────────────┘
```

```
┌─ Words in Signs: ──────────────────────────────────┐
│                                                      │
│   〜医院      〜いいん         〜 clinic              │
│   〜歯科      〜しか           〜 dental clinic       │
│   休診        きゅうしん        no consultation       │
│   診療時間     しんりょうじかん  consultation hours    │
│   営業時間     えいぎょうじかん  business hours        │
│   番号案内     ばんごうあんない  directory assistance/enquiries │
│   留学生課     りゅうがくせいか  international student section │
│                                                      │
└──────────────────────────────────────────────────────┘
```

```
┌─ Months: ──────────────────────────────────────────┐
│                                                      │
│  1月：いちがつ    5月：ごがつ      9月：くがつ        │
│  2月：にがつ      6月：ろくがつ    10月：じゅうがつ    │
│  3月：さんがつ    7月：しちがつ    11月：じゅういちがつ │
│  4月：しがつ      8月：はちがつ    12月：じゅうにがつ   │
│                                                      │
└──────────────────────────────────────────────────────┘
```

┌─ Dates (irregular): ──────────────────────────────┐

1日：ついたち　　**6日**：むいか　　**14日**：じゅうよっか

2日：ふつか　　　**7日**：なのか　　**20日**：はつか

3日：みっか　　　**8日**：ようか　　**24日**：にじゅうよっか

4日：よっか　　　**9日**：ここのか

5日：いつか　　　**10日**：とおか

└──┘

┌─ Time: ───────────────────────────────────────┐

1時：いちじ　　　**5時**：ごじ　　　**9時**：くじ

2時：にじ　　　　**6時**：ろくじ　　**10時**：じゅうじ

3時：さんじ　　　**7時**：しちじ　　**11時**：じゅういちじ

4時：よじ　　　　**8時**：はちじ　　**12時**：じゅうにじ

───

1分：いっぷん　　　　**6分**：ろっぷん

2分：にふん　　　　　**7分**：ななふん

3分：さんぷん　　　　**8分**：はっぷん

4分：よんぷん　　　　**9分**：きゅうふん

5分：ごふん　　　　　**10分**：じっぷん／じゅっぷん

└──┘

⇨まとめ2AI

Structure Drills

1. Say the following times in Japanese.

何時ですか。
なんじ

1.

2.

3.

4.

5.

6.

7. 8:18

8. 10:24

9. 3:21

10. 7:32

11. 9:56

12. 5:43

2. Carry on a dialogue with your partner as in the example:

a. デパート → Q：デパートは何時からですか。

A：10時からです。

Q：何時までですか。

A：7時までです。

```
┌─────────────────┐
│  A.M.   P.M.    │
│  10:00～7:00    │
├─────────────────┤
│  ○○デパート     │
└─────────────────┘
```

1. 郵便局
   ゆうびんきょく

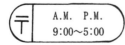

2. 銀行
   ぎんこう

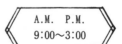

3. 図書館
   としょかん

   | 8：30a.m.～ 9：30p.m. |

4. ○○さんの国の銀行
   くに ぎんこう

   | ＜　？　＞～＜　？　＞ |

5. 午後の授業
   ごご じゅぎょう

   | ＜　？　＞～＜　？　＞ |

6. ○○の食堂
   しょくどう

   | ＜　？　＞～＜　？　＞ |

b.　**Q：デパートは何時から何時までですか。**
　　　　　　　　　なんじ

　　A：10時から7時までです。

Use the cues from a.

c.　**銀行＜閉まる＞**
　　　　　し

　→　**Q：銀行は何時に閉まりますか。**

　　　　A： {　**3時に閉まります。**
　　　　　　　　3時です。

1. 郵便局＜閉まる＞
   ゆうびんきょく

2. 昼休み＜終わる＞
   ひるやす お

3. 授業＜始まる＞
   はじ

4. デパート＜開く＞
   あ

5. 図書館＜閉まる＞

6. パーティー＜始まる＞

d. Give your own answers.

1) けさ・起きる　→　Q：けさ、何時ごろ起きましたか。

　　　　　　　　　　A：｜ 7時半ごろ（に）起きました。
　　　　　　　　　　　｜ 7時半ごろです。

2) 毎日・起きる　→　Q：毎日、何時ごろ起きますか。

　　　　　　　　　　A：｜ 7時半ごろ（に）起きます。
　　　　　　　　　　　｜ 7時半ごろです。

1. 日曜日・起きる　　　　　　　2. きょう・昼ごはんを食べる
3. きのう・うちへ帰る　　　　　4. きのう・寝る

3. Say the following dates in Japanese.

2月26日　→　にがつにじゅうろくにち

1. 11月15日	2. 1月5日	3. 6月1日
4. 7月8日	5. 5月6日	6. 10月3日
7. 3月10日	8. 9月24日	9. 4月18日
10. 8月7日	11. 12月9日	12. 4月20日
13. 9月2日	14. 3月4日	15. 10月19日

4. Look at Sharma-san's schedule and answer the following questions.

	SUN	MON	TUE	WED	THU	FRI	SAT
5 May			1 4:00 としょかんで 田中さんと べんきょうする	2	3 Trip 京都	4 京都、奈良	5 奈良
	6	7 6:30 リサさんの たんじょう日 パーティー	8	9	10 テスト 9:00〜12:30	11	12
	13	14 3:30 木村先生に あう	15	16 4:00 リサさんと えいがを見る	17	18	19 7:30〜 コンパ
	20 東京へ行く	21	22	23	24 国の 友だちが 来る	25	26
	27	28	29	30	31		

1. リサさんのたんじょう日はいつですか。
2. たんじょう日のパーティーは何時からですか。
3. 旅行はいつからいつまでですか。
4. 奈良にはいつ行きますか。
5. いつ田中さんと会いますか。
6. コンパはいつですか。
7. コンパは何時からですか。
8. いつ映画を見ますか。
9. いつ国の友だちが来ますか。
10. 20日に何をしますか。

5. Practise as in the example:

コーヒーが飲みたいです。
<small>の</small>

6. Practise as in the example:

a. 京都・行く → 京都へ行きたいです。
<small>きょうと　い</small>

  1. 国・帰る
<small>くに　かえ</small>
          2. 日本の大学・入る
<small>にほん　だいがく　はい</small>

  3. 4時・予約する
<small>じ　よやく</small>
          4. 家族・会う
<small>かぞく　あ</small>

  5. 日本の会社・働く
<small>かいしゃ　はたら</small>
          6. コンピュータ・使う
<small>つか</small>

b. 昼ごはん・食べる → 昼ごはんを ｜ 食べたくありません。
<small>ひる　た</small>　　　　　　（は）｜ 食べたくないです。

  1. 毎日・働く
<small>まいにち　はたら</small>
          2. 日本語・レポート・書く
<small>にほんご　か</small>

  3. 国・帰る
<small>くに　かえ</small>
          4. 東京・バス・行く
<small>とうきょう</small>

  5. 図書館・勉強する
<small>としょかん　べんきょう</small>
          6. あの人・この本・あげる
<small>ひと　ほん</small>

7. Carry on a dialogue with your partner as in the example:

食べる　＜何＞　→　Q：何が食べたいですか。
　た　　　なに
　　　　　　　　　　　　A：てんぷらが食べたいです。

1. 飲む　　　　　　＜何＞　　　　2. 日本で勉強する　＜何＞
　　の　　　　　　　　　　　　　　　　　にほん　べんきょう
3. 旅行する　　　　＜どこ＞　　　4. 会う　　　　　　　　＜だれ＞
　　りょこう　　　　　　　　　　　　　あ
5. 北海道へ行く　＜だれ＞　　　6. こんばん食事する　＜どこ＞
　　ほっかいどう　い　　　　　　　　　　　　しょくじ
7. あした出かける　＜何時＞
　　　　で　　　　　　なんじ

☆8. Make sentences as in the example:

a.　食べる　→　食べたかったけど、食べませんでした。

1. 買う　　　　　　2. 休む　　　　　　3. すわる
　　か　　　　　　　　　やす
4. 帰る　　　　　　5. 見る　　　　　　6. 母に相談する
　　かえ　　　　　　　　み　　　　　　　　　はは　そうだん

b.　食べる　→　食べたくなかったけど、食べました。

1. 起きる　　　　　2. 働く　　　　　　3. 勉強する
　　お　　　　　　　　　はたら
4. 会う　　　　　　5. 読む　　　　　　6. あげる
　　　　　　　　　　　よ

9. Practise as in the example:

レストランを予約する　→　レストランを予約したいんですけど。
　　　　　　よやく

1. あしたの午後、休む　　　　　2. この本を返す
　　　　　　ごご　　　　　　　　　　　　　ほん　かえ
3. 田中さんに会う　　　　　　　4. 5時に帰る
　　たなか　　　　　　　　　　　　　　　　　かえ
5. 国に電話をする　　　　　　　6. 4時から7時まで使う
　　くに　でんわ　　　　　　　　　　　　　　　　　つか

145

10. Carry on a dialogue with your partner as in the example:

Q：あした、ひまですか。

A：いいえ、＜日本語の試験だ＞。
にほんご　しけん

→　Q：あした、ひまですか。

A：いいえ、日本語の試験なんです。

1. Q：今度の日曜日、いっしょに秋葉原へ行きませんか。
こんど　にちようび　　　　あきはばら　い

A：すみません、＜日曜日は友だちのうちへ行く＞
とも

2. Q：国へ帰るんですか。
くに　かえ

A：ええ、＜母が病気だ＞
はは　びょうき

3. Q：郵便局へ行くんですか。
ゆうびんきょく　い

A：ええ、＜国の友だちに手紙を出す＞
くに　とも　てがみ　だ

4. Q：最近、専門の勉強をしませんね。
さいきん　せんもん　べんきょう

A：すみません、＜日本語の勉強が忙しい＞
いそが

5. Q：出かけるんですか。
で

A：ええ、＜　？　＞

6. Q：きのう、授業を休みましたね。
じゅぎょう　やす

A：すみません、＜　？　＞

7. Q：どうして日本語を勉強するんですか。
にほんご　べんきょう

A：＜　？　＞

11. Complete the sentences with the appropriate adjective.

a.　このかばんは小さいですが、重いです。
ちい　　　　　おも

1. タクシーは便利ですが、＿＿＿＿＿＿＿＿＿＿＿＿＿＿＿＿＿＿＿＿。
べんり

2. パーティーはおもしろかったですが、料理は＿＿＿＿＿＿＿＿＿＿＿＿。
りょうり

3. この本は難しかったですが、＿＿＿＿＿＿＿＿＿＿＿＿＿＿＿＿＿＿＿。
ほん　むずか

4. 私のアパートは古いですが、＿＿＿＿＿＿＿＿＿＿＿＿＿＿＿＿＿＿＿。
わたし　　　　ふる

b. **このカメラは小さいですから、便利です。**
べんり

1. 私のアパートは古いですから、＿＿＿＿＿＿＿＿＿＿＿＿＿＿＿＿＿＿＿＿＿。
わたし　　　　　　　　ふる

2. この本には漢字がたくさんありますから、＿＿＿＿＿＿＿＿＿＿＿＿＿。
ほん　　　かんじ

3. きのう、あまり寝ませんでしたから、＿＿＿＿＿＿＿＿＿＿＿＿＿＿＿。
ね

4. きょうは宿題がありませんから、＿＿＿＿＿＿＿＿＿＿＿＿＿＿＿＿＿。
しゅくだい

5. あの映画はよくわかりませんでしたから、＿＿＿＿＿＿＿＿＿＿＿＿＿。
えいが

Conversation Drills

1. Telephone number (GI. 2)

Practise in pairs, taking turns to use the telephone numbers below. A gives the number and B writes it on a piece of paper.

a.

A : 5 2 の 3 1 8 1 。	**52-3181**
B : 5 2 の……。	1. 95-6161　　2. (03)3291-9770
A : 3 1 8 1 。	3. 41-1005　　4. (045)203-1118
B : 3 1 8 1 。	5. 908-7820　　6. (0298)53-5109
5 2 の 3 1 8 1 ですね。↗	7. 3650-2525　　8. (0473)25-3742
A : ええ。	

☆b.　You can add an extension number.

A : 内線の１０５。 <small>ないせん</small>	**52-3181(内)105**
B : 内線の……。	1. 53-4100(内)210
A : １０５。	2. 908-7820(内)406
B : １０５。	3. (03)3911-6180(内)302
内線の１０５ですね。↗	4. (0298)53-5109(内)114
A : そうです。	

2. Asking for a telephone number (S-1)

a.　Asking an acquaintance

Ask for telephone numbers and fill in the chart given.
If you were unable to understand, use appropriate strategies.

a-1. A，B：not very close

> A：Bさん、井上医院の電話番号、わかりますか。↗
> いのうえ い いん　　でん わ ばんごう
>
> B：ええと、ちょっと待ってください。（Looking for the number）
> ま
>
> 　あ、52の3181です。
>
> A：52の3181ですね。↗
>
> B：ええ。
>
> A：どうもありがとうございました。
>
> B：いいえ。

a-2. A，B：友だち（friends）
とも

> A：Bさん、井上医院の電話番号、わかる。↗
>
> B：うん。ちょっと待って。（Looking for the number）
>
> 　ええと、52の3181。
>
> A：52の3181ね。↗
>
> B：うん。
>
> A：どうもありがとう。
>
> B：うん。

井上医院	52-3181	木村先生の研究室	
留学生センター		木村先生	
保健センター		鈴木さん	
宿舎の事務室		千葉大学	

☆b. Asking directory enquiries

Ask for the telephone number and write it down.

B：番号案内（telephone directory service）
ばんごうあんない

A：（Dialing 104）

B：はい、NTT 番号案内です。

A：あ、すみません。緑 町 の井上医院、お願いします。
みどりちょう　いのうえいいん　　　　　　　ねが

B：はい。少 々 お待ちください。
しょうしょう　ま

お待たせしました。

コンピュータでお知らせします。
し

「お問い合わせの番号は、～」＊
と　あ

緑町の井上医院　　＊This will be repeated until you ring off.

1. 新町の松見歯科
しんまち　まつみしか
2. 駅前のやまとタクシー
えきまえ
3. 緑町のスポーツセンター

---

3. Making a call and giving your identity (S-2)

Confirm whom you are calling, and if necessary, give your identity:

B：事務員（office clerk）
じむいん

A：もしもし。

B：はい。

A：あの、留 学生課ですか。↗
りゅうがくせいか

B：はい、そうです。

A：あの、情 報工学のシャルマですが。
じょうほうこうがく

B：はい。

~~~~~~~~~~ ：

留学生

your room number

your nationality

your course name

your university

留学生課

1. 宿舎の事務室
   しゅくしゃ じむしつ
2. 大学病院（of your university）
   だいがくびょういん
3. ～先生（your adviser）の研究室
   せんせい けんきゅうしつ
4. 留学生センター（of some other university）
   りゅうがくせい

4. Wrong number (S-3)

Practise with the entire class, using cards. Each student is given a card that matches another card, without knowing whose it is. Use your card to call others until the response and number match. When you succeed, give your identity; when you misdial, apologize using the pattern below. Continue by taking turns until you are successful.

A：もしもし。井上医院ですか。↗
　　　いのうえいいん

B：いいえ、ちがいます。「ノア」ですけど。

A：どうもすみません。まちがえました。

When you get the wrong number, try double checking the number:

A：あ、すみません。あの、５２の３１８１じゃありませんか。↗

B：いいえ、５１の４６７３です。

A：あ、どうもすみませんでした。

A：

| 井上医院 |
| 52－3181 |

B：

| 喫茶店「ノア」 |
| きっさてん |
| 51－4673 |

5．Making a medical appointment（S-2，S-4，S-5，S-6）

a.　Making a call and introducing a question politely

　　　　　B：病院（hospital）
　　　　　　びょういん

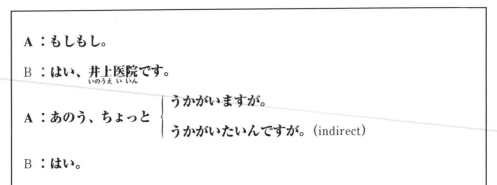

A：もしもし。

B：はい、井上医院です。
　　　　いのうえ い いん

A：あのう、ちょっと ｛ うかがいますが。

　　　　　　　　　　　うかがいたいんですが。（indirect）

B：はい。

b.　Enquiring about office hours

b-1．Asking if open or not

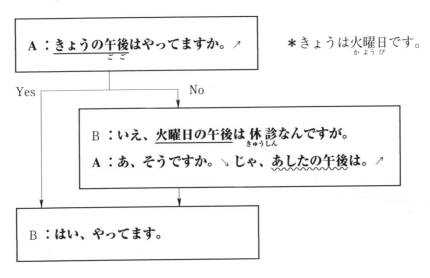

A：きょうの午後はやってますか。↗
　　　　　　ご ご

＊きょうは火曜日です。
　　　　　か ようび

Yes　　　　　　　　　No

B：いえ、火曜日の午後は休診なんですが。
　　　　　　　　　　　きゅうしん

A：あ、そうですか。↘ じゃ、あしたの午後は。↗

B：はい、やってます。

　　きょうの午後

1. あしたの午前中　　　2. あさって　　　3. 日曜日　　　4. 土曜日の午後
　　　　ご ぜんちゅう　　　　　　　　　　　　にちよう び　　　　　ど よう び

b-2. Asking how long they are open

A：何時から何時までですか。↗
　　なんじ
B：2時から5時半までです。
　　じ　　　じはん
A：2時から5時半までですね。↗
B：ええ。

c. Making an appointment

c-1. Asking for an appointment slot

（After giving necessary information）

A：じゃ、あしたの午後、お願いします。
　　　　　　　　　ごご　　ねが
B：はい。ええと、お名前は。↗
　　　　　　　　なまえ
A：＜your name＞です。
B：＜your name＞さんですね。↗
A：はい。

あしたの午後

1．土曜日の午前中　　　2．来週の月曜日　　　3．木曜日の夕方
　どようび　ごぜんちゅう　　らいしゅう　げつようび　　もくようび　ゆうがた

c-2. Confirming the time offered to you

B：それじゃ、4時15分に来てください。
　　　　　　　じ　ふん　き
A：はい、4時15分ですね。↗　よろしくお願いします。
B：はい。お大事に。
　　　　　だいじ

☆ 6. Making an appointment with your adviser (S-6)

You want to talk with your adviser about your thesis.

A：先生、論文のことで、ちょっとご相談したいんですが。
　　せんせい　ろんぶん　　　　　　　　　　　そうだん

B：はい。

A：いつがよろしいでしょうか。↘

B：あさってなら、いつでもいいですよ。↗

A：そうですか。じゃ、2時ごろは、いかがでしょうか。↘
　　　　　　　　　　じ

B：ええ、いいですよ。↗

A：じゃ、よろしくお願いします。
　　　　　　　　　ねが

B：はい。

あさって

1. あしたの午前中　　2. 今週の金曜日　　3. 来週　　4. 今月
　　　　ごぜんちゅう　　　こんしゅう きんようび　　らいしゅう　　こんげつ

7. Asking on the phone when shops/public facilities are open (S-4, S-5)

Practise with the entire class by using the notes given. Each student is given a note the contents of which are unknown to the others. Call the others asking about business hours and days when closed, using the following pattern, then fill in the chart below.

A：もしもし。

B：はい、松見デパートです。
　　　　まつみ

A：[Introducing a question politely]

B：はい。

A：あの、何時から何時までやってますか。
　　　　なんじ

B：[Telling the time]

A：あの、それから、休みはいつですか。
　　　　　　　　やす

B：[Giving the day they are closed]

A：どうもありがとうございました。

B：いいえ。

[松見デパート]

10：00 a.m.〜6：30 p.m.

（土・日）〜7：00 p.m.
　ど にち

定休日・水曜日
ていきゅうび すいようび

8. Role play

1. Make a medical appointment on the phone

   Practise with your teacher according to the following flow-chart, by using the dialogues in 5.

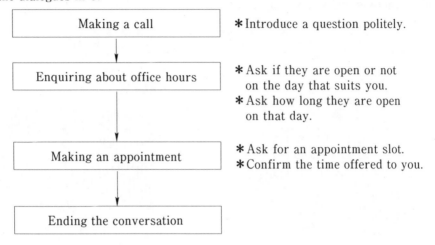

Making a call	*Introduce a question politely.
Enquiring about office hours	*Ask if they are open or not on the day that suits you. *Ask how long they are open on that day.
Making an appointment	*Ask for an appointment slot. *Confirm the time offered to you.
Ending the conversation	

2. Ask on the phone about office hours.

☆3. Make an appointment with your adviser for consultation about your thesis.

☆4. Ask directory enquiries for a telephone number.

Tasks and Activities

1. Listen to the tape. You will hear a series of telephone conversations.

   a. Where is the person calling ?

   1. _____   2. _____   3. _____   4. _____

   a 病 院
   びょういん

   b 図書館
   と しょ かん

   c 美 術 館 *art museum*
   び じゅつかん

   d デパート

   b. Fill in the blanks with appropriate time expressions.

   1. 休み　毎 週 （　　　）曜日と 祝 日　　　祝日 *national holiday*
   やす　まいしゅう　　　　　よう び　しゅくじつ

   2. 休み　毎週 （　　　）曜日と （　　　）曜日の午後
   　　　　　　　　　　　　　　　　　　　　　　　　ご ご

   3. （　　　）月 （　　　）日〜（　　　）月 （　　　）日

   4. （　　　）月 （　　　）日〜（　　　）月 （　　　）日

2. Listen to the tape. You will hear a series of conversations between the police and the suspects. A jewel was stolen from a shop. The police think it was stolen between 8 : 00 PM and 8 : 30 PM. Determine who does not have an alibi.

森さん
もり

[　　時　　分]
じ　　ふん

[　　時　　分]から
[　　時　　分]まで

[　　時　　分]から
[　　時　　分]まで

中村さん
なかむら

[　　時　　分]

[　　時　　分]から
[　　時　　分]まで

[　　時　　分]

上野さん
うえの

[　　時　　分]

[　　時　　分]から
[　　時　　分]まで

[　　時　　分]から
[　　時　　分]まで

3. Listen to the tape. You will hear a telephone conversation between Yamashita-san and Tanaka-san. Fill in Yamashita-san's schedule.

山下さんのスケジュール

	S	M	T	W	T	F	S	10			12	S	M	T	W	T	F	S

日	月	火	水	木	金	土
27	28	29	30 テスト(F) 10:30〜	31	1	2
3	4	5 → 京都へ旅行（A）	6	7	8 リーさんと 上野で 9:00	9
10	11	12	13	14	15	16
17	18	19	20	21	22	23
24	25	26	27	28	29	30

199× 11 NOVEMBER

A. 京都へ旅行
B. 田中さんと国立博物館へ行く
C. バースデーパーティー
D. ジョンさんと映画に行く
E. 田中さんから電話
F. テスト

国立博物館 *National Museum*

4．Follow the instructions in order to obtain advice regarding where you can have a pleasant holiday.

（スタート）

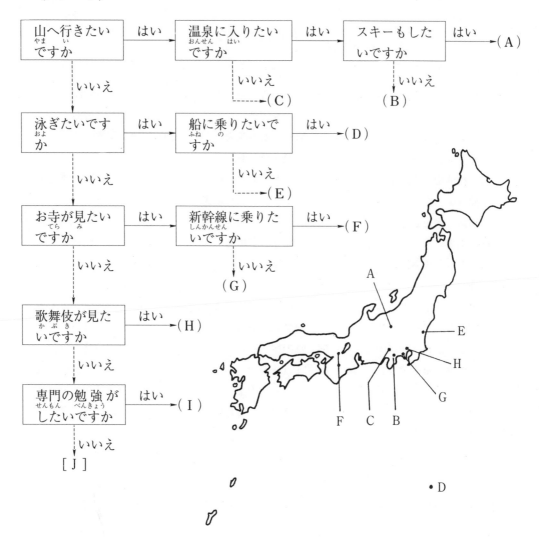

温泉　*hot spring*　　スキー　*ski*　　船　*ship*　　お寺　*temple*

新幹線　*shinkansen（bullet train）*　　歌舞伎　*Kabuki*

（A）：長野　（B）：箱根　（C）：富士山　（D）：小笠原　（E）：近くの海
（F）：京都・奈良　（G）：鎌倉　（H）：東京　（I）：大学　（J）：あなたの家

☆ 5. The following is a TV guide in a newspaper. Read the guide and answer the questions.

> Ⓝ：news　Ⓣ：weather forecast　Ⓢ：stereo　🔲：bilingual

NKK テレビ 2 チャンネル	時	KTB テレビ 5 チャンネル	まつみテレビ 7 チャンネル
00 🔲 7時のニュース　◇Ⓣ 30　ドラマスペシャル 　　「さようなら・グッド 　　バイ」江村英夫脚本 　　渡辺啓演出　小川圭子 　　本間雅子　金田一明 　　市川治　横山弘允 　　桜井由香　丹羽一順 　　清水あき　佐藤悠介	7 8	00 Ⓢ プロ野球～東京ドーム 　　巨人×広島 　　解説・長島茂太 　　実況・新谷清 　　ゲスト・大坪二男 　　リポーター戸村紀男 　　　　　　　山本淳郎 　▽大リーグ情報 8.54 Ⓝ ▽ Ⓣ	00　まんが水戸黄門 　　「スケさんの恋」 30　クイズ歴史入門 　　「今茨城がナウい」 　　小宮リカ　阿久津聡子 00　十手捕物帳 　　「大江戸仇討ち顛末」 　　加納祐介　西村康子 　　栃木紀子　◇54 Ⓝ Ⓣ
00　NKKニュース21 　　特集"帰ってきた白鳥 　　の親子"▽どうなる今 　　後の日米関係　54 Ⓣ	9	00　ブンちゃんのお笑いテ 　　レビ「スターの大失敗 　　発見」三田陽子 54　味の旅「長崎」	00 🔲 テレビロードショー 　　「スーパーマンX・本 　　当に最後の戦い」 　　（199X年イギリス） 　　チャールド・スター監
00　世界の旅「東南アジア 　　グルメツアー　インド 　　ネシア」 45　今日のスポーツ	10	00 Ⓢ ミュージックスタジオ 　　「ジャズの楽しみ」生 　　初登場！　日野照正 54　私の町の美術館	督　ファリスト・フォ 　　ード　バード・ファー 　　ガソン 54 Ⓢ 鉄道の旅トルコ

1. 映画が見たいです。何時から何チャンネルですか。　チャンネル *channel*
えいが み　　なんじ　なん
　　　　　（　　　）時（　　　）分から　　　（　　　）チャンネル
　　　　　　　　　　　じ　　　　　ふん

2. 英語のニュースが見たいです。何時から何チャンネルですか。
えいご
　　　　　（　　　）時（　　　）分から　　　（　　　）チャンネル

3. 野球が見たいです。何時から何チャンネルですか。　野球 *baseball*
やきゅう
　　　　　（　　　）時（　　　）分から　　　（　　　）チャンネル

4. あしたの天気が知りたいです。いま9時半です。何時から何チャンネルですか。
てんき し　　　　　　　　　じはん

　　　　　　　　　　　　　　　　　　　　　　　　　天気 *weather*

　　　　　（　　　）時（　　　）分から　　　（　　　）チャンネル

6．You want to go to the cinema. Look at the cinema guide and answer the following questions.

【シネマガイド】			
テアトルまつみ	スーパーマンX	8月1日～ 9月1日	9：20　11：20　1：20 3：20　5：20　7：20
まつみ 　ピカデリー	バットマンV	8月20日～ 9月14日	10：00　12：15　2：30 4：45　7：00
セントラル 　シネマ	ドラえもん アンパンマン	8月10日～ 9月2日	10：10　12：25　2：30 4：40
マツミプラザ	バットマンV	9月15日～ 10月14日	10：15　12：25　2：50 5：15　7：40 （土曜オールナイト）

a.　You want to go to see the movie "Batman V" on September 1st or 2nd.
Look at your schedule and decide which show is right for you.

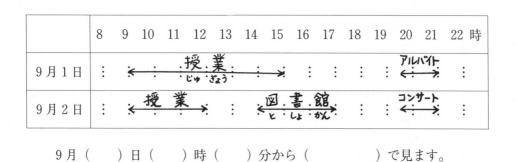

9月（　　）日（　　）時（　　）分から（　　　　　　）で見ます。

☆b.　The following is an exercise for two people. You want to see a movie with a friend but you don't have a cinema guide. Your partner has one. Call and ask him/her and decide to which movie you will see.

161

Lesson 8

許可を求める
きょ　か　　もと

Asking permission

● *New Words in Drills*

・is used only in Conversation Drills

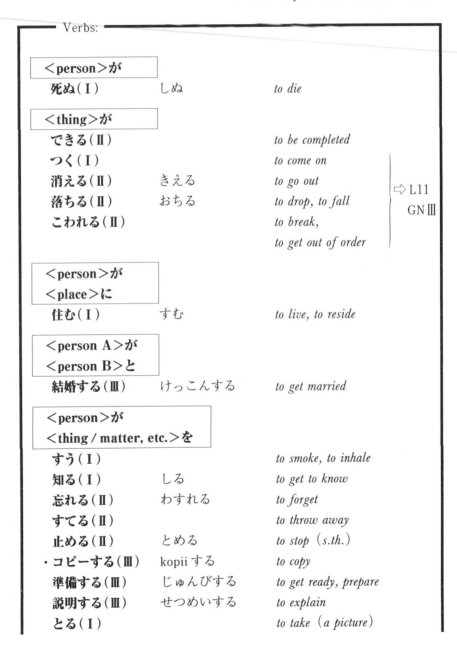

Verbs:

＜person＞が

死ぬ（Ⅰ）	しぬ	to die

＜thing＞が

できる（Ⅱ）		to be completed
つく（Ⅰ）		to come on
消える（Ⅱ）	きえる	to go out
落ちる（Ⅱ）	おちる	to drop, to fall
こわれる（Ⅱ）		to break, to get out of order

⇨ L11 GN Ⅲ

＜person＞が
＜place＞に

住む（Ⅰ）	すむ	to live, to reside

＜person A＞が
＜person B＞と

結婚する（Ⅲ）	けっこんする	to get married

＜person＞が
＜thing / matter, etc.＞を

すう（Ⅰ）		to smoke, to inhale
知る（Ⅰ）	しる	to get to know
忘れる（Ⅱ）	わすれる	to forget
すてる（Ⅱ）		to throw away
止める（Ⅱ）	とめる	to stop （s.th.）
・コピーする（Ⅲ）	kopii する	to copy
準備する（Ⅲ）	じゅんびする	to get ready, prepare
説明する（Ⅲ）	せつめいする	to explain
とる（Ⅰ）		to take （a picture）

> \<person\>が
> \<scheduled event / vehicle\>に
>
> | 遅れる（Ⅱ） | おくれる | *to be late* |
> |---|---|---|

Adjectives:

暑い	あつい	*hot*
寒い	さむい	*cold*
だめ（な）		*no good, not O.K.*

Adverbs and others:

・少し	すこし	*a little*
・早く	はやく	*soon, quickly*
・もちろん		*of course*
もう		*already*
まだ		*not yet*（＋*neg.*）
・また		*again*
・あとで		*later*
・次（の）	つぎの	*next*
去年	きょねん	*last year*

Other words:

ゼミ	zemi	*seminar*
・会議	かいぎ	*meeting, conference*
予定	よてい	*schedule, appointment*
・薬	くすり	*medicine*
店	みせ	*shop*
芝生	しばふ	*lawn, grass*
テニス	tenisu	*tennis*
天気	てんき	*weather*
エアコン	eakon	*air conditioner*
ヒーター	hiitaa	*heater*
ナイフ	naifu	*knife*
・クラス	kurasu	*class*
ミーティング	miitingu	*meeting*
車	くるま	*car*

● *Additional New Words in Drills*

```
┌─ Verbs: ─────────────────────────────────────────────────┐
│                                                           │
│  発表する（Ⅲ）    はっぴょうする    to present, to announce  │
│  出席する（Ⅲ）    しゅっせきする    to attend               │
│  欠席する（Ⅲ）    けっせきする      to be absent, to miss    │
│                                                           │
└───────────────────────────────────────────────────────────┘
```

```
┌─ Other words: ───────────────────────────────────────────┐
│                                                           │
│  実験          じっけん          experiment                │
│  約束          やくそく          promise                   │
│                                                           │
└───────────────────────────────────────────────────────────┘
```

```
┌─ Time words: ────────────────────────────────────────────┐
│                                                           │
│  ～週間        ～しゅうかん      ～weeks                    │
│  ～前          ～まえ            ～ago                      │
│  これから                        now                       │
│                                                           │
└───────────────────────────────────────────────────────────┘
```

```
┌─ Sickness: ──────────────────────────────────────────────┐
│                                                           │
│  顔色が悪い     かおいろがわるい   to look pale             │
│  熱がある       ねつがある         to have a fever          │
│  のどが痛い     のどがいたい       to have a sore throat    │
│  おなかが痛い   おなかがいたい     to have a stomachache    │
│  歯が痛い       はがいたい         to have a toothache      │
│                                                           │
└───────────────────────────────────────────────────────────┘
```

Structure Drills

1. Practise as in the example:

書きます　→　書く－書かない－書かなかった
　か　　　　　　か　　　　か

Ⅰ. 立ちます　　　乗ります　　　話します　　　入ります
　　た　　　　　　の　　　　　　はな　　　　　　はい

　　働きます　　　つきます　　　習います　　　閉まります
　　はたら　　　　　　　　　　　なら　　　　　　し

　　開きます　　　会います　　　すいます　　　休みます
　　あ　　　　　　あ　　　　　　　　　　　　　やす

　　貸します　　　買います　　　終わります　　始まります
　　か　　　　　　か　　　　　　お　　　　　　はじ

　　使います　　　死にます　　　出します　　　言います
　　つか　　　　　し　　　　　　だ　　　　　　い

　　持ちます　　　住みます　　　知ります
　　も　　　　　　す　　　　　　し

Ⅱ. 起きます　　　寝ます　　　　答えます　　　出かけます
　　お　　　　　　ね　　　　　　こた　　　　　　で

　　つけます　　　できます　　　消えます　　　落ちます
　　　　　　　　　　　　　　　　き　　　　　　お

　　変えます　　　開けます　　　閉めます　　　止めます
　　か　　　　　　あ　　　　　　し　　　　　　と

　　遅れます　　　忘れます
　　おく　　　　　わす

Ⅲ. 来ます　　　　します　　　　相談します　　　旅行します
　　き　　　　　　　　　　　　　そうだん　　　　りょこう

　　出席します　　欠席します　　結婚します　　　準備します
　　しゅっせき　　　けっせき　　　けっこん　　　　じゅんび

　　発表します　　予約します　　食事します　　　説明します
　　はっぴょう　　　よやく　　　　しょくじ　　　　せつめい

2. Look at the picture and make negative requests.

ここでたばこをすう

→　ここでたばこをすわないでください。

1. ごみをすてる　　　2. ここに車を止める　　　3. ここで写真をとる

4. 中に入る　　　5. まどを開ける　　　6. 教室で寝る

7. おふろに入る　　　8. 私の手紙を見る　　　9. いすの上に立つ

10. 押す

3. Make negative requests as in the example:

まどを開ける　→　まどを開けないでください。

1. まどを閉める
2. 英語で話す
3. テレビをつける
4. 電気を消す
5. この薬を飲む
6. このコンピュータを使う
7. この本をほかの人に貸す
8. 時間に遅れる
9. 約束を忘れる
10. 会議に欠席する

4. Practise as in the example:

テレビがついています。　　1. ＿＿＿＿＿＿＿。　　2. ＿＿＿＿＿＿＿。

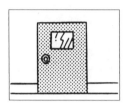 

3. ＿＿＿＿＿＿＿。　　4. ＿＿＿＿＿＿＿。

5. Look at the picture and make sentences as in the example:

お金　→　お金が落ちています。
かね　　　　　　お

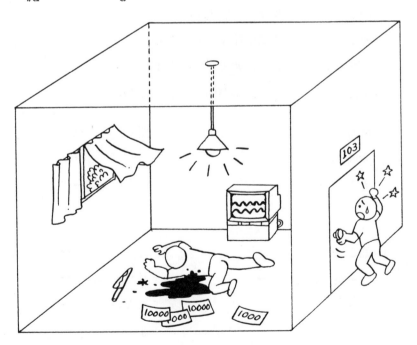

1. 人　　　　　　2. ナイフ　　　　3. テレビ
　ひと

4. まど　　　　　5. 電気　　　　　6. ドア
　　　　　　　　　でんき

6．Practise as in the examples:

1) Q：この本を読みましたか。　　　　　＜はい＞

　　A：はい、もう読みました。

2) Q：宿題をしましたか。　　　　　　　＜いいえ＞

　　A：いいえ、まだしていません。

1. この漢字を習いましたか。　　　　　　＜いいえ＞
2. あの映画を見ましたか。　　　　　　　＜はい＞
3. 木村先生の研究室に行きましたか。　　＜いいえ＞
4. レストランを予約しましたか。　　　　＜はい＞
5. 授業は終わりましたか。　　　　　　　＜いいえ＞

☆7．Practise as in the examples:

1) 始まる　　→　　始まっています。

　　授業が　　→　　授業が始まっています。

　　もう　　　→　　もう授業が始まっています。

2) 始まる　　→　　始まっています。

　　授業が　　→　　授業が始まっています。

　　＜ない＞　→　　授業が始まっていません。

　　まだ　　　→　　まだ授業が始まっていません。

1. 終わる　→　　　　　　　　　2. 開く　　　　→

　　映画が　→　　　　　　　　　　店が　　　　→

　　もう　　→　　　　　　　　　　＜ない＞　→

　　　　　　　　　　　　　　　　　まだ　　　　→

3. 知る　　　　　→　　　　　　4. 起きる　　　→

　　シャルマさんは　→　　　　　　リサさんは　→

　　もう　　　　　→　　　　　　　＜ない＞　→

　　　　　　　　　　　　　　　　　まだ　　　　→

5. 閉まる　　→

　　図書館は　→

　　大学の　　→

　　もう　　　→

6. 消える　　→

　　電気が　　→

　　事務室の　→

　　＜ない＞　→

　　まだ　　　→

8． Answer the questions, paying attention to the type of question.

1） Q：きのう新聞を読みましたか。

　　A：はい、読みました。

　　　　いいえ、読みませんでした。

2） Q：もうひらがなを習いましたか。

　　A：はい、習いました。

　　　　いいえ、まだ習っていません。

3） Q：山田さんは結婚していますか。

　　A：はい、結婚しています。

　　　　いいえ、結婚していません。

1. もう昼ごはんを食べましたか。
2. 三島由紀夫を知っていますか。

　　（三島由紀夫 a famous Japanese writer）

3. アパートに住んでいますか。
4. きのうテレビを見ましたか。
5. もうおふろに入りましたか。
6. 車を持っていますか。
7. 先週、図書館へ行きましたか。
8. もう日本語の辞書を買いましたか。

☆9. Practise the dialogue with your partner as in the example:

シャルマさん・結婚する ＜去年＞
→ A：シャルマさんは結婚していますか。
B：ええ、結婚していますよ。
A：いつ結婚したんですか。
B：去年です。

1. パーティー・始まる ＜6時＞
2. 子ども・寝る ＜8時ごろ＞
3. 山下さん・出かける ＜昼ごろ＞
4. リサさん・起きる ＜7時半ごろ＞

10. Practise as in the example:

あした休む → あした休んでもいいですか。

1. えんぴつで書く
2. 病院へ行く
3. ラジカセを借りる
4. コンピュータを使う
5. まどを開ける
6. ここにすわる
7. エアコンを消す
8. テレビをつける

☆11. Complete the sentences with ～てもいいですか and practise the dialogue with your partner. For the first two questions, cues are given in ＜ ＞.

＜午後休む＞
学生：ちょっと頭が痛いんですけれど、午後休んでもいいですか。
先生：ええ、いいですよ。

1. ＜あした出す＞
学生：まだ宿題ができてないんですけど、＿＿＿＿＿＿＿＿＿＿＿＿＿。
先生：だめです。宿題は今日中に出してください。

2. ＜ひらがなで書く＞

学生：この漢字はまだ習ってないんですけど、＿＿＿＿＿＿＿＿＿＿＿。

先生：ええ、いいですよ。ひらがなで書いてください。

3. 学生：ペンは持っていないんですけど、＿＿＿＿＿＿＿＿＿＿＿＿。

先生：ええ、いいですよ。

4. 学生：コピーをしたいんですけど、このコピー機を＿＿＿＿＿＿＿。

先生：いえ、学生は図書館でコピーしてください。

5. A ：あのう、少し暑いんですけど、＿＿＿＿＿＿＿＿＿＿＿＿。

B ：ええ、どうぞ。

6. A ：ちょっと寒いんですけど、＿＿＿＿＿＿＿＿＿＿＿＿＿。

B ：ええ。じゃ、私がつけましょう。

12. Complete the sentences, using とき.

子ども ＋ フランスへ行きました

→ 子どものとき、フランスへ行きました。

1. 大学 ＋ 毎日テニスをしました
2. 会議 ＋ ビールを飲まないでください
3. 病気 ＋ 何が食べたいですか
4. 元気 ＋ プールで泳ぎます
5. 寒い ＋ ヒーターをつけてください
6. 忙しい ＋ レストランで食事をします
7. 天気がいい ＋ せんたくします

13. Complete the sentences.

    1. 子どものとき、＿＿＿＿＿＿＿＿＿＿＿＿＿＿＿＿＿＿＿＿＿＿＿＿＿＿＿。

    2. 休みのとき、＿＿＿＿＿＿＿＿＿＿＿＿＿＿＿＿＿＿＿＿＿＿＿＿＿＿＿。

    3. 寒いとき、＿＿＿＿＿＿＿＿＿＿＿＿＿＿＿＿＿＿＿＿＿＿＿＿＿＿＿＿。

    4. ひまなとき、＿＿＿＿＿＿＿＿＿＿＿＿＿＿＿＿＿＿＿＿＿＿＿＿＿＿。

14. Answer the following questions, choosing from と，や，or か.

  1) Q：何を食べましたか。＜パン＋たまご＞
     A：パンとたまごを食べました。

  2) Q：部屋に何がありますか。＜いす＋つくえ＋テレビ……＞
     A：いすやつくえやテレビがあります。

  3) Q：いつ行きますか。＜あした／あさって＞
     A：あしたかあさって行きます。

  1. だれに手紙を書きますか。＜家族＋友だち……＞
  2. いつも何時に寝ますか。＜10時／10時半＞
  3. きのう晩ごはんは何を食べましたか。＜チキンカレー＋サラダ＞
  4. 誕生日に何をもらいましたか。＜時計＋花……＞
  5. 何曜日がひまですか。＜日曜日＋水曜日＞
  6. ○○へ何で行きますか。＜バス＋電車＞
  7. 日本ではどこへ旅行したいですか。＜京都＋北海道＋九州……＞
  8. いま、何が飲みたいですか。＜コーヒー／紅茶＞

Conversation Drills

1. Asking permission to enter （S-1）

a.　A student visits a teacher's room.

　　　Ａ：学生　Ｂ：先生
　　　　　がくせい　　せんせい

　Ａ：（knock-knock）

　Ｂ：はい。

　Ａ：失礼します。
　　　しつれい

　Ｂ：｛やあ。🚹
　　　　あら。🚺

　Ａ：あの、ちょっとよろしいですか。

　Ｂ：どうぞ。

☆b.　A student visits a friend's room.

　　　Ａ、Ｂ：友だち
　　　　　　　とも

　Ａ：（knock-knock）

　Ｂ：はい。

　Ａ：こんにちは。

　Ｂ：｛やあ。🚹
　　　　あら。🚺

　Ａ：ちょっといいかな。

　Ｂ：うん。何。↗
　　　　　なに

---

2. Asking permission to start a conversation（S-1）

📼

a. With a teacher 📠 🔼

A：学生　　B：先生
　　がくせい　　　　せんせい

A：すみません。

B：はい。

A：あの、ちょっとよろしいですか。

B：ううん。↘　いまはちょっと……。

A：あ、じゃ、けっこうです。<u>またにしますから</u>。

B：｛　そう。悪いね。♦
　　　　　　わる
　　　｛　そう。悪いわね。♦
　　　　　　わる

A：いいえ。じゃ、失礼します。
　　　　　　　　　しつれい

またにします

1. また来ます
　　　　き

2. またあとで来ます

3. 3時ごろ来ます
　　　じ

4. あしたにします

5. 来週にします
　らいしゅう

6. ＜time of your convenience＞にします

7. your choice

こんばん　あした　あさって　来週　次の週　また　あとで
　　　　　　　　　　　　　　　　　つぎ　しゅう

〜時ごろ　〜の朝　〜の昼　〜の晩　〜の午後　〜の曜日　etc.
　　　　　　あさ　　ひる　　ばん　　ごご　　ようび

---

b. Giving an appropriate reply

A：すみません。

B：はい。

A：あの、ちょっとよろしいですか。

Yes　　　　　　　　　　　　No

B：どうぞ。

A：＿＿＿＿＿＿＿。

B：あ、今はちょっと。
　　　　いま

A：＿＿＿＿＿＿＿。

3. Asking permission to be absent from class (S-2, S-3)

a. Announcing the topic

A：学生　　B：先生
がくせい　　　せんせい

A：あの、ちょっとよろしいですか。

B：｛ どうした。
　　どうしたの。

A：あのう、午後のゼミのことなんですが。
　　　　　　ご　ご

B：うん。

午後のゼミ

1. 午後のクラス　　　　　2. あしたのテスト

3. きのうの宿題　　　　　4. 次の授業
　　　　しゅくだい　　　　　　つぎ　じゅぎょう

5. 来週の実験　　　　　　6. 日本語のレポート
　らいしゅう　じっけん　　　　　　に ほん ご

7. 金曜日の会議　　　　　8. 水曜日のお約束
　きんよう び　かい ぎ　　　　　すいよう び　　やくそく

b. Giving the reason why you can't make it

A：実は、きのうからかぜで熱があるんです。
　　じつ　　　　　　　　　　　　　ねつ

B：そういえば、顔色が悪い｛ ね。
　　　　　　　かおいろ　わる　　　　わね。

かぜで熱がある

1. 頭が痛い　　　　　　　2. おなかが痛い
　あたま　いた

3. 歯が痛い　　　　　　　4. 気分が悪い
　は　　　　　　　　　　　　き ぶん

5. かぜでのどが痛い　　　6. other reasons

A 　　B 　　C

175

D  E

c. Asking permission by signalling what you want to do

A：**病院へ行きたい**んですが。
　　びょういん　い
B：うん。／ええ。

A：**ゼミ、休ん**でもよろしいでしょうか。
　　　　　やす

B：{ ああ ／ ええ }、もちろん { かまわないよ。♂ ／わよ。♀
　　　　　　　　　　　　　　　　かまいませんよ。

A：どうもすみません。

病院へ行きたい　　　**ゼミを休む**

1. 保健センターへ行きたい　　クラスを休む
　　ほ けん
2. この論文を読みたい　　　　コピーする
　　　ろんぶん　よ
3. 指導教官に会いたい　　　　きょうは早く帰る
　　し どうきょうかん　あ　　　　　　　　はや　かえ
4. ゼミに出席したい　　　　　日本語の授業を欠席する
　　　しゅっせき　　　　　　　に ほん ご　じゅぎょう　けっせき
5. 英語の論文を書きたい　　　このコンピュータを使う
　　えい ご　ろんぶん　か　　　　　　　　　　　つか

☆ 4. Asking permission（S-1，S-2，S-3）

Practise the student's part using expressions learnt.

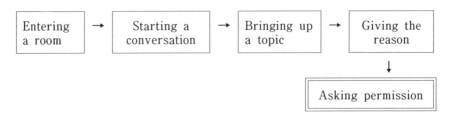

5. Giving a warning (S-4)

a.

Listen to the teacher's instructions and select the correct picture.

A：先生　　B：学生
　　せんせい　　　がくせい

> A：いまコピー機、こわれているから、使わないで。
> 　　　　　き　　　　　　　　　　　　　　つか
> B：はい、わかりました。

b.

Use the appropriate Japanese expressions.

It is prohibited to take photos in the museum. A guard tells you not to take photos.

→ 写真をとらないでください。
　　しゃしん

You are asked by a stranger, "May I smoke here?" You give a negative answer.

→ あ、すみません。ちょっと……。

1. In a bus, the driver tells the passengers not to put their hands out of the window.

2. In a cinema, a stranger asks, "Can I sit here?" Give a negative answer.

3. A doctor tells a patient not to smoke.

4. An instructor at the swimming pool says, "Please don't swim during the lunch break."

5. At a party, you advise your friend not to drink because s/he is going to drive later.

6. A teacher tells the students not to use dictionaries during the test.

7. A teacher tells the students not to speak English in class.

8. Your friend asks you, "May I use this dictionary?" Give a negative answer.

6. Asking permission (S-3)

a.

Examine the situations below and ask permission. Think of what to say according to the teacher's reply.

A：学生　　B：先生
　　がくせい　　　せんせい

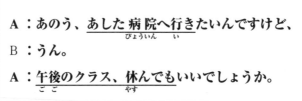

A：あのう、あした病院へ行きたいんですけど、
　　　　　　　びょういん　い

B：うん。

A：午後のクラス、休んでもいいでしょうか。
　　ごご　　　　　　　　やす

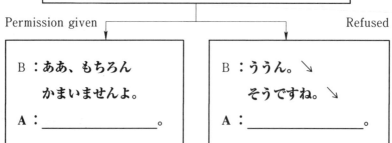

Permission given

B：ああ、もちろん

　　　かまいませんよ。

A：＿＿＿＿＿＿＿＿＿。

Refused

B：ううん。↘

　　　そうですね。↘

A：＿＿＿＿＿＿＿＿＿。

あした病院へ行く　　　午後のクラスを休む

1. これから病院へ行く　　　午後のクラスを休む

2. あした指導教官に会う　　　午後のクラスを休む
　　　しどうきょうかん　あ

3. 少し部屋でねる　　　　　　　午後のクラスを休む
　　すこ　へ や

4. 宿舎に帰る　　　　　　　　　午後のクラスを休む
　　しゅくしゃ　かえ

5. 午後、郵便局へ行く　　　　　授 業 に少しおくれる
　　ご ご　ゆうびんきょく　い　　　　じゅぎょう

6. あしたの朝、保健センターへ行く　授業に少しおくれる
　　　　　あさ　ほ けん

7. これから銀行へ行く　　　　　授業に少しおくれる
　　　　　ぎんこう

☆b.

Look at the situations and make appropriate dialogues as in the example.

A：あのう、<u>午後のゼミ</u>のことなんですが。
　　　　　ご ご

B：ええ。

A：<u>きのうからかぜで熱がある</u>んです。
　　　　　　　　　　ねつ

B：<u>そういえば、顔色が悪いですね。</u>
　　　　　　　かおいろ　わる

A：で、<u>これから 病 院へ行き</u>たいんですが、
　　　　　　　びょういん

B：ええ。

A：<u>ゼミ、休ん</u>でもよろしいでしょうか。
　　　　やす

B：ええ、もちろんかまいませんよ。

A：どうもすみません。

B：いいえ。<u>お大事にね。</u>
　　　　　　だい じ

A：ありがとうございます。

＊The underlined part 〰〰〰〰 might be changed.

きのうからかぜで熱がある

病院へ行きたい

午後のゼミを休む

1. けさから 頭 が痛い　　　　2. おなかが痛い
　　　　　　あたま　いた

　保健センターへ行きたい　　　宿 舎へ帰りたい
　　　　　　　　　　　　　　　しゅくしゃ　かえ

　きょうのクラスを休む　　　　午後のテストを休む

3. きのうから熱がある

　　薬を買いに行きたい

　　次の授業を欠席する

4. 母が病気だ

　　あした国へかえりたい

　　来週の発表を次の週にする

5. きょう国から友だちが来る

　　会いに行きたい

　　実験を来週にする

6. 月曜に指導教官と約束がある

　　東京へ行きたい

　　宿題を火曜に出す

☆7. Asking permission in general

Fill in the chart, choose a partner, and then carry on a dialogue.

	だれに(To whom)	何を(What)	どうして(Why)
ex. 1	先生	まどをあける	あつい
ex. 2	友だち	まどをあける	あつい
1			
2			
3			
4			

ex. 1

A：あの、すみません。　　　　　　　　B：はい。

A：ちょっとあついんですが。　　　　　B：ええ。

A：まど、あけてもよろしいでしょうか。　B：ええ、｛いいですよ。／どうぞ。

ex. 2

A：ねえ。　　　　　　　　　　　　　　B：何。↗

A：ちょっとあついんだけど。　　　　　B：うん。

A：まど、あけてもいいかな。　　　　　B：うん。いいよ。

A：ねえ。

A：ちょっとあついね。

A：あ、ありがと。 *(Oh, thanks.)*

B：何。↗
　　なに

B：まど、あけようか。

(Shall I open the window?)

8．Role play

1. You have had a headache since last night and you want to go to the doctor. Visit the professor's office and ask permission to be absent from the afternoon class.

2. Your professor will arrive from your country the following Monday morning. Ask permission to be absent from class on that day because you want to go to meet him at the airport (空港)
　　　　　　　　　　　　　　　　　　　　　　　　　　　くうこう

3. You want to use a photocopier in the office to copy your report. But your professor tells you you cannot use it because it is out of order. Then ask permission to go to the library to make a copy.

☆4. You have had a fever since this morning and you feel you need a good rest tonight. Telephone your friend and say that you cannot attend the party tonight.

☆5. Make up a situation of your own and make up a dialogue. Record the dialogue, then discuss the good and bad points of your performance in class.

Tasks and Activities

1. Listen to the tape and choose the corresponding pictures. Indicate whether the person was given permission or not.

1. _____   (permission given / not given)

2. _____   (permission given / not given)

3. _____   (permission given / not given)

4. _____   (permission given / not given)

5. _____   (permission given / not given)

a 使う
　つか

b 借りる
　か

c 帰る
　かえ

d もらう

e 質問する
　しつもん

2. The following is an exercise for two people. Each one is given a picture which differs from the other in some respects. Find the differences without showing the pictures by asking each other questions.

[A]

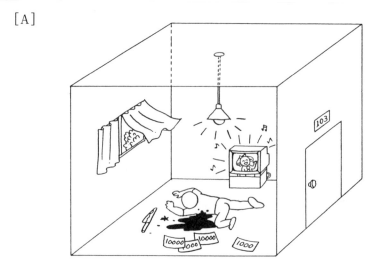

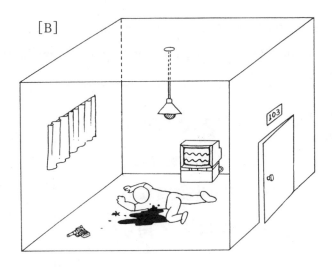

3. You have received a letter from Malaysia. Part of the letter is illegible because of an ink stain. Read the letter and try to find what the stained part contains.

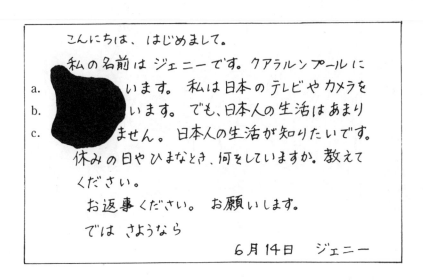

日本 にほん	日本人 にほんじん	生活 せいかつ	*life*	知る し	休み やす	日 ひ	何 なに
教える おし	返事 へんじ	*a reply*	お願いします ねが				

a. ＿＿＿＿＿ います

b. ＿＿＿＿＿ います

c. ＿＿＿＿＿ ません

4. a. You have to meet somebody named Ishikawa-san, whom you have never seen before. With the description below, identify him.

石川さん　あまり大きくない
たばこは すわない
ビールは 飲まない
黒い かばんを 持っている

☆b. Choose another person from the picture above and describe him/her to the class.

☆5. The following is a check list of things you may experience in Japan. Check your answers and see how you score.

あなたの日本経験度
にほんけいけんど

1	ふとんで	（2）	寝た	（1）	寝ていない
2	美容院／床屋へ	（2）	行った	（1）	行っていない
3	日本のお茶を	（2）	飲んだ	（1）	飲んでいない
4	なっとうを	（2）	食べた	（1）	食べていない
5	日本のふろに	（2）	入った	（1）	入っていない
6	日本語で電話を	（2）	かけた	（1）	かけていない
7	歌舞伎を	（2）	見た	（1）	見ていない
8	パチンコを	（2）	した	（1）	していない
9	日本の映画を	（2）	見た	（1）	見ていない
10	カラオケで	（2）	歌った	（1）	歌っていない

TOTAL

なっとう *fermented soybeans*　　歌舞伎 *Kabuki*

パチンコ *pinball game*　　美容院 *beauty salon*　　床屋 *barber shop*

カラオケ *singing to the accompaniment of a tape or video disk*

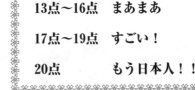

10点～12点	まだまだ
13点～16点	まあまあ
17点～19点	すごい！
20点	もう日本人！！

185

APPENDIX

◀ C.D. Check ▶

L 1

1. Listen to the dialogues a, b and c without looking at the drillbook, and choose the correct picture.

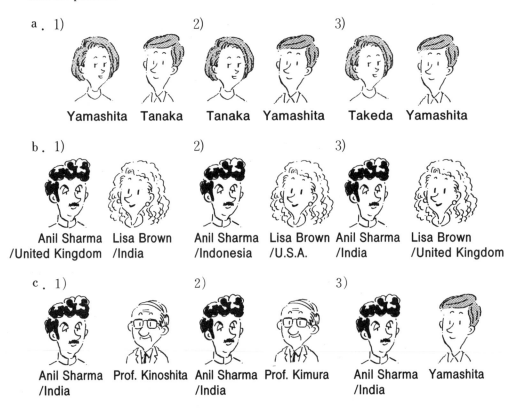

a. 1)
Yamashita Tanaka
2)
Tanaka Yamashita
3)
Takeda Yamashita

b. 1)
Anil Sharma Lisa Brown
/United Kingdom /India
2)
Anil Sharma Lisa Brown
/Indonesia /U.S.A.
3)
Anil Sharma Lisa Brown
/India /United Kingdom

c. 1)
Anil Sharma Prof. Kinoshita
/India
2)
Anil Sharma Prof. Kimura
/India
3)
Anil Sharma Yamashita
/India

2. Listen to the dialogues a, b and c, and choose the correct picture.

a. 1)   2)   3)

b. 1)　　　　　　2)　　　　　　3)

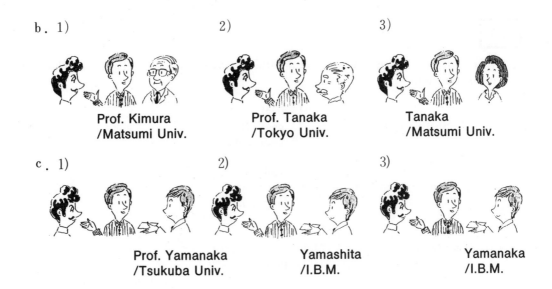

| Prof. Kimura /Matsumi Univ. | Prof. Tanaka /Tokyo Univ. | Tanaka /Matsumi Univ. |

c. 1)　　　　　　2)　　　　　　3)

| Prof. Yamanaka /Tsukuba Univ. | Yamashita /I.B.M. | Yamanaka /I.B.M. |

3. Listen to the dialogue and repeat Anil Sharma's part.

4. a. b. Listen to the model dialogues and get their meanings.

　　c. Listen to the dialogue and choose the correct passage.

　　　1) ロペスさんは大阪大学の学生です。国はブラジルで、専門は経済です。
　　　　　　おおさかだいがく　がくせい　　　　くに　　　　　　せんもん　けいざい

　　　2) ロペスさんの国はメキシコで、専門は経営です。大学は筑波大学です。
　　　　　　　　　　　　　　　　　　けいえい　　　　つくば

　　　3) ロペスさんは大阪大学の学生で、専門は経済です。国はメキシコです。

5. 6. Listen to the model dialogues and get their meanings.

L 2

1. Listen to the dialogues a, b, c and d without looking at the drillbook, and choose the correct answer.

   a. ♪ Sharma is going to the $\begin{cases} 1)\ \text{bank.} \\ 2)\ \text{post office.} \\ 3)\ \text{bookshop.} \end{cases}$

     ♬ Tanaka is going to the $\begin{cases} 1)\ \text{bank.} \\ 2)\ \text{university.} \\ 3)\ \text{hospital.} \end{cases}$

   b. Tanaka is going to the $\begin{cases} 1)\ \text{bank.} \\ 2)\ \text{bookshop.} \\ 3)\ \text{hospital.} \end{cases}$

   c. The professor is going to the $\begin{cases} 1)\ \text{library.} \\ 2)\ \text{post office.} \\ 3)\ \text{cafeteria.} \end{cases}$

  ☆d. Yamanaka is going to the $\begin{cases} 1)\ \text{hospital.} \\ 2)\ \text{supermarket.} \\ 3)\ \text{restaurant.} \end{cases}$

2. a. ♪, ♬ Listen to the dialogues, and choose the correct one.

    1)    2)   3)

3. a. Listen to the dialogue and choose the correct kind of mail and its destination from the following.

    1) U.K   2) U.S.A   3)  Germany

   b. Listen to the dialogue and choose the correct destination and its cost from the following.

    1) Indonesia   2) India   3) India
       ¥ 240   ¥ 260   ¥ 280

☆ c . Listen to the dialogue and choose the correct kind of mail and its destination from the following.

1)  U.K.　　　2) U.S.A　　　3) France

☆ d . Listen to the dialogue and get the meaning.

4 . Listen to the dialogues a and b and answer what the customer bought at the post office.

  a . 1) ８０円切手　５まい
　　　　えんきって
  　　2) ８０円切手　３まい
  　　3) ８０円切手　４まい

  b . 1) ８０円切手　５まい　／　はがき　３まい
  　　2) ８０円切手　３まい　／　はがき　５まい
  　　3) ８０円切手　３まい　／　はがき　３まい

5 . Listen to the dialogue and answer: how much did the customer pay at the post office?

  　　1) ４９０円
  　　2) ５１０円
  　　3) ５９０円

6 . Listen to the dialogue and get the meaning.

L 3

1. Listen to the dialogue and choose the correct picture.

1)   2)   3)

2. Listen to the dialogues a and b to choose the correct picture.

a. 1)   2)   3)

coffee   tea   coffee

b. 1)   2)   3)

3. Listen to the dialogue a and b to choose the correct picture.

a. 1)   2)   3)

Fried chicken set   Beef curry set   Tempura set

☆b. 1)   2)   3)

5. ♪, ♬ Listen to the model dialogues and get their meanings.

6. Listen to the dialogues a, b and c, and choose the correct answer.

    a. The price is   1) ￥1500   2) ￥1600   3) ￥1800

    b. The change is   1) ￥100   2) ￥200   3) ￥2000

   ☆c. Beef curry and coffee cost   1) ￥1000   2) ￥1150   3) ￥2000
       Tempura set and coffee cost   1) ￥1000   2) ￥1150   3) ￥850

L 4

1. Listen to the dialogues without looking at the drillbook, and choose the correct picture.

a. 1)　　　　　　2)　　　　　　3)

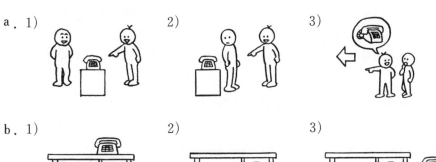

b. 1)　　　　　　2)　　　　　　3)

2. Listen to the dialogues without looking at the drillbook, and choose the correct picture.

a. What is she looking for?

1)　　　　　　2)　　　　　　3)

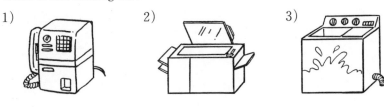

b. What is he looking for?

1)　　　　　　2)　　　　　　3)

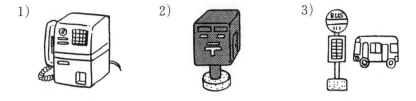

3. Listen to the dialogues and choose the correct answer.

a. Where is the washing machine?

　　1) on the 1st floor　　2) on the 2nd floor　　3) on the 3rd floor

b. Where is the telephone? — In front of

　　1) the coffee shop.　　2) the post office.　　3) the supermarket.

5. a. a-1, a-2 Listen to the expressions and repeat them.

   b. Listen to the dialogues and choose the correct answer.
      ♪ Where is Yamashita-san?
        1) on the 1st floor   2) on the 2nd floor   3) she doesn't know
      ♫ Where is Kimura-sensee?
        1) on the 1st floor   2) on the 2nd floor   3) he doesn't know

6. a. Listen to the dialogue and write the key word in hiragana.
                                   (   )

   ☆ b. Listen to the dialogues and get their meanings.

L 5

1. Listen to the dialogue without looking at the drillbook, and choose the correct picture.

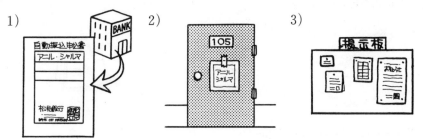

1)   2)   3)

2. a. Listen to the dialogue and choose the correct answer.

   ♪ 1) たきゅうびん   2) たっきゅびん   3) たっきゅうびん

   ♫ Long sound   1) あります。
                   2) ありません。

3. Listen to the dialogues a, b and c, and choose the correct answer.

   a. 1) じどはんばいき   2) じどうはんばいき   3) じどうはばいき

   b. 1) しゅだい   2) しゅくだい   3) しゅくうだい

   c. 1) dormitory   2) library   3) station

4. a. Listen to the model dialogues and get the meaning.

   b. Listen to the dialogue and choose the correct sentence.

   1) 女の人は保健センターを男の人に教えました。
   2) 女の人は保健センターを知りません。
   3) ほかの人は保健センターを知りません。

5. a. b. Listen to the announcement and fill in the blanks.

   ♪ (　　　　　) 号室のシャルマさん、(　　　　　) がありましたから、
      (　　　　　) に来てください。

   ♫ (　　　　　) は、(　　　　　　　　　) でございます。
      お降りの方は、お近くの (　　　　　) を押して、お知らせください。

7. Listen to the model dialogues and get their meanings.

L 6

1. Listen to the dialogues and choose the correct answer.

    a. What is Sharma receiving?

      1)   2)   3)

    ☆b. Where has it been left behind?

        1) in the cafeteria   2) in the classroom   3) in the computer room

2. Listen to the expressions and repeat them.

3. Look at the drillbook and listen to the model instructions.
    Then choose the number of the correct picture for each of them.

    a.   b.   c.   d.   e.   f.   g.   h.

4. Listen to the dialogue and choose the correct answer. What is he asked to write?

    1) name   2) address   3) student number

5. Look at the drillbook (p.128) and listen to the dialogue. Then correct the information about Sharma.

6. a. Listen to the dialogue and choose the correct answer. What is the problem?

    1) He doesn't understand Japanese.
    2) He doesn't have a ball-point pen.
    3) He doesn't have his seal.

    b. ♪, ♫ Listen to the dialogues and get their meanings.

☆8. Listen to the dialogue and choose the correct picture.

    1)   2)   3)

L 7

1. Listen to the dialogues without looking at the drillbook, and write the correct number in (　　).

　a. The telephone number is (　　　　　　　　　　).

　☆b. The extension number is (　　　　　　　　　).

2. a. Listen to the dialogues without looking at the drillbook, and choose who is asking whom for a telephone number.

　a-1.　1) 学生→学生(not very close)　2) 先生→学生　3) 友だち→友だち
　　　　　　がくせい　　　　　　　　　　　　　　せんせい　　　　　　　とも

　☆a-2.　1) 学生→学生(not very close)　2) 先生→学生　3) 友だち→友だち

　☆b. Listen to the dialogue and get the meaning.

3. Listen to the dialogue and choose the correct word.

　Sharma is making a call to $\left\{\begin{array}{l} \text{1) the hospital.} \\ \text{2) a coffee shop.} \\ \text{3) the university office.} \end{array}\right.$

4. Listen to the dialogues and choose the correct word and write the correct number in (　　).

　♪ He wants to call $\left\{\begin{array}{l} \text{1) the hospital.} \\ \text{2) a coffee shop.} \\ \text{3) the university office.} \end{array}\right.$

　♫ He dialled (　　　　　—　　　　　　).

5. Listen to the dialogues and write the answers in hiragana or numbers.

　a.　　Where is he making a call to?　　　　　(　　　　　　) 医院
　　　　　　　　　　　　　　　　　　　　　　　　　　　　　　　　　い いん

　b-1.　Is the hospital open today in the afternoon? (　　　　　)

　b-2.　What time is the hospital open?　　　　　(　　) 時～(　　) 時半
　　　　　　　　　　　　　　　　　　　　　　　　　　　　じ　　　　　じ はん

　c-1.　When is he going to the hospital?　　　　あしたの (　　　　)

　c-2.　What time is he going to the hospital?　　(　　) 時 (　　) 分
　　　　　　　　　　　　　　　　　　　　　　　　　　　　　　　　　ふん

☆6. Listen to the dialogue and answer the question in Japanese.

　When is she seeing her adviser?　　(　　　　　　) の (　　　) 時ごろ

7. Listen to the dialogue without looking at the drillbook, and write the appropriate word or number in (　　).

松見デパートは、朝（　　　）時から夕方（　　　）時半までやっています。
まつみ　　　　　　　あさ　　　　　　　　ゆうがた　　　　　　　じ はん

土曜と日曜は（　　　）時までやっています。（　　　　　　）は休みです。
どよう　にちよう　　　　　　　　　　　　　　　　　　　　　　　　　やす

L 8

1. Listen to the dialogues a and b without looking at the drillbook, and choose the correct picture.

a. 1) 　　2) 　　3)

b. 1) 　　2) 　　3)

2. a. Listen to the dialogue and choose who is asking whom for permission.

1) 先生　→　学生　　2) 学生　→　先生　　3) 友だち　→　友だち

b. Listen to the dialogues and choose the correct expression for the last part.

♪　どうぞ。　　―{ 1) 失礼です。
　　　　　　　　　 2) 失礼します。
　　　　　　　　　 3) 失礼しました。

♬　あ、今はちょっと。　　―{ 1) すみません。じゃね。
　　　　　　　　　　　　 2) すみません。じゃ、またね。
　　　　　　　　　　　　 3) すみません。じゃ、また。

3. Listen to the dialogues, and choose the correct situations.

a. この学生は、{ 1) あしたの午後
　　　　　　　 2) きのうの午後　}ゼミを休みたいです。
　　　　　　　 3) きょうの午後

b. 1) 　　2) 　　3)

c. どうして休みますか。

1) ゼミへ行きますから。

2) 図書館へ行きますから。

3) 病院へ行きますから。

5. a. Look at the drillbook and listen to the model dialogue. Then, eight dialogues a) to h) will be given. Listen to the dialogues and choose the number of the correct picture for each dialogue.

a.　　b.　　c.　　d.　　e.　　f.　　g.　　h.

6. Listen to the dialogues and choose the correct situations.

a. ♪ この学生は、
$\begin{cases} 1) きょう \\ 2) あした \\ 3) あさって \end{cases}$ $\begin{cases} 1) クラス \\ 2) 郵便局 \\ 3) 病院 \end{cases}$ へ行きたいです。

♬ この学生は、
$\begin{cases} 1) 今月 \\ 2) 来週 \\ 3) 来月 \end{cases}$ $\begin{cases} 1) 国へ帰りたいです。 \\ 2) 試験に行きたいです。 \\ 3) 病院へ行きたいです。 \end{cases}$

☆b. 1) この学生はこれからかぜで熱があるが、午後からゼミへ行く。

2) この学生はけさからかぜで頭が痛くて、いまから銀行へ行く。

3) この学生はきのうからかぜで熱があって、これから病院へ行く。

索　引（さくいん）　　　　Index

◉この索引の使い方

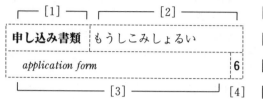

[1] the word
[2] the reading of the kanji
[3] the meaning of the word
[4] the number of the lesson

[あ]

アイスクリーム
ice cream — 3

アイスコーヒー
iced coffee — 3

IDカード
ID card — 6

会う　あう
to meet — 7

開く　あく
to open — 7

開ける　あける
to open (s.th.) — 5

あげる
to give — 3

朝ごはん　あさごはん
breakfast — 3

あさって
the day after tomorrow — 6

あした
tomorrow — 2

あそこ
there — 4

頭　あたま
head — 7

新しい　あたらしい
new — 6

暑い　あつい
hot (weather) — 8

あっち
over there (casual) — 4

あとで
later — 8

あの〜
that 〜 — 4

アパート
apartment, flat — 4

あまり
not so 〜 (＋ neg.) — 6

ある
to exist, to be — 4

あれ
that — 4

[い]

いい
good — 6

〜医院　〜いいん
〜 clinic — 7

言う　いう
to say, to tell — 5

医学　いがく
medical science — 1

イギリス
U.K. — 1

行く　いく
to go — 2

いくつ
how many? (things) — 3

いくら
how much? (money) — 2

いす
chair — 4

忙しい　いそがしい
busy — 7

痛い　いたい
painful — 7

一／1　いち
one — 2

一月／1月　いちがつ
January — 7

一万／10000　いちまん
ten thousand — 2

いつ
when? — 3

五日／5日　いつか
the 5th of the month 7

いっしょ（に）
together 3

五つ　いつつ
five 3

遺伝子工学　いでんしこうがく
genetic engineering 1

犬　いぬ
dog 4

いま
now 6

意味　いみ
meaning 5

いる
to exist, to be 4

印鑑　いんかん
seal 6

インド
India 1

[う]

上　うえ
on, above 4

うかがう
to ask 7

後ろ　うしろ
behind 4

うち
my (our) house/place 1

うるさい
noisy 6

[え]

エアコン
air conditioner 8

エアログラム
aerogram 2

映画　えいが
movie 2

映画館　えいがかん
cinema 4

営業時間　えいぎょうじかん
business hours 7

英語　えいご
English 2

駅　えき
station 2

駅前　えきまえ
area near the station 7

～円　～えん
~ yen 2

えんぴつ
pencil 4

[お]

おいしい
delicious 6

大きい　おおきい
large, big 6

大阪　おおさか
place name 1

おかえし
change＝おつり 2

（お）金　おかね
money 3

沖縄　おきなわ
prefecture name 1

起きる　おきる
to get up, to wake up 5

置く　おく
to put, to place 6

遅れる　おくれる
to be late 8

（お）酒　おさけ
alcohol, sake 3

教える　おしえる
to teach 3

押す　おす
to push, to seal 6

（お）茶　おちゃ
Japanese tea 3

落ちる　おちる
to drop, to fall 8

（お）つり
change 3

（お）手洗い　おてあらい
toilet 4

男の子　おとこのこ
boy 4

男の人　おとこのひと
man 4

おなか
stomach 8

お願いする　おねがいする
to request 7

（お）ふろ	
bath, bath room	5
（お）水 （お）みず	
water	3
重い　おもい	
heavy	6
おもしろい	
interesting	6
泳ぐ　およぐ	
to swim	5
オレンジジュース	
orange juice	3
終わる　おわる	
to end, to be finished	7
音楽　おんがく	
music	1
女の子　おんなのこ	
girl	4
女の人　おんなのひと	
woman	4

[か]

～階　～かい	
counter for floors (storeys)	4
会議　かいぎ	
meeting, conference	8
会社　かいしゃ	
company	7
階段　かいだん	
stairs	4
買う　かう	
to buy	2
返す　かえす	
to return, to give back	7
帰る　かえる	
to return, to go home	2
顔色　かおいろ	
complexion	8
化学　かがく	
chemistry	1
書く　かく	
to write	2
学生　がくせい	
student	1
学生証　がくせいしょう	
student card	6
学籍番号　がくせきばんごう	
student number	6

かさ	
umbrella	4
貸す　かす	
to lend, to rent	3
家族　かぞく	
family	7
～方　～かた	
how to ～	6
かたかな	
katakana	3
～月　～がつ	
～ th month of the year	7
金　かね	
money	3
かばん	
bag	4
カメラ	
camera	2
火曜日　かようび	
Tuesday	5
借りる　かりる	
to borrow, to rent	3
軽い　かるい	
light	6
カレーライス	
curry rice	3
カレンダー	
calendar	4
～側　～がわ	
～ side	4
環境科学　かんきょうかがく	
environmental science	1
漢字　かんじ	
kanji	2
かんたん（な）	
easy, simple	6

[き]

消える　きえる	
to go out	8
機械工学　きかいこうがく	
mechanical engineering	1
聞く　きく	
to listen, to hear	2
聞く　きく	
to ask	5
喫茶店　きっさてん	
coffee shop	4

切手　きって
stamp　　2

きのう
yesterday　　2

気分　きぶん
feeling　　7

九／9　きゅう，く
nine　　2

九州　きゅうしゅう
district name　　1

休診　きゅうしん
no consultation　　7

きょう
today　　2

教育　きょういく
education　　1

教室　きょうしつ
classroom　　4

京都　きょうと
place name　　1

去年　きょねん
last year　　8

きれい(な)
beautiful, clean　　6

銀行　ぎんこう
bank　　2

金曜日　きんようび
Friday　　5

[く]
九／9　く，きゅう
nine　　2

空港　くうこう
airport　　5

九月／9月　くがつ
September　　7

薬　くすり
medicine　　8

くだもの
fruit　　3

国　くに
country　　1

クラス
class　　8

来る　くる
to come　　2

車　くるま
car　　8

[け]

経営　けいえい
business administration　　1

経済　けいざい
economics　　1

掲示板　けいじばん
bulletin/notice board　　5

芸術　げいじゅつ
arts　　1

けさ
this morning　　4

消す　けす
to turn off　　5

けっこう(な)
fine　　6

結婚する　けっこんする
to get married　　8

欠席する　けっせきする
to be absent, to miss　　8

月曜日　げつようび
Monday　　5

元気(な)　げんきな
fine, healthy　　7

～研究科　～けんきゅうか
postgraduate course in ～　　6

研究室　けんきゅうしつ
seminar room　　1

言語学　げんごがく
linguistics　　1

建築　けんちく
architecture　　1

[こ]
～語　～ご
～ language　　2

五／5　ご
five　　2

(ご)いっしょ(に)
together　　3

工学　こうがく
engineering　　1

航空便　こうくうびん
airmail　　2

～号室　～ごうしつ
counter for room no.　　6

紅茶　こうちゃ
tea　　3

コース名　コースめい
course title　6

コーヒー
coffee　3

コーラ
cola　3

五月／5月　ごがつ
May　7

国際関係　こくさいかんけい
international relations　1

国籍　こくせき
nationality　6

ここ
here　4

午後　ごご
p.m., afternoon　7

九日／9日　ここのか
the 9th of the month　7

九つ　ここのつ
nine　3

午前　ごぜん
a.m., morning　7

こちら
here, this　1

こっち
here (casual)　4

小包　こづつみ
parcel　2

ことば
word　5

子ども　こども
child　4

この〜
this 〜　4

このへん
around here　4

ごはん
rice　3

コピー機　コピーき
copy machine　4

コピーする
to copy　8

困る　こまる
to be at a loss　5

これ
this　4

これから
now, from now　8

〜ごろ
about 〜　7

こわれる
to break, to get out of order　8

今月　こんげつ
this month　5

今週　こんしゅう
this week　5

コンパ
students' party　7

こんばん
this evening, tonight　4

コンピュータ室　コンピュータしつ
computer room　4

コンピュータ
computer science　1

[さ]

〜歳／〜才　〜さい
〜 years old　6

最近　さいきん
recently　7

サインする
to sign　6

魚　さかな
fish　3

酒　さけ
alcohol, sake　3

札幌　さっぽろ
place name　1

さとう
sugar　3

寒い　さむい
cold (weather)　8

サラダ
salad　3

三／3　さん
three　2

三月／3月　さんがつ
March　7

サンドイッチ
sandwich　3

[し]

四／4　し, よん
four　2

字　じ
letter, character　5

~時　～じ
~ o'clock　7

CD
compact disc　2

しお
salt　3

～歯科　～しか
~ dental clinic　7

四月／4月　しがつ
April　7

試験　しけん
examination　7

四国　しこく
district name　1

辞書　じしょ
dictionary　3

静か(な)　しずかな
quiet　6

下　した
under, below　4

七／7　しち，なな
seven　2

七月／7月　しちがつ
July　7

実験　じっけん
experiment　8

自転車　じてんしゃ
bicycle　5

自動販売機　じどうはんばいき
vending machine　4

死ぬ　しぬ
to die　8

芝生　しばふ
lawn, grass　8

～時半　～じはん
half past ~　7

閉まる　しまる
to close　7

事務室　じむしつ
general office　4

閉める　しめる
to close (s.th.)　5

社会学　しゃかいがく
sociology　1

写真　しゃしん
photograph　6

十／10　じゅう
ten　2

十一月／11月　じゅういちがつ
November　7

十月／10月　じゅうがつ
October　7

～週間　～しゅうかん
~ weeks　8

宗教学　しゅうきょうがく
theology　1

住所　じゅうしょ
address　5

十二月／12月　じゅうにがつ
December　7

十四日／14日　じゅうよっか
the 14th of the month　7

授業　じゅぎょう
class, lesson　6

宿舎　しゅくしゃ
dormitory, hall　4

宿題　しゅくだい
homework　5

受講届け　じゅこうとどけ
course registration form　6

出席する　しゅっせきする
to attend　8

準備する　じゅんびする
to get ready, prepare　8

奨学金　しょうがくきん
scholarship　6

しょうゆ
soy sauce　3

食事する　しょくじする
to eat, to have a meal　7

食堂　しょくどう
cafeteria, refectory　2

知る　しる
(to get) to know　8

～人　～じん
indicates nationality　1

新聞　しんぶん
newspaper　2

心理学　しんりがく
psychology　1

診療時間　しんりょうじかん
consultation hours　7

204

[す]

ずいぶん
quite, very — 6

水曜日　すいようび
Wednesday — 5

すう
to smoke, to inhale — 8

数学　すうがく
mathematics — 1

スーパー
supermarket — 3

少し　すこし
a little — 8

すてる
to throw away — 8

スパゲッティー
spaghetti — 3

スプーン
spoon — 3

スポーツセンター
sports center — 7

住む　すむ
to live, to reside — 8

する
to do — 2

すわる
to sit down — 5

[せ]

生化学　せいかがく
biochemistry — 1

政治　せいじ
politics — 1

生年月日　せいねんがっぴ
date of birth — 6

生物　せいぶつ
biology — 1

性別　せいべつ
sex — 6

説明する　せつめいする
to explain — 8

ゼミ
seminar — 8

0　ゼロ，れい
zero — 2

千／1000　せん
one thousand — 2

先月　せんげつ
last month — 5

専攻　せんこう
one's major, field of study — 6

先週　せんしゅう
last week — 5

先生　せんせい
teacher, professor — 1

せんたく機　せんたくき
washing machine — 4

仙台　せんだい
place name — 1

全部（で）　ぜんぶで
(in) total — 2

専門　せんもん
specialization — 1

[そ]

ソース
sauce — 3

相談する　そうだんする
to consult (with) — 7

速達　そくたつ
special delivery — 2

そこ
there — 4

そっち
there (casual) — 4

その〜
that 〜 — 4

それ
that — 4

それから
and, also — 2

[た]

体育　たいいく
physical education — 1

大学　だいがく
university — 1

大学院　だいがくいん
graduate school — 1

だいじょうぶ（な）
all right — 7

高い　たかい
expensive — 6

たくさん
many, much — 7

205

タクシー		
taxi	5	
出す		
to put out, to send	2	
出す		
to submit	6	
立つ　たつ		
to stand up	5	
宅急便　たっきゅうびん		
delivery service	5	
たな		
shelf	4	
タバコ／たばこ		
cigarettes	3	
食べる　たべる		
to eat	3	
たまご		
egg	3	
だめ（な）		
no good, not O.K.	8	
だれ		
who?	2	
誕生日　たんじょうび		
birthday	3	

［ち］

小さい　ちいさい	
small, little	6
チーズ	
cheese	3
チーズサンドイッチ	
cheese sandwich	3
ちがう	
to differ	7
近く　ちかく	
close to	4
地学　ちがく	
geology	1
チキンカレー	
chicken curry	3
千葉　ちば	
place name	1
茶　ちゃ	
Japanese tea	3
〜中　〜ちゅう	
during 〜	7
駐車場　ちゅうしゃじょう	
parking lot	4

注文する　ちゅうもんする	
to order	3
ちょっと	
a little, for a while	2
地理　ちり	
geography	1

［つ］

一日／1日　ついたち	
the 1st of the month	7
使う　つかう	
to use	5
次（の）　つぎ（の）	
(the) next	8
つく	
to come on	8
作る　つくる	
to make	6
つくえ	
desk	4
筑波　つくば	
place name	1
つける	
to turn on	5
つり	
change	3

［て］

手洗い　てあらい	
toilet	4
定食　ていしょく	
set meal	3
テープ	
tape	2
テープレコーダー	
tape recorder	4
出かける　でかける	
to go out, to leave	7
手紙　てがみ	
letter	2
できる	
to be completed	8
テスト	
test	5
哲学　てつがく	
philosophy	1
テニス	
tennis	8

206

デパート
department store 4

テレビ
television 2

天気　てんき
weather 8

電気　でんき
light, electricity 5

電気工学　でんきこうがく
electrical engineering 1

電子工学　でんしこうがく
electronics 1

電車　でんしゃ
(electric) train 6

天ぷら　てんぷら
tempura 3

電話　でんわ
telephone 4

電話番号　でんわばんごう
telephone number 5

[と]
ドア
door 4

どう
how? 6

東京　とうきょう
place name 1

どうして
why? 5

十／10　とお
ten 3

十日／10日　とおか
the 10th of the month 7

時計　とけい
watch, clock 2

どこ
where? 1

年　とし
age 6

図書館　としょかん
library 2

どちら
where? (polite) 1

どっち
where? (casual) 4

とても
very 6

どなた
who? 4

となり
next to 4

どの〜
which 〜? 4

土木工学　どぼくこうがく
civil engineering 1

トマトジュース
tomato juice 3

止める　とめる
to stop (s.th.) 8

友だち　ともだち
friend 1

土曜日　どようび
Saturday 5

とりのからあげ
fried chicken 3

取る　とる
to take 5

とる
to take (a picture) 8

どれ
which one? 4

ドレッシング
dressing 3

どんな
what sort? 5

[な]
内線　ないせん
extension 7

ナイフ
knife 8

中　なか
inside 4

長い　ながい
long 6

名古屋　なごや
place name 1

七／7　なな，しち
seven 2

七つ　ななつ
seven 3

何　なに
what? 2

何語　なにご
what language? 4

七日／7日　なのか
the 7th of the month　7

ナポリタン
spaghetti with tomato sauce　3

名前　なまえ
name　5

習う　ならう
to learn　3

何　なん
what?　1

何時　なんじ
what time?　7

何人　なんにん
how many? (persons)　3

何名（さま）　なんめいさま
how many? (persons) (polite)　3

[に]

二／2　に
two　2

二月／2月　にがつ
February　7

にぎやか（な）
lively, crowded　6

肉　にく
meat　3

二十四日／24日　にじゅうよっか
the 24th of the month　7

～日　～にち
counter for days　7

日曜日　にちようび
Sunday　5

日本　にほん
Japan　1

日本語　にほんご
Japanese language　1

日本酒　にほんしゅ
sake　3

日本人　にほんじん
Japanese (people)　1

荷物　にもつ
package　5

～人　～にん
～ people　3

[ね]

ねこ
cat　4

熱　ねつ
fever　8

寝る　ねる
to go to bed, to lie down　5

年齢　ねんれい
age　6

[の]

農学　のうがく
agriculture　1

ノート
notebook　3

のど
throat　8

飲む　のむ
to drink　3

乗る　のる
to ride, to get on　5

[は]

歯　は
tooth　8

パーティー
party　5

はいざら
ashtray　3

入る　はいる
to go/come in　5

はがき
postcard　2

はし
chopsticks　3

始まる　はじまる
to begin, to start　7

バス
bus　5

バス停　バスてい
bus stop　4

パスポート
passport　6

働く　はたらく
to work　7

八／8　はち
eight　2

八月／8月　はちがつ
August　7

発表する　はっぴょうする
to present, to announce　8

二十日／20日　はつか
the 20th of the month　7

花　はな
flower　4

話す　はなす
to talk, to speak　5

母　はは
(my) mother　7

早く　はやく
soon, quickly　8

払う　はらう
to pay　3

はる
to put, to stick　5

パン
bread　3

はんこ
seal＝印鑑（いんかん）　6

番号案内　ばんごうあんない
directory assistance　7

晩ごはん　ばんごはん
supper, dinner　3

[ひ]
ヒーター
heater　8

ビーフカレー
beef curry　3

ビール
beer　3

ピザ
pizza　3

美術　びじゅつ
fine arts　1

左　ひだり
left　4

ビデオ
video　2

一つ　ひとつ
one　3

一人　ひとり
one person　3

ひま(な)
to have time, to be free　7

百／100　ひゃく
one hundred　2

病院　びょういん
hospital　2

病気　びょうき
sickness, illness　7

ひらがな
hiragana　2

昼ごはん　ひるごはん
lunch　3

昼休み　ひるやすみ
lunchtime, lunchhour　7

広島　ひろしま
place name　1

[ふ]
〜風　〜ふう
〜 style　3

プール
swimming pool　5

二つ　ふたつ
two　3

二人　ふたり
two people　3

二日／2日　ふつか
the 2nd of the month　7

物価　ぶっか
prices　6

物理　ぶつり
physics　1

ふとん
futon, quilt　4

船便　ふなびん
seamail　2

フライドチキン
fried chicken　3

古い　ふるい
old　6

プレゼント
present　3

ふろ
bath, bathroom　5

〜分　〜ふん
〜 minutes　7

文学　ぶんがく
literature　1

文法　ぶんぽう
grammar　6

[へ]
〜ページ
counter for pages　6

べつべつ（に）	
separate (ly)	3
部屋　へや	
room	4
ペン	
pen	3
勉強する　べんきょうする	
to study	2
便利(な)　べんりな	
convenient	6

[ほ]

法律　ほうりつ	
law	1
ボールペン	
ball-point pen	6
ポークカレー	
pork curry	3
ほかの〜	
other 〜	5
ポスト	
mailbox, postbox	4
北海道　ほっかいどう	
district name	1
ホットコーヒー	
hot coffee	3
本　ほん	
book	2
〜本　〜ほん，ぽん，ぽん	
counter for long objects	5
本屋　ほんや	
bookshop	2

[ま]

〜まい	
counter for flat objects	2
毎月　まいげつ	
every month	5
毎週　まいしゅう	
every week	5
毎月　まいつき	
every month	5
毎日　まいにち	
everyday	2
前　まえ	
the front	4
〜前　〜まえ	
〜 ago	8

また	
again	8
まだ	
not yet (＋ neg.)	8
まちがえる	
to make a mistake	7
マッチ	
matches	3
待つ　まつ	
to wait	3
まど	
window	4
(満) 〜歳　まん〜さい	
〜 years old	6

[み]

ミーティング	
meeting	8
ミートソース	
spaghetti with meat sauce	3
右　みぎ	
right	4
短い　みじかい	
short	6
水　みず	
water	3
店　みせ	
shop	8
三日／3日　みっか	
the 3rd of the month	7
ミックスサンドイッチ	
mixed sandwich	3
三つ　みっつ	
three	3
見る　みる	
to see, to look at	2
ミルク	
milk	3
ミルクティー	
tea with milk	3

[む]

六日／6日　むいか	
the 6th of the month	7
難しい　むずかしい	
difficult	6
六つ　むっつ	
six	3

[め]

メニュー
menu — 3

[も]

もう
already — 8

申し込み書類　もうしこみしょるい
application form — 6

木曜日　もくようび
Thursday — 5

もちろん
of course — 8

持つ　もつ
to have — 6

もらう
to receive — 3

[や]

薬学　やくがく
pharmacology — 1

約束　やくそく
promise — 8

野菜　やさい
vegetable — 3

安い　やすい
cheap — 6

休み　やすみ
holiday — 5

休む　やすむ
to be absent, to rest — 7

八つ　やっつ
eight — 3

やる
to open — 7

[ゆ]

夕方　ゆうがた
evening — 7

郵便局　ゆうびんきょく
post office — 2

ゆっくり
slowly — 4

[よ]

八日／8日　ようか
the 8th of the month — 7

よく
well — 7

四日／4日　よっか
the 4th of the month — 7

四つ　よっつ
four — 3

予定　よてい
schedule, appointment — 8

呼ぶ　よぶ
to call — 3

読む　よむ
to read — 2

予約する　よやくする
to reserve — 7

四／4　よん，し
four — 2

[ら]

来月　らいげつ
next month — 5

来週　らいしゅう
next week — 5

ライス
boiled rice — 3

ラジオ
radio — 2

ラジカセ
radio cassette tape recorder — 4

[り]

留学生　りゅうがくせい
foreign student — 1

留学生課　りゅうがくせいか
international student section — 1

料理　りょうり
dish, food — 7

旅行する　りょこうする
to travel — 7

[れ]

0　れい，ゼロ
zero — 2

歴史　れきし
history — 1

レストラン
restaurant — 3

レポート
report — 7

レモンジュース
lemon juice   3

レモンティー
lemon tea   3

練習する　れんしゅうする
to practise   6

[ろ]

六／6　ろく
six   2

六月／6月　ろくがつ
June   7

ロッカー
locker   4

論文　ろんぶん
thesis   7

[わ]

ワープロ
word processor   5

わかる
to understand   5

忘れ物　わすれもの
something left behind   6

忘れる　わすれる
to forget   8

私　わたし
I   1

和風　わふう
Japanese style   3

悪い　わるい
bad   6

Compiled and Edited by:

General editor	Otsubo, Kazuo	大 坪 一 夫
Authors	Akutsu, Satoru	阿久津　　智
	Ichikawa, Yasuko	市 川 保 子
	Emura, Hirofumi	江 村 裕 文
	Ogawa, Taeko	小 川 多恵子
	Kano, Chieko	加 納 千恵子
	Kaiser, Stefan	カイザー シュテファン
	Kindaichi, Kyoko	金田一 京 子
	Kobayashi, Noriko	小 林 典 子
	Komiya, Shutaro	小 宮 修太郎
	Saegusa, Reiko	三 枝 令 子
	Sakai, Takako	酒 井 たか子
	Shimizu, Yuri	清 水 百 合
	Shinya, Ayuri	新 谷 あゆり
	Tochigi, Yuka	栃 木 由 香
	Tomura, Kayo	戸 村 佳 代
	Nishimura, Yoshimi	西 村 よしみ
	Hashimoto, Yoji	橋 本 洋 二
	Fujimaki, Kikuko	藤 牧 喜久子
	Ford, Junko	フォード 順子
	Homma, Tomoko	本 間 倫 子
	Yamamoto, Sonoko	山 本 そのこ
	Yokoyama, Noriko	横 山 紀 子
	Watanabe, Keiko	渡 辺 恵 子
Cover design		
Illustrator	Robles, Maria Elizabeth	ロブレスM.エリザベス
	Teshigahara, Midori	勅使河原　　緑

SITUATIONAL FUNCTIONAL JAPANESE
VOLUME ONE: DRILLS

1991年12月20日　　初 版第1刷発行
1996年 2 月10日　　第2版第1刷発行

著 者　　筑波ランゲージグループ
発行所　　株式会社 凡 人 社
　　　　〒102 東京都千代田区平河町 1 - 3 -13
　　　　　　菱進平河町ビル 1 F　電話 03-3472-2240
印刷所　　株式会社 イ セ ブ
　　　　〒305 茨城県つくば市天久保 2 -11-20
　　　　　　電話 0298-51-2515

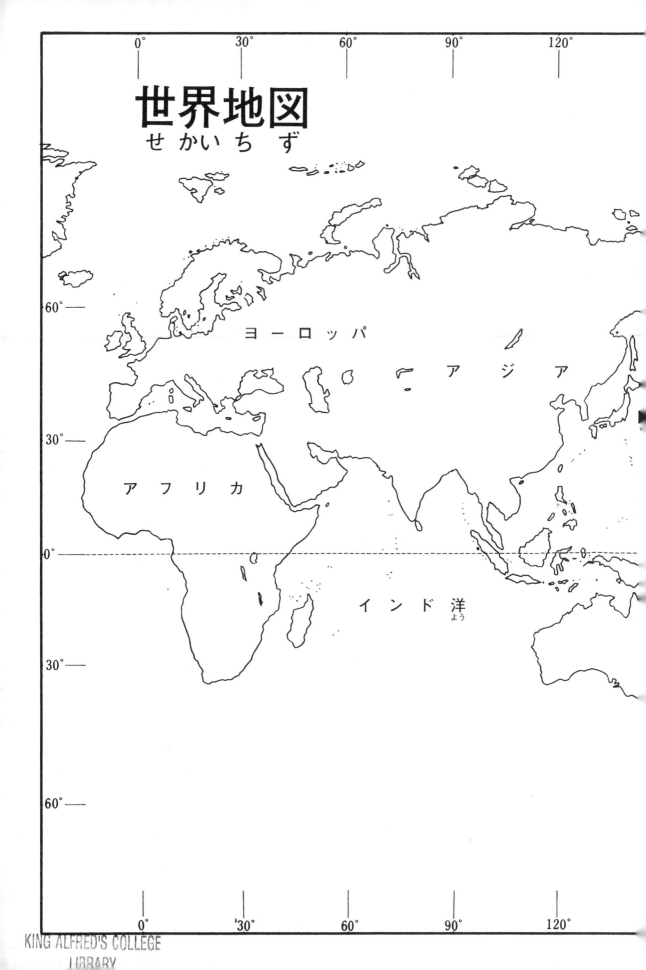

世界地図
せかいちず

ヨーロッパ

アジア

アフリカ

インド洋
よう